The Complete Book of
HOUSEPLANTS

The Complete Book of
HOUSEPLANTS

Galley Press

© M & P Boeken bv, Weert, 1985
World Book Promotion

© English translation Autumn Publishing Limited, 1986
English language edition produced by
Autumn Publishing Limited, 10 Eastgate Square,
Chichester, England.

Translation by Brian and Tricia Gohl
Editorial by Ingrid Goldsmid
            John Carden

Published in this edition by Galley Press, an imprint
of W H Smith & Son Limited
Registered No 237811 England
Trading as WHS Distributors, St John's House,
East Street, Leicester, LE1 6NE

Typeset by Avonset, Midsomer Norton, Bath, England.

ISBN 0 86136 664 6

Foreword

Many of the plants which we use to decorate and enhance our homes have particular requirements, so if you are to have the best results and greatest satisfaction from growing plants indoors you must be prepared to fulfil their needs. This can sometimes be more difficult than it would seem but there are times when it can also be easier.

One of the aims of **The Complete Book of Houseplants** is to explain how best to fulfil these requirements.

Attention is also drawn to other horticultural aspects. For example, details are given of materials and methods for potting and planting, sowing, cuttings, watering and so on, plus descriptions of hydro-culture, disease control, tools and equipment, pots, soils, etc.

Some of the subjects not always dealt with in other plant books are included in this book. In these chapters, attention is drawn to topics such as roof and balcony gardens, cultivation of vegetables and herbs in the home, and to bonsai.

The sections dealing with floristry will be of great interest to anyone with an interest and affection for plants and flowers. Not only is the art of flower arranging thoroughly dealt with but the use of freshly cut material for display is covered in detail. The drying of flowers, and the subtle methods needed to create dried flower pieces are also explained, in a step-by-step fashion. **The Complete Book of Houseplants** concludes with a series of plant descriptions that is almost encyclopaedic. The text has been kept short and concise, but the quality of information is of a high standard. The plants in this large section are arranged under several natural headings such as succulents, foliage, or flowering plants.

This book is full of beautiful, full colour illustrations which show in great detail different methods of potting, propagation, flower arranging and working with dried flowers.

The comprehensive coverage of the many different aspects of plants and flowers in the home, makes **The Complete Book of Houseplants** informative and enjoyable reading for beginner and expert.

Contents

Flowering plants need good light.

Below:
A living curtain imparts a distinctive atmosphere.

Decorating your home with plants

Plants in the living room: placement, plant furniture, plant cases, flower windows

The use of plants

Why should a room without plants be so dull? You can furnish a living room with the finest furniture, the most beautiful carpets, and yet a vital element can be found to be lacking. Everything remains static. Nothing changes. This can certainly not be said, however, when plants are present. A plant is changing constantly, it grows larger, it produces blooms. Plants make a room look softer, giving it a more-friendly atmosphere. Take care not to over-do things, for you may become slaves to the needs of your plants — and this cannot be right.

On the other hand, do not be afraid to use large plants — they are not necessarily more difficult than smaller varieties. When planning your house, allocate enough space in different situations for a variety of plant containers; in this way you will have many more options than window sills crowded with small pots.

Window sills naturally make the best situations for plants because of the light. They can also make some of the most attractive displays. A sill filled with fire-red geraniums in white pots is eye-catching and provides a completely different effect to the singly placed geranium, dotted here and there on their saucers. But filling the sill with begonias or ferns would be equally effective — provided, of course, you remember to consider the growth requirements of each species.

Choosing the best positions

There are probably features in your house that you would like to conceal — such as pipes across a wall, and the use of a plant as a screen could provide the answer. In this case the location is dictating the position of the plant.

However, if you have just bought a beautiful palm from a florist and are wandering around the room looking for a

Above:
Larger plants need not stand on the window sill.

Below right:
An attractive composition can still be attained with less light.

suitable spot, then clearly the plant is the determining factor.

Whatever your starting point, always try to create harmony in your living room, with plants and furnishings complementing each other; the total 'atmosphere' will usually be successful thanks to the overall effect that your plants provide.

Window sills

We have already mentioned that window sills can provide the best conditions for indoor plants. If a sill is too narrow for plants, it is usually still possible to do something about it, perhaps by installing a wider timber shelf or building-in ceramic tiles. Tiles always make sense wherever water is likely to be used, as spillage can cause no harm. Where heating elements or panels are located below a window, then the sill can still be extended, provided slits or holes are made in the shelf for the heat to disperse freely.

An extra shelf could be built-in, half-way up a window opening, to provide more space for pots. With both sill and shelf full of plants you would hardly need curtains!

Choose plants according to the shape of the window. An Ivy (Hedera) *or Passion Flower* (Passiflora) *trained up the frame can accentuate the curvature of a bow-topped window. A tall, thin Cactus would better suit a narrow, upright window.*

Right:
Variegated Dieffenbachia (Dumb Cane) needs a plain background.

Below:
Linear leaves of Cordyline complement joints of panelling.

A variegated plant shows up best against a plain background. Avoid floral wallpaper or other complex backgrounds.

Consider placing the second shelf somewhat higher than the centre of the frame, and let hanging plants become your curtain. Ivy *(Hedera)*, Spider plant, *Chlorophytum* or Goldfish plant, *Columnea* are ideal for this purpose.

Plants as room dividers
Sometimes a room is divided with a cupboard or screen, but plants can often be used with equal effect, as a fresh, living screen.

Start by determining your requirements of height and length, and whether plants are to be grown in pots or troughs. Sketch your ideas on paper, trying different combinations of size and shape.

If you have sufficient space for a green partition, you could install a row of substantial pots with plants such as *Ficus Banjamina*, which can grow quite large, but which can still be controlled by regular pruning.

Where space is more confined, climbing plants such as Ivy *(Hedera)*, *Rhoicissus*, *Cissus* or *Philodendron scandens* can be planted in elongated troughs and trained upwards on lattice screens. It may be feasible to install wires between the trough and ceiling to provide an almost invisible support.

Nephrolepis fern provides a pretty contrast to the stark background.

Right: *Bird's nest fern (Asplenium) forms an interesting contrast with its surrounds.*

12

The Spider Plant, Chlorophytum, doesn't mind low light levels, and so can be used away from the window.

Where there is insufficient natural light from windows, then the installation of special 'growing lights' would be beneficial.

Specimen plants

Attractive and unusual plants, especially those of larger sizes may be placed on their own to display their features to their best advantage. Norfolk Island Pine *(Araucaria),* House Lime, African Hemp *(Sparmannia)* and many Palm species are frequently seen as 'specimens'. Good plant specimens immediately catch the eye when one enters a room, and should therefore always be in pristine condition. 'Spotless' may seem an odd way of describing a variegated plant (such as Dumb Cane *Dieffenbachia*), but any plant prominently displayed should be free of yellowed, brown-edged or diseased foliage. Healthy large ferns can make beautiful displays, especially when mounted on a pedestal.

Space for hanging plants

If you've run out of space for plants, then how about suspending them? A variety of hanging pots and containers can be bought, suiting all tastes and situations. Just

Pedestals and stands carrying heavy plants are dangerous if you have young children who are still crawling and who pull themselves up on furniture.

remember that the container must be large enough, and that it should not leak, or should be provided with a 'drip tray' or saucer.

Attractive wire baskets can be bought for use in- or out-doors. These baskets must be lined with a layer of sphagnum moss to retain the compost and plants. For indoor use, the addition of a plastic sheet between the moss and compost is necessary, to control drainage.

Plant hanger bases can easily be made by drilling three holes into the sides of plant-saucers and attaching copper chains or wires of the appropriate length. Always ensure that hooks for any hanging container are securely attached either to the ceiling or to a beam capable of carrying the full weight of the plant, pot and damp soil. Containers should not be hung so high that a ladder is needed for watering.

Since warm air in a room rises, it follows

Left:
Plant displays like this need plenty of light.

The choice of plants to be used in hanging pots is wide. For an area that is not too dark, do try Maidenhair Fern (Adiantum), Creeping Fig, Ficus pumila and Ivy (Hedera). A basketful of Chlorophytum always looks good. In a bay window, a cascade of the white flowers of the Campanula isophylla 'Alba' can be sensational.

that hanging containers usually dry out faster than those at lower levels, and the plants transpire more. For this reason, porous clay pots should not be used.

Logically, hanging containers look best when planted with hanging plants — stiff, upright-growing plants tend to look incongruous.

An ever-changing scene

With care, forethought and handling, a plant will thrive in the correct environment. But it must be remembered that a healthy plant keeps on growing, and will eventually reach a stage where it has outgrown either its pot, or its allotted space. When this happens the plant must be replaced with a smaller one of the same species, or try something different. Overgrown plants can be re-potted in larger containers, and tried in a new position.

Flowering plants provide a changing spectacle. They are commonly removed from view after blooming, most especially those species that do require a rest period. As plants and their needs vary through the year, so the challenge to the keen indoor gardener involves the growing and positioning of suitable plants to provide a continuous floral or foliage effect. The micro-climate in a home changes too, and plants may well have to be moved if their situation becomes too hot or cold.

Terrariums

Plant cases (or terrariums) have a wide appeal, and are available in a variety of shapes and sizes — some look like miniature conservatories, complete with framed and glazed panels, while others are more basic, comprising simply a plastic tray with a raised transparent plastic lid. Some are so small they can hardly be termed 'cases', while larger modern terrariums are almost room-sized.

Propagating trays

Trays with transparent lids, commonly called 'propagating trays', are used for sowing and weaning seedlings, and for rooting cuttings. Young plants are sensitive to temperature fluctuations and drying out.

Propagating trays provide protected conditions for them. Modern propagating trays with electric 'bottom-heat' are a great aid to germinating many otherwise-difficult seeds, especially during the colder months.

A variety of indoor plants can be grown from seed. This can become a most satisfying hobby. African violet *(Saintpaulia)*, *Primula,* Geranium, Sensitive Plant *(Mimosa pudica)* and *Aralia* are but a few examples.

Fern cases

A fern-growing cult developed in England during the late 19th century following the

Plant cases with flowering plants such as African Violet (Saintpaulia) *or certain Begonia types in full bloom are a pleasure to see. Dead flowers must be removed regularly before they can turn mouldy, and so infect other parts of the plant.*

Below:
Nevregelia carolinae tricolor.

Right:
Banana plants grow fast, but will need lots of space.

publicity given to the earlier findings of Dr Nathaniel Ward that many tropical and other difficult plants could be grown successfully in glass containers indoors, with minimal attention. Their popularity was such, that 'Wardian cases' became an unmistakeable feature of Victorian furnishing at all levels of society.

Most of the great variety of fern types that were introduced to enthusiastic home-growers would not have survived outside their glass enclosures.

In those days the cases were themselves works of art, and were often miniature replicas of large conservatories or 'Crystal Palaces'. Unfortunately not many examples have survived.

Make your own fern case

The chances of obtaining an antique Wardian case are slim, but this is no reason not to make one's own version, for year-round pleasure. A tropical fish tank or old glass battery case with panes of glass for lids prove highly satisfactory.

For a more authentic version, choose wood or metal for the frame, with insertable glass panes. Glass is more transparent than plastic, and allows water to run off faster. Where possible, roofs should have a slope of at least 60 degrees, so that condensation will run down the walls rather than form heavy droplets, as is the case when horizontal lids are used.

Establishing a terrarium

The principle of a terrarium is that of a closed system, whereby the same moisture in the container is circulated continuously via the soil and plant.

After planting, water is applied lightly, and the lid or door closed. As the plants transpire (lose water through evaporation) the water vapour condenses on the glass and the droplets roll down into the soil, where they are again absorbed by the plant roots.

Before starting to plant up a terrarium, ensure that the glass walls are spotlessly clean; when establishing a bottle garden or other container with a small entrance, use a funnel or roll of cardboard to introduce the soil, so that sides remain clean.

Initially a drainage layer must be placed across the base; clean gravel, mixed with charcoal, or charcoal alone is best, about 2cm (¾ in) deep in small containers, and up to 5cm (2ins) deep in larger cases

containing several plants. Follow this with a layer of moist, light, potting compost, at least 5cm (2ins) thick, and up to 10cm (4ins) deep in larger containers where larger plants are being planted. When planting, try not to disturb the drainage layer.

Excess moisture is difficult to remove, so the compost should not be too damp, and the first watering of plants should be very light, preferably using a fine spray.

Plants for terrariums

Dwarf ferns are perfect subjects for terrariums, with their humid atmosphere. The lack of temperature changes suits them particularly. Suitable species include: Maidenhair fern (*Adiantum*), Holly fern (*Cyrtomium falcatum*), *Nephrolepis cordifolia* 'compacta', and the Button fern, *Pellaea rotundifolia*.

Apart from dwarf ferns, you could use other small plants such as Sweet Flag, *Acorus gramineus, Selaginella* and the small-leafed Ivy types.

Terrarium plants should be pruned regularly as they become larger before, hopefully, they start crowding each other

Mini-domes are ideal for cuttings.

You could use a plant case to start off herbs and seedlings, for later planting out in the garden.

A more unusual idea is to keep a case of fly-catching plants. Carnivorous plants need the protected climate of a terrarium; but will appreciate being fed live flies occasionally. There are several species: Venus flytrap (Dionaea), Butterwort (Pinguicula), Sundew (Drosera), Pitcher (Sarracenia).

Napenthes alata, a carnivorous plant.

too much. In this way they can give pleasure for many years.

Flower windows

In a broad sense, any window still containing a row of plants is a 'flower window'. More correctly, a 'flower window' comprises an extended sill specially adapted to provide good facilities for the growing of flowering plants.

You can usually develop a window feature within a normal window frame, provided it is not too small. Its height should be at least 1.25m (4ft) and should not be narrower than 90cm (3ft). A trough is then made (or bought), to fit the width of window, at least 20cm (8ins) deep, and between 20cm–40cm wide (8ins–16ins).

When a window extends down to the floor, a trough may be let into the floor to a depth of 50cm (18ins) or deeper; however, such a trough with adequate drainage and with soil-heating cables would have to be deeper still.

The trough should be filled with moistened Irish peat into which the plants in their clay pots are placed. Generally, individual pots are more convenient for watering; where the plants are planted directly into the trough their roots can become tangled which is a disadvantage if one wishes to replace one or more of the plants.

If a heating cable is to be installed in the base of the trough, over the drainage layer, it should be covered with a 5cm (2ins) layer of sand before the peat is inserted.

Do you need a plant window?

Most plants prefer to grow together in a group. Consequently, when several compatible plants are grouped together in a trough in a warm, light window they would feel extremely comfortable, and would all grow profusely.

The main disadvantage of having a window crowded with flourishing plants is, of course, that the room will start to lose its natural light. So it would not be advisable to turn all your windows into plant displays!

Better to choose one window that is most suitable climatically for the types of plant you wish to grow. A hot, south-facing window, for example, is only really suitable for cacti and succulents, unless you are prepared to shade the plants during the hottest hours of each day.

A tropical window

The climate in a plant window can be regulated to an extent; you can create a tropical climate by installing a transparent partition to 'sandwich' the plant area between the room and the window panes. Frequently in modern houses and offices, plant windows are an integral part of the building, and may extend from floor to ceiling, and troughs may be let into the floor. The great advantage of these custom-built growing areas is the amount of light they provide for plants, and so large-sized plants can be grown. These may be termed 'built-in' plant windows.

Externally projecting plant windows are sometimes seen, usually glazed, and metal-framed. They provide optimum light conditions, but are obviously more expensive to install. The larger external plant windows could well require the expertise of a specialist, both for the choice of plants and for the installation of heating, ventilation and humidity control.

Practical tips

To return to the conditions in your own home, in which you can create your own 'tropical paradise', provided, of course, you observe certain fundamentals. You must be able to reach all parts of the display and window area, so that the condition of both the soil and plant can be regularly monitored.

The plant trough itself should not be so wide that you cannot reach the window to clean it. If the trough is let into the floor, it is more convenient if there is a space between trough and wall, so that you can stand while cleaning the glass. Whenever possible, try to prevent plant foliage from touching the glass; in winter the cold can cause considerable damage, and in summer the foliage can easily scorch.

In winter do not let your plants become trapped between the curtains and window-panes, excluding them from the room's warmth, and creating a refrigerator for your plants. Double glazing does solve this problem to a great extent.

Plants for a flower window

The correct choice of a plant for a flower window is naturally dependant on the window size, its 'climate' and the amount of light it gets and, of course, on your own preferences.

Seemingly difficult houseplants, that appear weak and unhealthy in one part of the house, could well thrive in a well-lit window.

North-facing windows are not ideal for flowering plants, which generally prefer lighter and warmer situations. Many foliage plants are more tolerant of lesser levels of light. Hardy varieties for a north-facing plant trough include *Cissus, Dracaena, Dieffenbachia, Fatsia, Hedera, Peperomia,* and some ferns.

A south-facing plant trough can be planted with any from the following selection: Croton *(Coadiaeum)*, Shrimp plant *(Beloperone)*, *Campanula isophylla,* varieties of Geranium, and most succulents.

Eastern and western windows will provide conditions for a range of plants that are similar — notably *Asparagus, Begonia, Caladium, Camellia, Cyclamen, Anthurium* and *Hoya carnosa.*

Colourful cacti in full bloom.

Below: *Cyclamen.*

17

Plants in the work area, bathroom, bedroom

Top:
Plants can enhance the bedroom.

Below:
Plants being used for colour contrast.

Plants that need a dormant period after flowering could be kept in a cool bedroom; Clivia and African House Lime (Sparmannia) should flower well after a cool dormancy, and many other types will also enjoy the lower temperatures.

Plants in other rooms

Most decorating with furnishings and plants is concentrated in the living area, where most of our 'living' and entertaining is done, but most of us spend a great proportion of our working lives away from home, and may miss the surrounding greenery.

Is this really necessary? Plants can be used in offices, shops or hospitals as a decorative element; we can also surround ourselves with living greenery in rooms other than the living room at home.

How can this be applied in, say, the bathroom, where the climate tends to be humid, either hot or cold, and does not suit many plants?

Most bedrooms could accommodate a few plants — unless, of course, the idea does not appeal to you. Much of our lives is spcnt in our bedrooms — mainly asleep, it is true — but it is nice to wake up to fresh greenery.

A bedroom's cooler and fresher atmosphere is quite different climatically from the bathroom. Plants that find the warmer living room conditions excessive may well be happier in a bedroom.

Another important work area in the home is the kitchen. Whatever its size, every kitchen must have a window, where you could keep some potted herbs.

A garden room, sun-room or conservatory form another category. Attached to the house, they are designed specifically to suit the needs of plants.

Left above:
A mixed succulent group highlights a corner.

Left below:
A plant in a dark hall will not grow well.

Below:
A successful mixed arrangement needs imagination.

Plants in the work area

Pleasant working conditions

Indoor plants are not only found at home. They are evident in almost all public buildings, offices, shops and arcades, and hotels, contributing greatly to the appearance and feel of our surroundings.

The use of plants may start unintentionally: a lonely little plant may be seen on a secretary's desk; this may be followed by the Director receiving a trough of plants for his birthday, and before you know it, plants are growing everywhere!

Today it is usual for architects to make provision for 'greenery' during the design stage of a building.

Plants for the work environment must be chosen with the specific conditions of each room or passageway in mind. Nothing looks worse than unhealthy plants, struggling to survive in the wrong conditions.

Caring for office plants

The plants in a working environment provide 'atmosphere', which can have a direct influence on productivity. It is important, therefore, to make sure that plants are looked after. This is done by providing the most favourable climatic and growing conditions — that is, the fundamental growth requirements of light, air, temperature, moisture and feeding.

Light

During office hours, blinds or sunshades are adjusted according to the weather; but what happens at week-ends?

In many cases, plants brought into a commercial environment start to deteriorate as soon as they arrive. A good example of this is in a new shop, where beautifully planted troughs have been placed in prominent positions inside the shop. In almost all cases, a shop's interior is too dark for the plants, and they soon show their intolerance, by dropping leaves, stretching or growing smaller new foliage.

It is well known that people work better in an environment with 'greenery'. The restful effect of plants helps to reduce stress.

Indoor plants can be grown in dark places provided that special 'grow-lights' are installed, to give the correct lighting. An ordinary spotlight is of no use — initially, the lighting effect appears good, but the type of light is so different from sunlight that plants receive no benefit and soon deteriorate.

Lighting is dealt with more fully in the chapter on 'The climate in your home'.

A draughty affair

When entering a building, attractive plant displays provide an important first impression. These can be found in the entrance halls, or reception areas, of hotels, hospitals, offices or flats. But the little draughts that blow in and flutter the leaves every time the door is opened, can be very harmful to the plants. In fact, draughts are probably one of the main causes of plants 'going-off', even though they are otherwise well cared for.

It is therefore important to choose tougher plant species for entrance halls and passages; large plant cases, plant windows or possibly screens could provide protection.

Moisture in the air

With central heating, floor coverings and closed windows the air in modern buildings is now much drier. A tiled floor and lots of

plants would help lessen this dryness. Keeping an eye on the atmospheric humidity benefits plants and humans alike, dry air is unhealthy for both.

A room's atmosphere can be made more humid by placing bowls of water around the room, especially above radiators and by installing fountains and water settings together with plants; nothing helps more to reduce the dryness in a room than lots of plants, especially foliage varieties.

The daily watering of pot-plants also helps maintain the humidity, as does the occasional syringing or light spraying with water of the foliage of many tropical plants.

There is no water shortage with an automatic system.

Suitable for office conditions?
Plants that will be happy in an office environment must be chosen according to their ability to tolerate a uniform temperature throughout the year. Plants such as Clivia, that require a dormant period after flowering, should not be kept permanently in an office, for neither time nor facilities exist to cater for this dormant period. Without this natural slowing down, such plants can never be at their best.

Who does the watering?
Indoor plants must receive reliable attention, regularly if they are to survive. It is simply not enough to leave the care of the plants in an office to chance, where someone gives them a dash of water when they think of it, or when the foliage is drooping visibly. In a small office, there is usually no problem, but as the number of employees increases, the responsbility for watering the plants presents difficulties! Either everyone presumes that someone else has watered the plants and therefore it is not done, or the reverse happens and the plant has too much water!

The logical solution to plant care in a larger office is to enter into a contract with a local

florist, who can keep the plants in prime condition. This way the staff need not worry about it. A large company will probably employ the services of a specialist plant-maintenance contractor to care for all of their plant displays.

Choosing the right plant
If you are looking for plants to enhance your environment, you must choose carefully. First, try not to include those plants that have special needs. These include plants such as Croton (*Codiaeum*), that will not tolerate a dry atmosphere, and soon shed their foliage. Second, plants that dislike too much moisture don't do well amongst plants that like an occasional spraying with water.

Flowering plants are yet another matter. They look attractive whilst flowering, but don't bloom throughout the year. During the non-flowering period, they may require different treatment, very often involving removing them from the display. Cyclamen are such plants — beautiful whilst in bloom, but not a permanent plant for the office.

Large pots
For office displays, ignore most of the smaller plant types usually planted alone in little pots. Watering becomes a problem if there are too many small containers dotted about.

*A pair of matching pots with Philodendrons gives a lush effect, especially if plants are of different size.
If different types of plants in different sizes and shapes of pot are placed in a group, the effect is not always harmonious.
Compare this to a dining-room table surrounded by six different chairs.*

Below:
Sensitive plant
(Mimosa
pudica).

Below right:
*Norfolk Island
Pine*
(Araucaria).

Bigger plants in larger pots are initially more expensive, but will prove more economical in the long run. Think of the pleasure you will have by making the right choice of plants for your office.

Solitary specimens

Plants with special features are best displayed on their own. The Screw pine *(Pandanus veitchii)*, is such a plant; as it grows larger it looks fantastic, but needs more space as the fine-toothed edges of its leaves are razor-sharp and a hazard to the unwary.

Many plants do not like being touched or handled, and are best kept away from passageways and desks. Plants with soft foliage are more sensitive and liable to damage than those with leathery leaves.

The Sensitive Plant *(Mimosa pudica)*, is an extreme example, whose leaves fold together when touched.

Plant troughs are the best solution for the work environment, and the correct choice of plants is important. Don't try to cram in as many different plants as possible; rather limit the planting in each trough to a few

complementary species (you could well use more than one plant of each type for a more spectacular display).

A work area will usually have more space than other rooms for larger plants. Plants large enough to be placed on their own include: Ficus benjamina; Ficus lyrata; Monstera delicosa; *Kentia palm* (Howea); Philodendron selloum; Grevillea robusta; *Cordyline species. Many smaller plants are also suitable: Stagshorn fern* (Platycerium); *Birdsnest fern* (Asplenium); Dieffenbachia; Dracaena; Fatsia.

Plants in the bathroom

A warm and humid atmosphere

The bathroom provides a suitable environment for plants that grow naturally in humid rainforest conditions. They thrive in the moist atmosphere that results each time anyone has a bath. If you have had no previous success with plants in your bathroom, then possibly your choice of plant type has been wrong. For example, drought-loving succulents will not tolerate a humid situation; they also need plenty of light, and bathroom windows are often small. But the beautifully flowering *Cyclamen* doesn't survive either — as *Cyclamen* prefer a uniformly cool climate. However, if you choose a Birds nest fern *(Asplenium)*, success is guaranteed. Another fern, *Nephrolepsis*, also enjoys warmth and humidity, as do many *Philodendrons* and *Cyperus*.

If you have a broad window sill in your bathroom, then you could fill it with Geraniums or Begonia during the summer, whilst they are in bloom. Although they are only temporary plants they can be enjoyed for a relatively long period.

A fern or similar plant placed on a shelf in front of a mirror can create a very good effect. And don't fill all the flat surfaces with toiletries; save a spot for an attractive pot containing *Spathiphyllum*. This is a useful plant that looks good even where there is not much light. With the humidity of a bathroom, it should bloom throughout the year. Is your bathroom too small? There's always space for a hanger or two, with Ivy, *Cissus, Scindapsus* or *Philodendron scandens*. In a larger bathroom you could try one of the taller-growing plants such as *Cyperus*, palms or *Philodendron*.

In warmer weather, you can occasionally soak houseplants, up to their pot-rims, in tepid water and syringe the foliage.

You must be careful when using aerosol sprays in a bathroom. They can be very harmful to plants. So when you spray, ensure that there is adequate ventilation.

Left below: *Green plants enliven a white bathroom.*

Plants needing less light and high humidity should be happy in a bathroom.

Left:
Cissus discolor

*Summer colour
for the window
sill:*

Begonia

Streptocarpus

Geranium

Spathiphyllum

Plants in the bedroom

Clivia miniata

Sparmannia
(African Hemp)

Hedera helix
'Ivalace'

It is not advisable to turn your bedroom into a conservatory. You and your plants would then be competing for the same oxygen; at night, without light, the plant's assimilation process stops, so they stop giving off oxygen. But respiration continues as always, so oxygen is still being taken in, oxygen that you need too! A few plants would not be harmful, but a jungle would be! Let fresh air in whenever the weather allows.

Blooms of a yellow Oleander.

A cool situation

Many plants would be more than happy with the climatic conditions normally found in a bedroom — usually somewhat cooler and less dry than the living areas of a home.

Cool customers

Plants preferring cooler conditions have usually originated in cooler climatic areas of the world, and include plants such as bamboo *(Bambusa)*, Norfolk Island Pine *(Araucaria)*, Ivy *(Hedera)*, *Fatsia japonica*, *Aucuba* and *Ligustrum*. The *Ligustrum*, or privet, is the same one used for hardy hedges, but it is just as happy in a cool interior.

Bedrooms tend to be fairly cool, and for this reason the air is also relatively humid. Ferns generally appreciate this climate. *Sparmannia* would also be happy in a bedroom as it likes light, sun and fresh air,

and could stay here throughout the year or possibly during its dormant period, from October to January. It requires a temperature of about 10°C (50°F) during winter to produce a good spring show of flowers.

Sitting out the winter

The African Hemp *(Sparmannia)*, is one of many popular plants that also need to rest in a cool place after their flowering period. A bedroom-type climate would suit most of these; in this category we can include *Clivia, Bougainvillea, Cyclamen, Geranium* and *Pelargonium*, and *Hibiscus*. All these plants can be given sheltered positions outside during summer.

Other plants that need cool, light, protected conditions during winter only, include *Euonymus japonica*, Bay tree *(Laurus)* and Oleander *(Nerium)*.

Plants in the kitchen

A separate environment

You can use plants in a kitchen in the conventional way to freshen and brighten its appearance, but you can also try creating something original and different.

Because the kitchen is furnished and fitted in a different and more fundamental way than other rooms in the house, it seems logical to use kitchen 'foliage' which is attractive and functional.

On the menu

Which plants would be most suitable for putting on a kitchen window sill? As most people are concerned with food in a kitchen, a natural first choice would be plants that could be used in cooking.

Herbs are the obvious example. If you start sowing seeds of herbs early in the year, you can start using them indoors long before herbs are ready for picking out of doors. These same herb plants can be used throughout the summer, provided you don't crop them too vigorously, and give them the chance to grow out again.

Many of the useful herbs that are normally grown out of doors, such as chives, parsley, celery and thyme can be grown on a kitchen sill, where they are to hand when needed.

Larger growing herbs such as sage, tarragon, and rosemary are not as happy indoors, and are also more awkward because of the larger sized pots they need. It's probably better to grow these on a balcony or in the garden.

What other edible plants could be kept in a kitchen? Fruiting vegetables, such as peppers, tomatoes and dwarf cucumbers can be successful. Herbs and vegetables need a good light, but not direct sunlight. They have to grow and fruit in a relatively short season, so need good potting soil, and pots of adequate size.

Worried about forgetting to water? Plants in the kitchen are always on view, and so

It is wise to keep several plants of each herb that you use frequently. You can then take sprigs from one plant while the others are recovering.

are frequently the best-cared-for plants in the house!

Endless variety

The arrangement on the kitchen window sill should be as variable as the meals you prepare. After all, you don't choose the same menu day after day. The window sill show can reflect the changing seasons with the 'useful' green colours coming and going, and blending with the ornamental.

It seems a pity to throw out the healthy green top of a pineapple, when it could form a nice plant in a shallow pot. The tops of carrots placed in a shallow tray of water soon form a fresh green clump. A piece of sweet potato in shallow water makes an interesting climber, while a sprouted onion in water can sometimes develop a stem and flower.

After a long winter, everyone starts looking forward to salads; a window sill is a good spot for sowing seed of mustard and cress in small trays for their succulent sprouts.

Many of the fruits and vegetables we eat are very decorative. How about showing off the golden-brown colours of a bunch of onions, or the dramatic purple aubergines? Most fruits are very decorative in a bowl,

Above the cooker is not a good place for plants.

Shadelovers only on cupboard tops!

Plants for a kitchen should have leathery leaves as plants soon collect a greasy layer from all the cooking. Tougher leaves are easier to clean than tender or hairy foliage.

in the kitchen or living room. Ripening tomatoes on the window sill are also colourful.

What to plant them in?

In a kitchen, normal ornamental pots would look wrong. With all the utensils around, you could try some interesting containers.

A little thyme plant in a tea-pot standing next to chives in a gravy-boat; an enamel mug with a parsley plant side-by-side with a pineapple in a soup bowl. You can plant directly into these containers, but must be very careful not to over-water as they have no drainage holes. Alternatively, keep the plants in clay pots and place these inside the outer 'utensil' of your choice.

'Ordinary' houseplants can obviously also be grown in the kitchen. But remember that the temperature in a kitchen is usually more variable than in other parts of the house. While you are cooking temperature and humidity will be high, but it will be much cooler for most of the day. There are also the clouds of steam and grease-droplets from cooking, which need regular cleaning from the plants' leaves. All this is worthwhile, because of the advantages of having greenery in your kitchen.

27

Plants in the conservatory or garden room

A small garden room can be most attractive.

A garden room with double-opening doors is extremely convenient and helps extend the house into the garden. Early sunshine can be let in, while it is still cold outside. If your terrace extends from the garden room, you can use it for a barbeque even if it looks as though it is going to rain.

A special room for plants

Breakfasting in the conservatory, among the plants, can make a very pleasant start to the day.

Let's look at the garden room — or conservatory, in more detail. It is usually a room attached to the house, adapted for the needs of growing plants, but is also intended as a peaceful recreational space. Walls are generally made of glass, and the roof either wholly or partly of glass or glassfibre.

The sun can keep a glassed structure warm throughout the year, with a little help during the winter from some form of heating. If you are fortunate enough to own a house with a built-on conservatory, then you and your plants are very lucky.

However, if there is space against a sunny wall, then this could be a good site for a garden room, especially if you can provide direct access from the house. This is necessary, if you want to make the most of your new amenity and enjoy looking after all your new plants.

You should be aware that, in spite of the glass roof, such structures can reduce the amount of light entering the adjoining room. The roof structure, whether it is to carry glass panes or glassfibre sheets, must be strong and firmly attached to the house. A sloping roof is better than a flat roof, not only to allow rain and snow to run off, more rapidly, but also to allow condensation forming on the underside to run down the walls, rather than drip all over the place.

Furnishing the conservatory

As a floor covering, carpets are the most impractical because of the moisture and high humidity. Rush matting, although attractive in a green and leafy setting, would probably soon get mouldy. The most practical solution to use a floor covering of one of the man-made materials, which are not affected too much by moisture. A smooth vinyl floor covering is extremely practical, and water resistant, and comes in a wide range of patterns. Carpeting especially made for bathrooms and outdoor situations is probably the best solution, as it looks good and tolerates damp. Ceramic tiles, quarry tiles, cobbles, bricks, or stone paving can also be used, but they are sometimes expensive.

Tables and chairs made of natural materials, such as wood, bamboo or cane, look best amongst green foliage. Cast-iron (or alloy) garden furniture is equally suitable. The high humidity will damage normal household furniture.

Temperature in the conservatory

The type of plants you want to grow will determine the amount of heat you will need, especially during the cooler months. If the conservatory is being used as an extra room, then normal room temperature is adequate. If your home has central heating, then you can probably extend the system, add extra radiators, and ideally, a separate thermostat.

The sun will warm a conservatory faster than the rest of the house, but in winter it will be necessary to watch the temperature (and weather), to avoid wide fluctuations. If central heating is not available there are many suitable greenhouse heaters. These include electric fan heaters, enclosed tubes, coal or wood-burners, and gas or paraffin heaters. Whichever heater you use, make sure that the temperature remains above 10°C (50°F).

Planting

Plants feel at home in a conservatory, because they prefer being with other plants. Together, they can create a micro-climate which improves their growth. Provided the various conditions such as temperature, humidity, etc., are right, growth should be rapid. Vigorous growth of foliage also requires strong root development, so make sure that plants are put in large enough containers. It is sometimes better to 'plunge' plants in individual pots into a larger trough, filled with peat, creating an attractive group. If you feel confident, plant your selection directly into a trough

containing potting soil. Plants in larger, single pots can be moved quite easily, and perhaps placed outside during summer.

Direct planting

Some conservatories are constructed so that plants can be planted directly into the soil, either at ground level, in raised beds, or as part of an ornamental feature (pond, waterfall, etc.). If the soil is well prepared and manured in advance, growth should be vigorous and healthy. Creepers or vines are also most effective and tropical foliage plants can soon reach 'jungle' proportions!

Older conservatories in many parts of the country contain magnificent plant specimens planted directly into the soil many years ago. They require regular pruning to keep them within the bounds of their 'environment'.

Plants for a conservatory

Collectors sometimes turn a garden room into a 'desert', with cacti and succulents. Or a tropical jungle can be created, where bromeliads and orchids grow on tree-trunks and hang from baskets. Some plants will have to be protected from the full sun by installing screens, roller blinds or venetian blinds. It is always useful to see how nurserymen keep the sun off their glasshouses.

Climbing plants can be grown to create shadier conditions in a conservatory: Black-

A garden room can be fitted out as an 'orangery'. These were common in old country houses. Oranges and other frost-tender plants in pots or tubs can be over wintered in a light frost-free place. Temperatures do not have to be high. In summer the pots are placed outside again, and you have full use of your garden room right through summer.

*Ipomoea
(Morning
Glory)*

*Good light
encourages
healthy growth
and blooming.*

*Turn a garden room
into a 'tea-room' by
providing a small table
and a few cane chairs.
A dainty tea-set and a
small vase of flowers on
the table will capture
some 'olde worlde'
charm and appeal to
family and friends alike.*

eyed Susan *(Thunbergia)*, Passionfruit *(Passiflora)*, Grape vines, Morning Glory *(Ipomoea)*, *Cobaea* and *Gloriosa* will all grow vigorously indoors but a frame or lattice will have to be provided for them to climb up. The disadvantage of this shading method is that it can't be 'rolled-up' when too dark so regular pruning will probably be necessary.

Unusual plants such as banana *(Musa)*, Acacia and Eucalyptus will thrive in a garden room.

Hanging indoor plants thrive in a garden room and it doesn't matter if some water is spilled during watering.

Once a garden room is established it is sure to become a favourite room for all the family to relax in.

Arrangements in containers

A modern, fresh arrangement.

Plants like company

Groups of plants make a natural display in all rooms. Plants like one another's company and, as with people, it should be 'good company'. To plant a cactus and a fern in the same pot is asking for trouble. A cactus needs lots of sun and little water, while a fern needs shade and plenty of moisture.

When it comes to choosing plants for a group display it is necessary to look closely at the needs of the plants in terms of light, water and temperature. This way it is possible to avoid mixing totally incompatible plants (such as the cactus and fern).

When a compatible selection of plants is grouped together they not only look better, but also grow better than similar plants in individual pots.

Plant troughs as screens

If plants are being used as a screen, it is more practical to plant or plunge them alongside each other in an elongated trough. Obviously it is easier to move one container than several separate pots.

Troughs have more space

It is advisable not to get too carried away and overfill the container. The plants must not be so close together (particularly in the early stages) that they have no room to grow. They must be able to develop.

A newly-planted trough may well look sparse, with space around each plant but within a few months these plants will have filled out, forming an attractive display.

Where do plants prefer to be?

Plants can be left in their own pots and plunged into a trough filled with peat. Thirstier plants can easily be given extra water, and plants can be removed or repositioned. The surrounding peat must be kept moist. When the plants in such a trough feel at home, their roots soon grow through the drainage holes of the pot into the peat.

Once rooted-through they are no longer easily transplanted. If the roots become too thick and constricted then the pot will have to be removed. Smash the pot carefully and take out the pieces without damaging the root ball.

Plants can naturally also be planted directly into a trough containing compost. This should be deep enough to allow the roots to expand freely.

Provision must be made for drainage of surplus water. If water cannot escape it will stagnate and cause water-logging of the soil.

A thick layer of broken clay pots (crocks), or crushed stone form a suitable drainage layer. Ideally, the container should have drainage holes, and a drip-tray to collect surplus water. However, this is not always practical, especially when dealing with large troughs.

Never place a plant container directly onto any good surface, whether the container has drainage holes or not, as condensation is likely to mark the surface, and on wooden furniture can cause permanent staining.

A small container of plants given as a present will not look good forever. Within a month or so the Begonia might finish flowering, and the Ficus pumila *growing rampantly! So larger containers must be found for these plants. Florists plant up the pots for immediate effect only! In most cases, the plants are too close together and in too-shallow pots. Replanting in a more spacious container will extend their life.*

Below: *Peperomia and the lower Pellaea.*

A useful tip: insert a hollow plastic tube through the soil to the bottom of the pot; check occasionally with the aid of a pocket torch, and if water is visible, then the plant is definitely too damp. Slight moisture indicates correct watering, and if it appears bone-dry, then water should be given.

Which plants to group together?
One container full of the same type of plant can look stunning. Many fern species enjoy being grown together as this is how they grow in their natural habitat. A large bowl or pot of Maiden-hair fern *(Adiantum)* grown as a large cluster, and displayed on an antique pedestal, can be spectacular. A few *Nephrolepsis* ferns planted in a long trough of compost, will soon start increasing, and new plants will fill and cascade over the container. This is unlikely to happen in a smaller single pot.

A shallow copper bowl filled with African Violet, of a single colour matching a colour scheme, can be another attractive feature. A show like this doesn't last forever, but is still worthwhile.

Don't overdo the colours
When deciding to plant-up a mixed bowl, bear in mind that too many colours will detract from the overall effect.
If you have a container that could accommodate 10 plants and is planted with 10 different ones, then the appearance may be anything but harmonious! It would be

Left:
*Chlorophytum
bichetii*

*Sansevieria
trifasciata
'Golden
Hahnii'*

better to plant, for example, one large *Ficus benjamina*, a few green *Sanseveiria*, a few variegated *Chlorophytum*, and a few pieces of trailing *Ficus pumila*. This provides variation in size, colour and leaf form. All of them are tough plants which should grow happily together for a long time.

When too many variegated plants are used in the same display, the effect can seem 'overdone'. A green background with variegated and pale-foliaged plants as highlights is always successful.

Timely replacement
A plant display is spoiled if it contains seedy, sick or unsightly plants. Plants that have finished flowering should be stored out of sight, and ailing plants nurtured away from the display.

The container may be too wet or dry for the plants; perhaps they are infected with some disease or have been attacked by some pest. The message is simple: remove unsightly and sick plants, and find out the cause of the problem so it can be rectified.

Keep them in check
When plants start growing well, it is necessary to think about trimming and pruning, especially the faster-growing plants that can overshadow the slower growers. Simply cut off unwanted trailers of Ivy; Mother-in-law's tongue *(Sansevieria)*, is not pruned, but surplus plants have to be removed.

It is surprising how many people have started their own houseplants from someone else's cuttings. In these cases you can look with pride at any large and healthy example, knowing that you have grown it yourself!

Happy families
Some people collect stamps or coins, and others collect plants. As a stamp-collector may specialise in one country, so a plant-collector may choose a particular plant family, or types of plant requiring similar conditions. Different plants of the same family in a trough can look attractive, and would probably have similar growth needs and habitats. A trough containing a range of dwarf-growing ferns, for example, would be interesting and look good, as would a dry tree-trunk bearing a collection of Bromeliads.

The range of plants that can be collected is almost limitless.

Potting your own houseplants

Pots and materials

Containers come in all shapes and sizes.

The needs of an indoor garden

Before using indoor plants to decorate your home, think carefully about their basic needs and buy the things which will keep plants healthy.

Start an 'indoor garden' by planting young plants in pots or troughs filled with potting compost. Make sure that the containers can hold enough soil for healthy root growth. The potting mixture should contain all the different nutrients that a plant needs to grow and remain healthy.

Preparing a potting mix from scratch is not easy as many different chemicals need to be added in precise proportions, and various ingredients such as peat, sand or loam. Luckily, you can buy a wide range of ready-mixed potting soils at any garden centre. These should have a suitable 'structure' to encourage healthy root development.

Hydroponic culture is another system for those who want to experiment, and want to cut down on plant maintenance. By using this method, all the nutrients that the plant usually gets from the soil are supplied by water.

This way you don't have to use potting soil with all its associated problems!

Terra cotta (clay) pots

There is an infinite variety of pots. The common red clay pot is today replaced by the lighter, tougher and cheaper plastic pot. Interest in clay pots has not only waned because of cost or brittleness, but because of the disadvantage of their porous walls.

Fresh air can easily penetrate the porous walls and stimulate root development. The air does not reach much further than the outer layers of the root ball, so most of the new growth happens here. Consequently, the pot soon becomes too small.

Another problem with porous walls is that water given to the plant is absorbed by the pot, and evaporates rapidly, often leaving harmful salts deposited on the pot, which can look unsightly and, more important, can cause rotting of the roots.

But clay pots do have some advantages. Excess water evaporates quickly, so there is little chance of over-watering becoming a hazard to plants. The colour of a clay pot can be an indicator of the moisture-level in the pot; with practice, you will be able to tell at a glance whether the plant needs water — a light colour indicates lower moisture and darker shades show that adequate moisture is present.

Plastic pots

Plastic pots are ideal for the home gardener. They are light, strong, easy to keep clean, and plants grow well in them.

However, their walls are non-porous, so that problems can arise through over-watering, as water is not lost through the walls. Over-wet soil could cause roots to rot, especially if the plant is a slow grower.

Pots made of 'styrofoam' probably have more disadvantages than advantages; their insulating properties are good, and so keep the soil temperature constant. Unfortunately, the material is brittle, and pieces are easily broken off. As a plant's root ball expands it can also 'burst' the pot. Smaller styrofoam pots are easily blown or knocked over as are troughs.

It is best to stick to plastic or conventional materials for containers.

Make your own containers

With some imagination you can make containers from everyday materials. For instance, a plant-trough constructed

Grow-bags can be bought, or you can make your own.

too hard to drill through, or you don't want it damaged, then you can place an extra-thick drainage layer of grit, 3–5cm (1½–2ins) deep across the base of the pot.

If you choose glass pots or bowls, remember that plant roots prefer growing in the dark, so you might have to paint the outside of the container. In fact, a bit of paint can be used to brighten up many less-attractive pots.

Wooden troughs

Functional plant troughs can easily be made from a few planks. The great advantage of making one's own troughs is that they can be 'made-to-measure'.

For a solid, long-lasting trough, hardwood at least 2.5cm (1in) thick should be used. A trough needs to be at least 25cm (10ins) deep, so try to obtain planks of at least this width for easier working.

Cut the planks to the required size, and use copper corner brackets and brass screws to hold everything together. Drill holes through the base plank for drainage.

To ensure that air can reach the underside, which promotes healthy root development, raise the trough on blocks. A 'drip-tray' may be necessary under the trough if dripping moisture may cause damage.

The inside of a new trough should be given a coat of wood-preservative (non-toxic to plants), followed by a coat of bitumen-based paint. An alternative is to line the trough with a plastic sheet.

Grow-bags

Even houseplants can be grown in grow-bags. They can be bought at nurseries and garden centres, but it is possible to make your own. Use a piece of thick, black plastic sheet, about 75cm×125cm (2½ft×4ft). Fold the sheet lengthways and sew the long sides together. Then move the seam to the underside of the tube, and sew one short side, to create a 'bag'. Apply a strip of adhesive plastic over the seams to prevent leaking. Fill the bag with a good potting soil and tie the opening with string. Cut 3 or 4 X-shaped slits on the upper side and fold the ends inwards to create the planting holes.

of bricks, lined with tar-paper, or a basket with a plastic liner?

Decorative pots can also be made from terra cotta sewerage pipes, chimney pots, and a variety of plastic and metal trays and tins.

The first requisite of a plant container is drainage. If the container is intact, holes will have to be drilled through the base of the pot. If the proposed pot is

A glazed pot needs good drainage.

Below:
A handsome plant deserves an unusual pot.

Left:
A suitable pot can be found for every interior.

Selecting containers

For the best results with your house-plants, select pots that suit the plants, and make sure that the plants are in the right situation. Most orchids will not tolerate wet soil, but grow well in a pot with many extra-large drainage and air holes in the sides, and a very porous growing medium. Any good garden centre sells these pots and mixes. There are, of course, other pots and baskets suitable for growing orchids.

Lilies and palms have completely different needs — they are better in a container in which they can stretch their roots, so do best in narrower, upright containers.

Rhododendrons and azaleas, on the other hand, prefer a shallow, wide container because they have a shallow root system.

Before making your own containers, here are a few tips. Putting castors under large containers makes for easier maintenance, allowing you to turn and move them regularly. Turning towards the light prevents plants becoming lopsided.

The drainage holes in any large containers are best situated in the sides, directly above the bottom ridge. Holes made in the bottom weaken the container. When planning to keep many large containers in a room, you must decide whether the floor or window sill will be able to withstand the additional weight. It is obvious that the least damage will be done if the containers and potting mixtures are kept as light as possible.

If you have small children or cats in the house, there is the possibility of the containers being knocked over. This can be prevented by group planting in larger containers or troughs, or in pots which can be installed in some type of holder. Hanging baskets, out of reach, provide another solution.

Look carefully before you throw things away. You might well find some suitable plant containers among your 'rubbish'!

Here are a few suggestions:
Tins: Coffee tins, biscuit tins, tea tins, etc.
Baskets: With plastic lining, baskets make

Even a dinner service can come in useful.

Kitchen 'pots' to brighten the kitchen.

excellent plant containers. Washing baskets, self-service (supermarket) baskets, picnic hampers. A very useful moveable container can be made from a supermarket trolley.

In the kitchen: Cake tins, vegetable racks, buckets, and bread bins.

Toys: Pull cars, doll's prams and baby baths.

Building materials: chimney pots, sewer pipes (these come in unusual shapes), guttering pipes and naturally, with a plastic lining, bricks.

Various: Battery cases, water tanks, plastic barrels cut in half, aquariums and styrofoam packing.

Re-potting

When you first buy plants from a florist or nursery, the containers are fine, but after a while they become too small. The roots begin to grow through the drainage holes or to show on the surface of the soil. This can result in the roots functioning less

efficiently, and proper growth being impaired. The plant then often takes on a characteristic pale colour. If you have been over-generous with watering, your plants may have to be re-potted, as the excess moisture in the soil causes the roots to rot. Plants may not survive if the necessary steps are not taken to correct the problem. All that is necessary is to re-pot into fresh potting soil, having pruned back the plant to compensate for root loss.

If an existing clay pot turns green with algae or gets a white crust of lime on it, the plant will have to be re-potted. Such a pot should not be used again, even as drainage 'crocks' for other pots.

Cacti and succulents do well in glass pots.

Amaryllis with trailing ivy.

Soil mixtures

You can make up your own potting soil mixture.

Select your soil

The ultimate success of an indoor garden depends on using the right potting mixture. The potting soil must contain all the ingredients that a particular plant needs for strong, healthy growth. The various nutrients must be present in the correct proportions, and enough air and water must be able to reach the roots.

Good potting soil must satisfy many criteria. 'Good potting soil' is a variable concept, because what might be perfectly good for one plant might not suit another at all. The choice of a potting mixture must therefore be based on the needs of the particular plants that you want to grow. No matter what plant you choose, don't simply fill the container with soil taken from your garden or the local park. This soil may suit garden plants, but why not have the correct nutrients for pot plants and in the right proportions. More importantly, garden soil often contains diseases which could easily infect new plants. Most garden soils are far too 'heavy' for use in pots, and provide poor drainage and aeration.

Types of potting soil

A wide range of potting soil mixtures are available from nurseries and garden centres. There are special mixes for ferns, cacti and orchids. It is therefore not easy to generalise about potting mixes.

For most plants the soil should not be too fine. The roots of houseplants can only anchor themselves securely in soil that has a good structure. It must also contain enough humus, as this retains moisture which is essential in the dry indoor atmosphere. A darker coloured potting mix indicates a higher humus content, but it is not true that black potting soil is better than brown.

A potting mix with a high clay content is unsuitable for the majority of pot plants. You can test the quality of a potting mix by rolling it between your fingers. If it sticks together in little balls, then it contains a high percentage of clay.

Sand is essential in a potting soil. It keeps the soil loose and aerated, and allows roots to push through it easily. It is worth taking some trouble to find out the quality of the various available potting mixtures as some are better than others.

Potting soil mixtures

If you are an experienced houseplant grower you can make up your own mixtures, tailoring them to suit the needs of specific plants. The easiest solution is to choose one of the many mixtures from the local garden centre.

The most widely accepted potting mixtures are based on 'John Innes' formulae, which specify different proportions of loam, peat and sand, with nutrient additives, for different uses (such as seed compost, and different composts for indoor and outdoor plants). These mixtures are made up by many firms, as are a variety of brand name houseplant mixtures, usually with peat (Irish or sedge peat) as their main component. These general mixes will serve the needs of a wide range of indoor plants, as they are light, airy, contain the major nutrients, and retain moisture well. Feeding will have to be undertaken after a while, as peat is not a food-rich base.

Some plants are not happy in a general potting soil. For example, *Anthuriums* need a coarse medium, containing sphagnum moss or shredded bark. *Rhododendron, Azalea, Gardenia* and *Erica* species grow best in a mixture rich in garden peat — they are very sensitive to any chalk or lime in the mix.

Orchid potting mixtures

The orchid family is large, and varies from little ground-orchids growing in open fields to tropical tree-orchids, which grow on tree

Sand loosens the mixture.

Various potting soils can be bought at a nursery. The nurseryman can advise on which mixture is most suitable for a specific group of plants. He can, for example, supply specific mixtures for cacti, ferns or orchids.

The needs of individual plants, and how to adjust the soil mixtures, or growing conditions will become familiar to you quite quickly. Lime-loving plants will soon show their dislike of an acid soil, and acid-loving plants will never grow well in a chalky soil.

Good potting soil is crumbly and dark brown in colour.

Fern roots are useful in a potting mixture for orchids.

branches, high above the ground, i.e. epiphytes. It is therefore essential to find out about the growing habits and origin of any orchid you want to grow. Many tropical orchids, such as *Cattleya*, can be grown on pieces of bark, and have spectacular flowers, but must be kept at the right temperature. Hardier species, such as *Cymbidium*, are relatively easy to grow in a normal greenhouse, and require a very coarse rooting medium, made up from any of a variety of materials, including bark chips, stone chips, charcoal, styrofoam pieces, osmunda fibre, 'lumps' of dry manure or compost, etc. The 'coarseness' of the mix is more important than the actual ingredients. Other species need a more 'composty' mix, with a high humus content.

Cactus and succulent soils

Desert plants exist under conditions of low humidity and soils lacking in humus. Desert soils are often sandy, but can be rock-hard and are not always poor in mineral nutrients. It is wrong to include compost or manure in a potting soil for true desert cacti; they are happiest in a well-drained sandy loam such as John Innes composts with extra sand.

Smaller, more fleshy succulents, such as *Crassula, Sedum,* and *Echeveria* prefer a soil with slightly more compost, and need more regular watering.

There is another section of the cactus family which occurs naturally in more humid tropical conditions. These are epiphytic cacti, growing on the trunks of trees, and have showy flowers, as for example, the Christmas Cactus (*Schlumbergia*), or the *Epiphyllum* group, both of which have flattened, thin stems that look like leaves. These plants like a peaty soil, rich in humus.

Specific mixtures

There are other groups of plants that also need particular growing mediums to thrive. *Bromeliads* are one of these. Typical *Bromeliads* are epiphytes, clinging to the trunks of trees in tropical rain forests. Therefore, they require high humidity, and a light, well-drained mixture, rich in humus. A suitable mixture would be coarse peat moss, fern root, dry manure lumps, and coarse leaf-compost, oak or beech are good, with coarse river sand. *Bromeliads* that grow naturally in the soil such as

When making up a soil mixture, it is important that the components are well mixed. This is easy when small quantities are mixed. For larger amounts, spread each item in a thin layer over the previous item, with washed river sand applied last. The spread components are then turned repeatedly, until mixed completely. Water lightly, then allow the heap to stand for a few days before use.

In certain instances clay or loam (or garden soil) may be used in a mixture. If these ingredients have not been bought from a nursery, but dug up yourself, they run the risk of containing diseases. These will have to be eliminated by sterilisation. Sterilise small amounts of soil by spreading a layer onto a baking tray, and heating in an oven for an hour at 100°C (212°F). Keep the kitchen ventilated during this process, as ammonia fumes may be released. After cooling, allow the soil to stand for about two weeks, to allow all water vapour to escape.

Above:
*Components for
a Bromeliad-
mixture.*

From top:
*Beech compost;
River sand;
Peat moss;
Rotted manure.*

Pandanus (Screw Pine), or *Ananas* (Pineapple) require a heavier mix, with more loam. Ferns and other riverside plants are happiest with a permanently-moist, light mix, with a high humus content.

Palms have a very 'stiff' root system, and are best planted in a loamy, well-drained mix, not over-rich in humus. Smaller and slower-growing palms, such as the Parlour Palm *(Neanthe bella)* and *Cocos weddeliana* enjoy a lighter mix, with compost or peat added.

Seed sowing

The requirements of seedlings and cuttings are completely different from those of established plants. They need a mixture where tender young roots can develop freely. For seedlings, the amount of nutrient in the soil is of lesser importance, as their stay in the seed trays is not long.

When sowing seeds, make sure that the top 1.5cm (½in) of soil is finely sieved to remove all lumps. If the compost has clay or loam in it, the addition of peat and river sand will lighten it.

Soil mixture for cuttings

The most common way of increasing many houseplants is by taking cuttings. Yet another soil mixture is needed for this. A safe, general mix for cuttings is equal parts Irish peat and washed river sand, well mixed and placed in a pot or tray although perlite or vermiculite are also used.

The river sand promotes the development of *callus* at the base of the cutting. Too much sand can, in fact, produce all *callus* and little or no root! Rooting of most cuttings is greatly encouraged when heating cables are present in the soil. Humidity should be kept high, but drainage must be good.

Storing potting soils

It is always useful to have a supply of potting soil handy at all times, to avoid having to keep on making up small mixes each time you have a plant to pot up. The potting soil should be stored in such a way that its good properties are not lost. If it is stored under too-damp or too-dry conditions, its air and water-holding capacities could be impaired. This could result in water draining straight through the mix, without being absorbed at all. With a

damp, sticky mix, the water can stand on the surface, and prevent air from penetrating the soil. Refuse bins make ideal storage containers, as do larger plastic bags, but allow a certain amount of air to enter, by punching a few small holes in the sides of the bag.

Components of potting mixtures

It is always useful to know the characteristics of the component materials in a potting mixture:

Leafmould: Partially rotted leaves of deciduous trees, especially oak and beech, which are slightly acidic, high in humus, and a good soil conditioner.

Loam: Reasonably fertile topsoil of varying quality and composition.

River sand: Sometimes called 'sharp sand'. River sand should have been 'washed' to remove impurities and very fine grains. Sand lightens a mixture and aids drainage and aeration.

Peat moss: Brown fibrous peat (Irish Peat) has a low food value, but is water-retentive, and a good soil conditioner and lightener. Used as a base for houseplant mixtures.

Sedge Peat: A finer, very dark material, with a high humus content. Also a good conditioner.

Fern fibre: (Osmundo fibre), derived from roots of certain ferns, is used in coarse mixes, for epiphytic Orchids and Bromeliads.

Sphagnum moss: Living moss, kept green for a long while by watering. Used for lining baskets and for rooting of certain plants on vertical 'beds' or poles.

Drainage and potting up

New clay pots should be thoroughly soaked in water before use.

The importance of drainage

Healthy plant growth depends on good drainage. Over-wet soils are inadequately aerated, and roots can soon start rotting, with disastrous consequences for the plant.

Traditionally a drainage layer is put in the bottom of a container, made up of broken clay pots (crocks) or crushed stone, to keep the drainage holes unblocked. This practice is becoming less common today, particularly when using peat-based composts, which drain uniformly. Pots are simply filled with the mix, and after the first watering no compost escapes via the drainage holes.

Preparing for transplanting

At some stage, a healthy plant is going to become too large for its container, and will need to be re-potted into something larger. This is easy enough if you have your new pot and the other necessary materials. Generally, the best time for transplanting is spring and early summer.

First, you need a working surface, where it won't matter if you make a mess, and where everything can be gathered together, before you begin. You will need the right sized pots, a suitable potting soil, drainage crocks or stone chips, a watering can and a sharp knife.

Young plants require a slightly larger pot than they were originally in, but if the new pot is too big then root development may be too rapid. This can produce excessive foliage at the expense of blooming, or evenly-spaced branching.

New terra cotta pots should be soaked in water for some hours before being used, so that the porous clay can absorb enough moisture not to dry-out the newly-potted plant. Clay or plastic pots that have been used before must be cleaned well, to eliminate any chance of contamination from fungus or insect eggs. Scrubbing with washing soda is effective, but the pots must be thoroughly rinsed to prevent damage to new roots.

Young plants are re-potted into a slightly larger pot.

Use a sharp knife to loosen the roots.

Tapping the pot on the bench should free the root ball.

Work fresh soil around the sides of the roots.

Removing the old pot

Before removing the plant from its pot, give it a good watering or, better still, stand the pot in a basin of water until air bubbles cease to appear from the soil-surface. The root ball, which is now thoroughly moist can be removed from the pot without breaking up. Root-damage must be kept to a minimum, so that the plant is not set back in any way.

For the best results follow this procedure. Loosen the roots from the side of the pot with a sharp knife, place a flat hand over the soil-surface, with the stem between the index and middle fingers. Turn the pot upside down and tap the underside of the pot to loosen the root ball. If this does not work, tap the (inverted) pot rim against a firm surface and, in most cases, the root ball will be freed. But if the roots are still firmly attached to the pot, then the chances are that the roots are growing through the drainage holes. In this case it is best to gently break the pot, or cut it open carefully.

When re-potting fully mature plants, it is advisable to remove some of the existing root ball to make space for fresh potting soil (which will give the plant a boost). To reduce the size of the root ball, loosen some of the soil gently and tease out some of the roots. A portion of these can be cut off with a sharp knife, and the plant then placed in the container, and soil pushed down this newly-created space.

Drainage in pots and troughs

In any plant container, it is essential to ensure that surplus water can be drained away, otherwise root damage will occur after a while through a lack of oxygen reaching the roots. Therefore, when re-potting make sure that moisture can pass through the soil, and that it can also pass out of the container.

Clay pots normally have a central drainage hole, which can be kept open by placing a piece of broken pot (crock or shard) over the hole, to prevent soil from blocking it. Remember that earthworm casts are a common cause of blocked drainage holes. Plastic pots usually have several drainage holes, so have less trouble with blockage, and can simply be filled with a peaty-type potting mix.

Waterlogging of troughs can be overcome to some extent by placing a layer of clay pellets or crushed stone across the base. The best thing is to have adequate drainage holes, and to use drip-trays to catch the surplus moisture.

Filling the new pot

Place just enough potting soil in the new pot (over the drainage layer), so that when the root ball of the plant is placed onto it, its top surface lies about 1.5cm (½in) below the rim of the pot. Hold the plant firmly in this position with one hand, and fill-in around the sides of the pot with potting soil up to the surface of the root ball and lightly over it. Tap the pot lightly on the work surface to settle the soil, and then water thoroughly. If necessary, top up any subsidence with potting mix, but make sure that there is at least a depth of 1.5cm (½in) below the rim, to facilitate watering and avoid spillage and mess.

The roots of houseplants are seldom seen. If they become diseased or damaged, this is reflected in the condition of the above-ground foliage; it is then often too late. During re-potting, you have the opportunity of examining the roots. Remove any diseased or damaged sections with a sharp knife.

A sturdy work bench is useful when working with plants.

Re-potting cacti

The re-potting of a prickly cactus can be a tricky business, and you will have to devise ways of protecting your hands. With smaller plants, leather gloves may be adequate, but larger plants will have to be 'wrapped' with cloth or pads of crumpled newspaper. If the plant is firmly rooted it can sometimes be loosened by pushing up through the drainage holes with a stick or pencil.

Remember that cacti have sensitive roots, and can rot easily so do not water at all for a week or more after transplanting.

A plant in bloom or in bud is expending considerable energy for the formation of flowers and seeds. At this stage, plants would find it difficult to recover from the trauma of being transplanted. It is better to wait until after the flowering or fruiting.

Hydroponics

Indoor gardens without soil

For most people the time spent caring for plants is pleasurable but for others it is a tedious chore! When a plant's daily attention is neglected the results soon show in deteriorating growth or poor blooming.

If you find plant maintenance tedious, hydroponic culture can provide an answer. In this system, the normal potting soil is replaced by a nutrient solution, and this does away with a great deal of maintenance work.

Time-consuming transplanting can be forgotten, and watering is only necessary at intervals of two to four weeks. In fact, this system is so effective that hydroponically-grown plants grow far better than plants in normal soil. It is therefore not surprising that hydroponic troughs, in spite of their higher initial cost, are becoming popular, particularly in larger organisations.

Background facts

The basis of modern indoor hydroponics was started some thirty years ago by a Swiss, Gerard Baumann. He undertook extensive tests with plants in water, and after 10 years was able to market the first modern 'hydro-troughs'. Initially, it was only commercial firms that expressed an interest in the new system, which obviously cost more than conventional plantings. This time-saving was obviously attractive for offices and factories where time is valuable.

The private individual has only recently 'discovered' hydroponics. The variety of special pots and troughs designed for this water-based system, which are available from modern garden centres, confirm this new interest.

What exactly is hydroponics?

As with all living things plants must have food to grow and develop. Nourishment is usually obtained from the soil but not always. It is quite feasible for the essential plant nutrients to be dissolved in water and for this to be absorbed by the plant. This is the basis of hydroponics.

Naturally, there is a little more to the practice than simply filling a pot with nutrient-rich water and dropping the plant into this. First, some form of 'anchorage' must be provided for the roots. Next, it is important that the root system is adapted to hydroponics. Roots that have developed to absorb nutrients from the soil will not normally be able to function in a more liquid environment. Therefore, conventionally grown plants cannot suddenly be converted to being grown on the hydroponic system.

*When nurserymen
produce new plants for
hydro-culture, they often
grow the cuttings (or
seeds) in individual,
highly absorbent blocks
of peat. Rooting is
generally quicker than in
water, and there is no
problem with
transplanting. 'Water
roots' can be easily
developed when the
rooted blocks are
established in hydroponic
containers.*

Clay granules for anchorage

Under normal growing conditions, a major
function of the roots is to provide a firm
anchor-hold in the soil, and so keep its
stems upright. In the hydroponic system the
supporting role of the soil is replaced by an
inert medium, such as gravel, vermiculite,
or baked clay pellets. These pellets were
originally only used in the building
industry, but are now produced extensively
for the hydroponic industry. They are able
to absorb moisture and the nutrient
solution, and release it slowly. The spaces
between the granules ensure that more than
enough air can reach the roots. All the
conditions for healthy root development are
thus present.

Pots and troughs for hydroponics

A 'hydropot' or trough is different from a
normal pot. A water-permeable inner pot
must stand, to about a third of its depth, in
a lower tray of nutrient solution, and these
two pots are contained in an outer
waterproof pot or trough.

There are many newly-developed pots and
casings for indoor plant growing — cone-
shaped, plastic inner pots are very
practical, and were specially developed for
hydroponic use. Similar pots are made of
softer plastic materials, but have the
disadvantage that they don't last as long as
the plastic cones, and their walls are likely
to be penetrated by the roots.

Air can reach the roots through the slits
and holes in the bases of these inner
containers. Adequate aeration is essential
for healthy growth.

You can buy matching outer containers for
the cone-shaped inner pots that were
developed for this system. It is just as
effective to use an earthenware jar, bowl or
vase as a water reservoir.

Plastic flower-troughs, moulded in one
piece are the best choice for outer cases,
and don't leak, unlike many 'joined'
troughs made up of separate sections.

Exterior containers of steel or clear glass
are not to be recommended. The nutrient
solution, when it comes into contact with
metal, could react and give off vapours
harmful to the plants. In such a case, an
additional inner trough of plastic or glass
would be needed, to keep the solution from
making contact.

If transparent glass containers are used,
another problem arises. The light that

reaches the water results in a growth of
green algae, which is unsightly and
unhealthy. You can get around this
problem by using a second container inside
the first, and filling the space between with
brown clay granules. Sunlight can also be
excluded from the interior of a glass trough
by painting the outside, but this doesn't
look attractive.

Aiding the system

In a hydroponic system, it is usually
enough to supplement the water at intervals
of two to four weeks. To determine the
optimum period, a water level indicator is a
useful accessory.

Most models of level indicator consist of a
transparent, enclosed glass tube containing
a calibrated float, intended to coincide with
markings on the tube.

The instrument is pushed down between the
clay pellets so that its base touches the
bottom of the water reservoir. It must be
long enough for its vital upper section to
project above the surface of the pellets. The
float and indicator then rise and fall
according to the water level and this level
can be directly 'read' on the instrument. So
when the arrow indicates the minimum
level water must be added until the
maximum level is reached.

The addition of water to a larger
hydroponic trough is normally done
through a 'filler tube'. This is a vertical
plastic tube or pipe installed when the clay
pellets are put in, and extends from the
base of the reservoir to the surface, with a
plug to close off its opening. Thus, when
water is added, it is fed directly to the
water reservoir.

In hydro-cultural systems, clay pellets take the place of soil in providing anchorage for roots.

Some plants are more difficult to adapt to hydro-culture. In these cases, roots must be allowed to gradually redevelop, with normal watering, until new roots are well established in the hydro-culture medium.

Planting without soil

The 'planting up' of 'hydro-plants' is not simple. It is best to use one of the specially adapted pots. The first step is to add a layer of clay pellets which is thick enough, so that when the base of the plant's root ball is resting on it, the top is just below the rim of the pot. Lightly loosen the outer roots and then fill in all the spaces with clay pellets. But be careful that the fine root tips are damaged as little as possible.

The potted up plants are then placed either individually into outer pots, or grouped in a trough (the former is easier). If the specially developed hydro-pots are used, then all you have to do is insert the inner pot into its outer container. If the outer pot is a bit big the surplus space can be filled with clay granules. Now you can pour water with its dissolved nutrients into the outer reservoir pot, until the lower third of the inner pot is immersed.

If the plants are being grouped in a trough, then each plant must be surrounded by clay granules up to just below the rim of the outer trough (it is in this medium that the filler pipe should be installed). It can look attractive if you replace the surface layer of clay granules with a layer of natural stone chip or other crushed stone.

Feeding via the water

'Hydro-plants' take up nutrient requirements via their water supply. This food supply must be dissolved in the water in exact proportions. Good garden centres will stock carefully formulated and balanced nutrient mixtures for hydroponic use, in the form of tablets, powders and liquids. Normal houseplant fertiliser is not suitable for hydroponic use.

When a 'hydro-plant' suffers a deficiency in a certain nutrient, it will develop the appropriate symptoms (as in the case of soil-grown plants), either of foliage colour change, or deviant growth.

An excess of nutrients is usually indicated by stagnant growth, smelly water and white deposits on the clay granules. To rectify this problem, you should first remove the 'polluted' water and replace it with fresh solution. As the clay granules will have absorbed the 'too-strong' solution everything will have to be removed and replaced and the plant's roots will need careful rinsing.

Watering

The nutrient solution in the reservoir of the outer container, initially covering a third of the depth of the inner container, is gradually absorbed by the plants. This change in levels is indicated by the water level indicator. After two to three weeks it is possible that the water level will drop to below the level of the inner pot. At this stage the water needs topping-up. If it is left too long then plants will start showing symptoms of drought. Early topping-up is not a good thing as during the cycle of growth and water-replenishment the air should reach beneath the inner pot to aid the plant's respiration.

Smaller hydro-pots, without filler-tubes, are best topped-up by simply pouring the nutrient solution through the clay pellets. If the container has a fitted filler pipe remove its plug and pour the water down the tube until the correct level is indicated on the water level indicator.

Periodic refreshment

A hydroponic tank needs cleaning out about once every six months. First, empty the water reservoir in the outer container. In larger containers (that cannot be easily tipped over) the usual methods of draining are siphoning, via the filler tube, or with the aid of one of the modern, plastic hand-operated pumps. After draining the solution is replaced by fresh water which is then also removed. After this, a new nutrient mixture can be added.

If tap water has a high lime content, it is a good idea to boil the water first, to allow some of the excess lime to settle-out in the kettle. Freshly collected rainwater (from a heavy downpour) is also suitable.

Which plants?

Generally, hydroponic culture is suited to virtually all houseplants. Even water-shy cactus types can be grown in hydro-pots. You cannot, however, simply take a plant that is growing in soil, put it in a hydro-pot, and expect success. Plants normally require a period of adjustment, as roots that have developed in potting soil will not function in a nutrient solution.

Plants that have been propagated and grown in a liquid medium, have developed a root system adapted to this form of nutrition. Anyone who has grown cuttings in water will have seen such roots. They are thick and soft, and have long and fine root-hairs. Hydroponically-grown plants depend on such roots for their food absorption.

Soil-grown plants can be transformed into hydro-plants' but the root system has to be developed slowly, via a biological route, into a 'hydro-culture' root system.

Commercial hydroponic pot plant growers use expensive installations to develop their 'hydro-plants' and this explains why they usually cost more than other indoor plants. This is also a good reason for trying your hand at producing your own hydro-plants.

Your own 'hydro-plants'

The simplest method of starting-off new plants is by cuttings, especially healthy tips, of the plants you want. Cut each piece, using a very sharp knife (or razor-blade), just below a bud (or eye) and about 5–10cm (2–4ins) in length. Place the cuttings in a glass or jar of water, immediately after cutting. Some plants will start rooting fairly quickly but others may take several weeks.

If the jars with cuttings are placed in a warm, light situation, rooting will be encouraged. Once the roots have started forming you will need to start adding very diluted nutrient to the water to sustain the 'new' growing plant. As the roots develop further, the cuttings can be transferred to hydro-pots, and clay granules carefully placed between and around the young root system.

Converting plants to hydro-culture

It is possible to take healthy young plants (up to 2 years old) that are growing in potting soil and convert them into plants adapted to hydroponic growing methods. This is how to do it:

It is obvious that plants grown hydroponically will not do well in a smoky or stuffy atmosphere, or in a climate that lacks humidity. In these respects, hydro-plants do not differ from 'ordinary' pot-grown houseplants. As far as watering and ventilation are concerned the same rules apply as for any other plant.

Remove the selected plant from its pot, and rub the root ball between your hands to loosen the soil. Wash the root ball thoroughly in a bucket of water (not ice-cold) to remove all traces of soil.

The plant can now be planted in a hydro-pot.

The existing normal feeding roots of the plant are gradually replaced by roots able to exist in the 'watery' environment. Do not become alarmed if, during the transition period, leaves turn yellow or fall off. Whilst this is often unavoidable, given enough moisture, most plants will survive this process.

Semi-automatic watering

For the plant lover who finds the idea of converting to hydroponic culture too daunting, semi-hydroponic methods may be the answer. With such a system the plant stays in its own soil and pot but the water is fed to the plant from below, so that watering is limited to perhaps once per month, and then only a dash. It is also easy enough to convert existing plants gradually to the new system. There are several semi-hydroponic systems available. Some are based on water reservoirs, some on wicks (between pot and water), and others on capillary watering. The simplest of these consists of a special synthetic 'capillary' mat, on which the plants are placed. They root through the base of the pot onto the mat and only the mat is watered.

With more regular watering, some potting mixes may remain too damp. This is not good for the roots, which prefer to alternate moisture with a bit of drying out. This, of course, is also important for aerating the roots. It is more difficult to establish an exact water-to-air balance in soil than in an inert medium, such as perlite or clay granules.

Special pots and troughs

Various plant containers have been developed for the different hydro-cultural systems. In most cases it is simpler to buy a container with plant at a garden centre. These usually have full instructions so all you have to do is find a suitable spot at home.

Do look at the range of pots and self-watering devices at a large garden centre, to give you some idea of the scope for experimenting with this system.

Is hydro-culture the answer?

If you are going to make comparisons between different growing-systems you should first consider the merits and disadvantages of water-based growing systems.

Advantages	Disadvantages
Hydro-plants need little maintenance.	Hydro-cultural systems are expensive initially.
Plants have a better chance of survival, as they have a constant nutrient and water supply.	Hydro-plants are not as readily available as normal plants.
Plants usually appear healthier and more lush, with the more intensive feeding.	Because of the lack of maintenance, contact is lost with the plant.
Disturbances from transplanting do not occur.	

A simple method of automatic watering can be arranged in a watertight vase or jug. Fill the lower third of the jug with brown clay granules, and insert a filler tube and water level indicator. Over the clay, and penetrating to the bottom of the jug, lay a piece of nylon mat. Fill the rest of the pot with soil and plant the plants. Water in the normal way, through the soil, for the first three months and then via the filler tube. This way the water arrives directly at the base, where the plant will have developed coarser 'water roots'. For best results, the water level should be about 1.5cm (½in) below the soil.

The climate in your home

Even a small window sill can be used for plants.

Light

Imitating nature

All living things, including plants, need food, water, light and fresh air, to stay alive. Nature takes care of most of the needs of plants that grow outside, with a little help from us! The situation is reversed indoors. Here the climate is governed by the whims of the occupants, and the 'captive' plants have no choice but to accept whatever conditions exist. The air may be smoky or stale, and the central heating turned up or down at will.

If you want plants to share your home you will have to take into account the plants particular needs, and try to create a climate where the plants are happy and grow well. This may need a bit of organising, and some knowledge of plants and their growth.

It is not always easy to simulate natural conditions. You must water the plants at the right times, the air should be fresh but not excessively dry, and the temperature must be controlled. As a reward for your care and diligence, your home will become more pleasant with its flourishing greenery.

To a certain extent plants change the 'climate' in your home by adding to the humidity and giving off oxygen, thereby helping to improve the air you breathe.

Sunlight as a source of energy

Plants derive their vital energy requirements from the inexhaustible supply of sunlight. While the sun is shining, and the temperature is not too low, there is a complicated chemical process taking place in the green leaves of plants. Within the cells that make up a leaf are millions of minute grains of chlorophyll, which are green and give the leaf its colour. Here, with energy absorbed from sunlight, the plant combines carbon-dioxide with nutrient-rich water from the roots, to create sugars. In this process, oxygen is released from the leaves back into the atmosphere,

and the sugars are distributed to other parts of the plant, and used for growth. During the day, the plant makes more sugar than it can use at once, and converts the surplus to starch, which it stores. This whole process is called photosynthesis. At night, when this process cannot take place, the starches are converted back into sugars, to allow the plant to continue growing. This is why healthy plant growth needs alternate periods of light and dark, in the right proportions. The quality and intensity of the light is very important.

The sunlight through your window

The majority of houseplants need good light conditions, if they are to remain

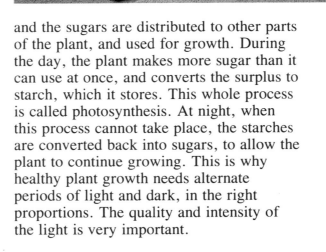

Some plants need less light than others.

Plants in the home are a comfort to its inhabitants.

healthy. This does not mean that they have to have full sunlight shining directly onto their leaves. Full sunlight through a pane of glass can cause the temperature to reach levels far higher than a plant can withstand. Most rooms have places out of direct sunlight where there is still enough indirect light. If the only convenient place for keeping plants is in full sunlight, then precautions will have to be taken to prevent scorching of the foliage. This can best be done by using sun-filter curtains or Venetian blinds. Glass only allows certain parts of the sun's rays to pass through it, and during the winter months, the intensity of light would be insufficient for healthy

plant growth. In these cases, the plants tend to become pale and spindly, and become more susceptible to disease and pest attack. Obviously plants that come from hot, sunny climates are usually the first to suffer when conditions are too dark.

Lack of natural light in a room can be corrected by installing special 'grow-lamps'.

Artificial sunlight

An ordinary light bulb, such as the one in your reading lamp, cannot be used as a substitute for sunlight. The energy it gives off is largely heat energy (infra-red), which plants cannot use in their growth-processes.

Many houseplants have the unfortunate habit of growing towards the light, which leaves you with a view of the back of the foliage, and the plant becomes lop-sided. This can be countered by regularly turning the pot a few degrees at a time. This trick should not be tried with budding or flowering plants, as they are likely to drop their blooms after being moved. The problem can sometimes be solved by placing the plants against a pale background, or by placing a lamp behind them, so that the light is not only coming from one direction.

Plants which are lit by normal light bulbs develop weaker, stretched stems, and diminishing foliage. What plants need is ultra-violet light, a constituent of sunlight, which is available in special light bulbs and fluorescent tubes. These tubes emit a very hard light and are commonly used, together with normal fluorescent tubes, for general lighting. They have to be located fairly close to the plants to be of any benefit, so are best installed as part of the display. These grow-lights are available from larger garden centres and electrical suppliers. Other more specialised and more expensive light sources, such as mercury vapour lamps, sodium lamps, etc. can be used, but need expert advice before use.

Light requirements of different plants
The amount of light needed for healthy plant growth varies according to the type of plant. Plants such as *Hedera, Aspidistra* and *Philodendron* need relatively little light, while begonias and cacti are happiest with the maximum light possible.

In the next page you will find a chart showing the comparative amounts of light needed by the better-known plant groups. The 'Lux' rating is used by lighting experts as a measurement of light intensity, so the higher the figure the stronger the light. Now you will have to determine the light intensities in various parts of your home, then think in terms of what light each of

A Clivia needs strong light for blooming.

A plant lamp can make even a dark corner suitable for plants.

A Sansevieria is happy with little light.

A plant lamp can also replace sunlight.

your plants needs. What might be an adequately lit spot for one could be a dark corner to another.

A rough indication of the light intensities in different rooms in your home can be obtained by using a photographic light-meter. You can then compare these readings with the light requirements indicated in the chart, and so find the best locations for your plants.

Cacti and succulents need plenty of light for healthy growth.

Comparative light requirements

An indication of the 'Lux' light requirements of the main houseplant groups

800 Aspidistra, Fatshedera, Fatsia, Hedera, Maranta, Neoregelia, Nephrolepsis, Philodendron, Raphidophora, Spathiphyllum *(non-flowering)*, Syngogium.

1000 Aechmea *(non-fl)*, Aglaonema, Anthurium, Billbergia *(non-fl)*, Chamaedorea, Chlorophytum, Cissus, Clivia *(non-fl)*, Cordyline, Cryptanthus, Cyperus, Dieffenbachia, Dizygotheca, Dracaena, Nidularium, Sansevieria, Saxifraga, Schefflera, Tradescantia, Vriesia, Zebrina.

2500 Aechmiea *(in flower)*, Ananas, Anthurium *(in fl)*, Aphelandra, Begonia *(non-fl)*, Billbergia *(in fl)*, Cactus *(non-fl)*, Croton, Hoya, Peperomia, Spathiphyllum *(in fl)*, Yucca.

5000 Aphelandra *(in fl)*, Begonia *(in fl)*, Cacti *(in fl)*, Clivia *(in fl)*, Hoya *(in fl)*.

It is essential for plants to have alternating periods of light and dark. If grow-lamps were left on all the time, photosynthesis would continue without a break, and result in growth-deformities. Some hours of darkness are needed as a 'rest' period, when other growth processes occur. There are no general rules for the exact number of hours of dark or light; foliage plants are usually pretty adaptable. The hours of light and dark are more critical for many flowering plants, such as Chrysanthemum, Azalea, Poinsettia and Kalanchoe, and commercial growers frequently have to adjust the hours of light or dark artificially.

This group will tolerate fairly low light conditions.

57

Air

Importance of fresh air to plants

Plants breathe continuously, day and night. During this process they absorb oxygen which they need for respiration, where starches are converted into sugars providing energy. This energy is used by the plant to perform its many functions. It may sound strange, but plants have many different 'jobs' to do. The growth of shoots, roots and leaves requires energy; even the opening and closing of flower-buds takes energy, as do the tendrils of vines looking for support, or leaves turning to face the light.

Plants don't have lungs; all parts respire. To allow the roots to breathe there must be enough fresh air in the potting soil. Watering houseplants supplies the soil with a certain amount of the air it needs. Air can also enter the soil via the walls of clay pots. The above-ground parts of the plant absorb the necessary oxygen through minute openings in the leaf and soft stem surfaces. This can only occur when the air contains enough oxygen, and is not too polluted or smoky. Dust or other pollutants block the pores on the leaves which restricts the oxygen uptake.

The rate of respiration is not constant. As the temperature rises, so does the respiration rate. During very low temperatures respiration almost ceases. Whereas, during high temperatures, the demand for sugars (to convert into energy) may be greater than the quantity which the plant can produce. This is the time to help your plants to cool off a bit, by shading or syringing.

Tropical plants growing in our somewhat darker climate may have problems with respiration and photosynthesis, with a subsequent lower sugar assimilation.

The imbalance can be corrected by providing artificial lighting to stimulate photosynthesis. When the plant converts sugars to energy, the products given off are carbon dioxide and water vapour.

Fresh air indoors

Fresh air is of vital importance to your plants indoors. Smoky and stale air may not contain enough oxygen resulting in 'stressful' respiration for the plant. This polluted air may also allow less sunlight through, which could result in reduced photosynthesis.

It is impossible to keep a room dust-free. Whenever you settle back into an armchair a fine cloud of dust is released; whenever a door is opened dust is blown up and around from all the surfaces. And, of course, there is the dust created by sweeping and cleaning! Some of this dust comes to rest on the leaves of plants, and blocks the pores which the plant needs for the uptake of oxygen and carbon dioxide and the release of other products. It is therefore necessary to clean a plant's leaves regularly. Do this by syringing the foliage with water about once a fortnight. The same effect can be obtained by placing the plants out in the rain (provided it is not too cold). Large-leaved plants can easily have their foliage rinsed off by hand, with a soft cloth or sponge. Make sure that the plant is allowed to dry off after washing, to prevent mildew or other fungus infection.

Fresh air is of vital importance to your indoor garden.

Letting the fresh air in

To obtain maximum pleasure from an indoor garden you will have to air your house regularly. This isn't only necessary for the plants' healthy growth, but also for the health of your homes' occupants. But be careful! Plants are susceptible to sudden changes in temperature, and draughts. In the summer, when the air has been warmed to a moderate temperature by the sun, airing can be done by opening windows and doors. This is not possible in winter, when the differences between internal and external temperatures are too great for plants. However, you can open a window in an adjoining room, to allow the air to warm-up first, before reaching your plants. If you have a lot of plants, you might think about installing an air-conditioner, which heats up fresh air before blowing it into the room.

Water

Evaporation

Lime, nitrogen and other nutrients cannot be absorbed by the plant's roots in a dry state. They need to be dissolved in water. The minerals present in a good potting mixture need to be in a soluble form before they can be absorbed. Some of the water taken up by the plant is used within the plant. Some is passed through the system and evaporated into the air through the leaves (this process is called transpiration). When the temperature increases, so the amount of water lost by evaporation increases accordingly. Thus, in hot weather, the rate of transpiration may exceed the rate at which the plant can absorb water, in which case the plant starts to wilt. If the water supply in the soil is also inadequate, wilting may become extreme, and the plant could die. Drooping leaves are a sure sign that either the plant is too hot or is lacking water.

Applying water

Since it doesn't rain indoors, your plants are totally dependant on you for the water they receive. The easiest way of watering a few plants is with a small watering can. The biggest danger to houseplants is being given too much water. Misplaced kindness, by way of watering even when the soil is already damp, results in water-logging, and consequent lack of root aeration. Plastic or glazed containers dry out more slowly than clay pots, and so are more prone to over-damp soil where the roots cannot function properly.

Too much watering could mean the end for your houseplants! At first their leaves may droop, then drop off, or wither, and then the plant dies.

You can save a plant from water-logged soil, if too many roots have not already rotted. First, remove all the soggy soil

A reservoir of water against a radiator panel is a useful way of increasing humidity.

Cacti are perfectly adapted for drought conditions.

Plants in small pots can be watered via their saucers.

Regular syringing with water reduces transpiration, and so reduces the task of the roots.

from around the roots, and cut off rotted parts. Then add drainage material to a pot and replant with a light soil. Keep watering to a minimum until there are signs of recovery.

Common-sense watering

The water needs of a plant depend on certain variable factors, so that there cannot be any definite rules regarding the frequency of watering or the amounts needed. Plants with large leaves will need more water than those with small leaves as they have a larger leaf surface area, and will therefore lose more water by transpiration.

There are certain plants that have developed means of trapping or conserving moisture, so as to lose it as slowly as possible. Some have hairs on their leaves, to trap any moisture and hold on to it. Others have developed ways of making the

leaf surface as small as possible in times of drought by rolling up their leaves, folding them together, or letting them droop. Some plants deliberately drop their leaves. Cacti are in a class of their own: they don't have any leaves, and what may appear to be leaves are usually modified stems. These adaptations certainly work and these plants survive on very little water.

The climate in your home also plays a role in influencing watering frequency, by its affect on the rate the soil dries out, and the rate at which the plant needs to absorb moisture from the soil. In a warm, dry atmosphere, plants will transpire more than in a cooler, moist atmosphere, and will consequently need more water.

Practical judgment

You will have to learn by experience when a plant needs water. Use your eyes and fingers. If the plant's leaves are drooping

Plants with plentiful foliage transpire more than those with fewer leaves.

and the soil feels dry, then the plant needs water badly. Another way of determining whether a plant needs water is by feeling the weight of the pot. When the pot feels light it lacks moisture, whereas pots that contain moisture will feel proportionately heavier.

Feeling the soil surface with your fingers is still the most reliable way of checking on the degree of moisture in the soil.

Other water-testing methods

If you can't trust your own senses to tell you when a plant needs water you'll have to use other methods. A moisture-meter, purchased from a garden centre, can be used to determine the exact soil-moisture content, simply by pushing the probe into the soil. A cheaper, but somewhat less efficient method of judging the moisture content of the soil, involves the laying of strips of newspaper onto the surface of the soil. If they absorb moisture, then the plant doesn't need water; if they stay dry, then water the plant.

Thorough soaking

If your plants are drooping, despite regular watering, perhaps each dose is not enough to reach all the roots. It is better to give a thorough soaking less frequently than too little too often.

However, you do have to be careful of overdoing the soaking. The water that ends up in the saucer or drip-tray isn't doing the plant any good. In fact, too much watering can be harmful by washing out too many of the nutrients dissolved in the soil-mix. Excess moisture is usually present at the expense of soil air and so the roots suffer. If you occasionally stand the plants in a basin of water up to their rims, and wait until the soil surface turns moist, then you can be certain of a thorough soaking.

Holiday watering

Whenever you have to leave your home for a few days, watering your plants can be a problem. During milder weather give them all a good soaking before you leave and again when you return. Don't leave them standing in bowls of water while you're away as roots can soon start rotting. You may find on your return that some plants are very dry and that when you water them it simply runs straight through the pot without being absorbed by the soil at all. The cure for this is to immerse the pot in a

basin of water for a while and wait for air-bubbles to stop rising from the root ball. After removal from the water, and having been allowed to drain, the plant should present no more problems.

Types of water

The quality and taste of water differ from place to place. The main reason for the differences in chemical content lies in the predominant rock and soil types of the region: chalky, acid moorland, sandy, etc.

Today, most homes are connected to a 'mains' water supply, which has been purified or treated to some extent against harmful organisms, but will still bear the characteristics of local geology. Thus, it may have a high lime content (hard water), be fairly saline, or, in some areas, slightly acidic. Some plants are less tolerant of specific chemical excesses or shortages in the soil (and water). For example, rhododendrons and other acid-loving plants react to hard water by reduced growth-vigour and some yellowing of foliage.

Plants in the countryside get all their water from the rain, and this is also a suitable source for houseplants. It should be clean though, and in towns and industrial areas it is often polluted. Before collecting rainwater from a roof, let the shower first wash off the worst impurities. Rainwater of reasonable purity is preferable to mains water for houseplants as it is not likely to contain excesses of any particular chemical. Be careful of using river or stream water as this could also be polluted, or even be harder than your tap-water, if it runs over chalk.

Water temperature

Whatever its source, the water you use on your houseplants shouldn't be ice-cold, straight from the tap. Watering with cold water cools down the potting soil and the roots do not function as efficiently as they should. Keep a bucket filled with water in a warm place, and as long as you keep it topped-up, you will always have a supply at the correct 'room-temperature'. If you use this method of storing water in a bucket, and the local water is 'hard', you can reduce this effect by suspending a cloth bag filled with peat into it for a few days. Some of the lime in the water will be 'drawn out' by the peat, and the water will be more neutral by the time you use it on your plants.

If the soil is very dry stand the pots in water.

Root damage during transplanting cannot always be avoided. Damaged roots cannot absorb water, so watering should be adjusted accordingly. Be less generous than usual for the first few weeks after re-potting. After re-potting plants may transpire at their normal rate, but will wilt if their roots are not fully functional. Light syringing could be beneficial by helping to reduce the transpiration rate, and so give the roots a chance to develop.

Houseplants enjoy a light sprinkling of rain when the weather is not too cold.

Maintaining humidity

Many of the common houseplants have tropical origins where the climate is always humid and never too cold. The warm, dry atmosphere in our homes is hardly what they're used to! Although most types are able to adapt to conditions in our homes their natural preferences should be borne in mind. This applies particularly during winter when the central heating is turned up and the humidity in the air can drop below 25%. You can increase the indoor humidity by placing bowls of water round and about, and the closer to heaters and radiators the better. In a warm room the water evaporates and increases the humidity.

Special humidifiers which are attached to the sides of radiator panels are more efficient. Because of their closeness to the heat-source, these reservoirs of water can evaporate quite quickly.

With moisture-loving plants in a drier room, you can place their pots inside larger pots and fill the surrounding space with peat. This is then kept damp and the moisture, which peat retains well, slowly evaporates and increases the humidity around the plant.

A similar humidifying effect for individual plants can be achieved by placing the plant on a stand which is then placed in a shallow container of water, so that the rising evaporated moisture benefits the plant.

Benefits of syringing

We have already mentioned that syringing is good for the removal of dust from the surface of leaves. Spraying and syringing with water has another useful purpose. Some of the sprayed moisture can be absorbed by the plant, some runs off to aid watering, and some evaporates into the air to benefit the humidity level.

Remember that droplets of moisture staying on the leaves after spraying can act like a magnifying glass when the sun in shining, causing scorching, with the resultant ugly yellow marks. Avoid this by spraying early in the morning, before the sun has any strength, or spray only on cloudy days.

Plants in bloom should not be syringed as the blooms could be adversely affected.

Some of the more harmful pests, such as red spider mite and scale insects, prefer dry conditions; regular syringing of susceptible plants can discourage infestation.

Water is best applied to the soil surface. In this way it can gently percolate down through the soil taking with it air and nutrients for the roots. Do not water your plants each time by filling their drainage saucer with water, as it could result in stagnation around the roots. Only moisture-loving plants should ever have water standing in their saucers.

Tropical foliage loves regular syringing with water.

Temperature

A comfortable temperature

The main living processes in a plant — photosynthesis and respiration — are only possible where there is enough light and warmth. On the other hand, if the temperature is too high, the plant loses more moisture through its leaves that its roots can absorb. This causes wilting and, in the worst cases, can kill the plant. So what you need for indoor conditions, is a reasonable compromise between what plants need, and what you want for a comfortable existence. These needs are not always fully compatible!

One plant may be happy with a temperature of 15°C (58°F), while another would prefer 20°C (68°F), while a comfortable temperature for people in the room may be between these two. There are other plants that do not want a constant temperature, but prefer a lower heat during their 'rest' period.

Dont't be put off by these problems. The better known houseplants are those that

Most plants are happy with a temperature of around 20°C (68°F).

All plants, including houseplants, are sensitive to wide temperature fluctuations. Therefore, if you go away for a few days during winter don't turn down the central heating too much. If someone is looking after your house, ask them to keep the temperature at the level that you usually have it.

Cacti prefer full light and relatively high temperatures.

In imitating nature you must consider the balance between warmth and light.

have long shown their adaptability to a range of home conditions, and will tolerate the same temperatures that peope find most comfortable. The indoor temperature is more dependant on the weather during summer, when doors and windows are open. During winter, with continuous central heating, daytime temperatures will average 16°–22°C (60–70°F), and at night between 10° and 15°C (50–58°F).

Relative warmth and light

In nature both warmth and light come from the sun. When the sun is high in the sky it is warm and light outdoors. On a cloudy day it is somewhat cooler and darker. This indicates how in nature light and warmth are directly related.

This also applies in your home or office, where a balance between these two factors should be maintained in an attempt to imitate nature as closely as possible.

Even houseplants of tropical origin will not survive in a situation where the relationship between light and heat is unbalanced. Turning up the central heating to give the plants a 'bit more heat', without also considering the light conditions, is not necessarily beneficial as the balance between photosynthesis and respiration may be impaired.

In summer plants need to be protected from the direct rays of the sun through glass window panes where a great exaggerated heat build-up can occur.

Many houseplants require a cooler 'dormant' period during winter prior to spring flowering. Place these in a cooler room and reduce watering. In this rested state they can store energy needed for the demanding processes of blooming and fruiting.

Feeding

The main plant foods

All plants need regular and adequate feeding. Those plants in containers with various potting mixtures will use up the available nutrients after a while. Therefore, to keep your houseplants in good condition, and growing well, you need to add nutrients to the soil on a regular basis. The three main chemicals vital to plant growth are nitrogen, phosphorous and potassium. These are known by their respective chemical symbols of N, P and K (and always in this order). Fertilizer mixtures bought from a garden centre will have the formula of the contents printed on the package stated as a percentage of each of the three chemicals present. For example, if the formula is printed as 7-6-9, then this indicates 7% of nitrogen (N), 6% of phosphorous (P), and 9% of potassium (K).

The N-P-K ratio in different fertilizer mixtures will vary. Plants that need a high proportion of nitrogen for healthy leaf growth need a fertilizer with a high first number in its formula. Likewise, a high potassium content is indicated with a high last number. It is useful to remember that nitrogen stimulates the growth of the green parts of plants, and phosphorous promotes healthy blooming.

Trace elements

Besides the three main feeding elements, N-P-K, there are other chemicals that are equally important for healthy growth but are needed in lesser quantities. These chemicals are called micro-nutrients (or trace elements). They include iron, zinc, manganese, magnesium, copper, sodium, boron, and molybdenum.

A lack of one or more of these trace elements in the soil or potting-mix can result in growth irregularities. For example, a lack of iron can result in yellow leaves with green veins. It is often difficult to isolate the missing chemical when growth is abnormal, but there are also many typical symptoms for chemicals in short supply (and also where they occur in excess).

The assortment of fertilizers

Do not be put off by what at first seems a very complicated subject. Most houseplants do perfectly well on the fertilizers that have been specially formulated for them. These are available from any nursery or garden centre. Some fertilizer mixtures are formulated for a particular group of plants (e.g. roses, cacti, or hydrangeas).

Plant foods, or fertilizers, that are produced in chemical factories are called inorganic fertilizers. Many plant growers prefer to use 'natural' or organic fertilizers, and can make their choice from a range of products. Always effective, well matured cow manure is safe and clean to use. Keen growers can still make use of a 'manure barrel'.

Fertilizer application

Because a plant needs regular feeding to sustain its growth, it doesn't follow that it would grow better if you were to give it larger doses of nutrient.

If too much fertilizer is put into the potting soil, it can result in disturbance of the plant's water metabolism whereby the roots are unable to absorb water freely, which causes wilting and eventually death. Conversely, too much fertilizer could overstimulate a particular process. Take, for example, the too vigorous and stretched appearance of plants given too much nitrogen.

It is always better to apply nutrients regularly, in small doses, rather than give bigger doses less frequently. Plants that are growing well and are healthy can be given small amounts of fertilizer about once every fortnight during the summer months.

Plants that are 'resting' after blooming, or are in a more dormant state during the cooler months should not be fed.

Houseplants during the holidays

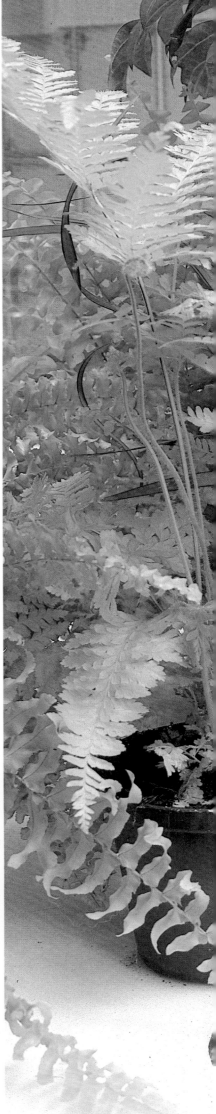

Correct preparation

It is possible to keep your plants alive while you are away on holiday, without having to ask a friend or neighbour to come in and water them.

With careful planning and preparation you could leave your plants to look after themselves for as long as two to three weeks.

To start with, remove all blooms and buds from the plants to help conserve energy and so that less water needs to be absorbed.

Then place the container in a bucket of water and allow the soil to absorb all the moisture it can. You can tell that the soil is saturated when air-bubbles stop rising from the soil.

Remove the plant from the water and envelop it carefully with a large, clear plastic bag which you have blown into, to open it fully. Tie-up the opening securely to seal the bag. The water that transpires from the plant's foliage cannot escape from the bag and so condenses on its walls. The relative humidity remains high so that additional water is not needed. This 'greenhouse' effect can be used for shorter periods with many houseplants, but would be too humid as a permanent habitat.

When using this method you must make sure that the leaves of the plant do not touch the sides of the bag. If they do, the chances are that they will start rotting fairly soon. Sticks may be inserted into the soil to help keep the bag fully opened. For the best results, place the plants in a light place, but not in direct sunlight.

Capillary watering

The use of 'wicks' to provide plant pots with water can be the answer for those who are frequently away for short periods.

Various designs of 'self-watering' pots are available from garden centre, and you can also experiment with your own adaptations.

Capillary watering aids may take the form of matting, on which the plants are stood and the end of the mat is hung into a container of water. Provided the soil in the pot can make contact with the damp mat it will form part of a capillary chain as the plant uses up the moisture in the pot.

Another method involves inserting fibreglass or other fibre wicks through the drainage holes in the base of containers, with their other ends suspended in a container of water. The plant pot needs to be placed on a stand next to or over the water, but not touching it. The rate of water uptake will depend on the thickness of wick, and the rate at which the plant uses up water. If water rises too fast, remove some strands from the wick.

A temporary 'mini-case' limits water-loss.

With some experimenting you can develop your own temporary watering system.

Window sill, balcony and roof garden

Instead of being limited to conventional containers other interesting materials can be used. Some new, some salvaged. For instance, there is a range of unusual shapes found in salt-glazed earthenware pipes, especially the junction pieces. Further searching and salvaging can result in 'treasures' amongst old, larger-sized cast iron water and gas main pipes, couplings, junctions and branches. More interesting forms may have to be set in concrete, for stability. Old chimney pots and pipes are also worth collecting as pots and for their interesting shapes.

Plants on the roof, balcony and window sill

Colourful pots need regular maintenance.

Forethought and planning

To say that plants should be placed or grown in every possible space would be over-stating the case. Careful planning will ensure that everything is not simply hidden by a great green mass, and let you enjoy the contrasts that plants can bring to the home. Become aware of all the choices open to you, and try not to limit your thinking to the 'conventional' only.

It makes sense to examine the under-utilised areas around your home. Are they neglected because of inaccessibility or perhaps through lack of effort on your part? Look critically at the potential of a small balcony for providing a new floral display, or a flat roof area which could become an outdoor 'lounge'.

You must also make sure that the pleasure of your newly-created feature is not spoiled by some technical error. It would be terrible to find out, too late, that the new roof garden is too heavy for the roof!

The correct choice of plants is as important as ever. A balcony or roof are probably more exposed and windy than ground-level situations, while plants on a patio or sheltered corner might get a great deal of heat.

After a difficult or under-used spot has been transformed into an attractive feature, it can give the creator a great sense of satisfaction knowing that the careful planning and preparation has all been worthwhile.

A long tradition

There is nothing new about the use of plants to decorate and enhance buildings and living areas. Even in Roman and earlier times men were busy gardening in pots and containers and using them to enhance buildings and decorate courtyards.

Much later, with the blossoming of the European 'gardening arts', the custom of placing plants in containers on corners,

next to steps, on pedestals at entrance doors or gates became established. Containers were themselves often 'works of art' and highly decorated. It also gave the opportunity to display especially attractive shrubs or trees, by placing them at strategic spots in gardens.

The traditions of decorative planting are still practised all over the world, and some countries are renowned today for their bright floral features — Swiss and Italian window boxes, or French verandah displays. Older horticultural practices, such as the keeping of plants in 'orangeries', can still be seen today. The basic principles still apply, and our modern equivalents extend to a whole range of plants from warmer parts of the world, which provide attractive displays outdoors during summer, but must be brought indoors during cold weather.

Detailed planning is necessary

Exotic plants can be used when you want to create garden features where plants are not usually found. However detailed planning is needed when creating, for example, a roof garden.

Here, all the factors that normally apply when planting, seem more difficult or

An attractive shady corner, complete with strawberry pot.

unfavourable. A roof top is probably exposed and the wind blows too much, and it doesn't seem as if there is enough depth or soil . . . and it will dry out too fast . . . and the weight will be excessive . . . etc. A worse situation would be hard to find.

Yet, carefully chosen materials, good preparation, and an adaptable selection of plants, can go a long way towards success. You should also consider the problems of maintenance at this early stage. There will be many demands on the gardener, but the results will be well worth the effort. But in your enthusiasm do not give yourself more work than you can manage by putting plants on every available surface.

Sometimes you will need to disregard a seemingly suitable spot for plants. As an example, think of the mini-balconies built outside the upper floor windows of many older houses. These were intended as fire-escapes, and are likely to be part of the architectural decoration of the building's façade. In such a case it would often be aesthetically better not to put in flower boxes or pots.

Nevertheless, there are many instances where small balconies, sills and ledges are decorated with plants to great effect.

75

Outdoor materials

*A showy
Trichocereus.*

*Agapanthus is a
good tub plant.*

*Home-made
troughs can be
made to any
design.*

Outdoor containers

You usually have a clear idea of the containers to use for indoor plants. So what type of container should be used for outdoor plants? Pots used for indoor plants are not always practical or strong enough for the tougher outdoor conditions. These are more likely to be bumped, moved about, or have to carry a heavier load of plant plus soil. Weather conditions are tougher too, and winds can blow lighter containers over.

So what is really needed for outdoors are sturdy, weatherproof containers, that are stable and secure on the ground, and will withstand weather and storm conditions and man-handling. A major problem with outdoor containers is too rapid drying out of the soil. There are, however, various means of reducing this.

Larger terra cotta and other ceramic pots should have relatively broad bases, for stability, and smaller pots are better if they are wider than they are high. Glazed interiors or exteriors are desirable, to help reduce evaporation through otherwise porous walls. Glazing, or sealing with paint also eliminates the unsightly deposits of salt so often seen on unglazed pots. If you have an attractive pot or trough that is not sealed, you can easily apply a coating yourself (on either the interior or exterior). Ask your local paint supplies expert for a suitable paint or sealer, making sure that it is safe to use with plants.

Apart from the widely used ranges of plastic and other synthetic containers, there are a number of less usual containers. For example, moss-lined hanging baskets, made of wire or wood, and which can be 'fully' planted, both on the surface and through the undersides, to form a rounded mass of colour, if various annual flowering plants are used. The effect is spectacular, but requires very regular watering, especially on hot days.

The various self-watering troughs used for indoor plants, although expensive, can be used equally effectively for outdoor situations, especially when you consider that watering is the most important chore. The two disadvantages of these containers are that plastic becomes brittle after a while and, because they have a water reservoir, cannot be left outdoors when there is a chance of freezing. They are, of course, ideal for planting up with annual flowers and then being stored over winter. Some ceramic pots with holes or pockets in their walls for plants can look attractive, such as herb and strawberry pots, and smaller bulb and crocus pots.

Then there is the whole range of 'other' materials which were never intended as pots, but which are extremely useful. Tins and drums, for example, are found in all shapes and sizes and many can be used as instant containers once their tops are removed. Many similar drums, both square and round, are made of good quality plastic and those in the 4–5 gallon (25 litre) range can be made into many useful tubs, with tops removed, cut in half, or cut lengthways as a trough. Cutting and drilling of drainage holes is easily done with normal woodworking tools.

Soil mixtures and drainage

Drainage outdoors
To prevent a build-up of water in containers outdoors, it is essential that excess water can drain away freely. Make sure that all containers have drainage holes of adequate size. If they block, poke a stick or wire up through them. When planting-up an outdoor pot or trough, place pieces of pot-shard over the drainage holes to keep them open before filling the container with soil. If the container is raised off the ground slightly, on bricks or strips of wood, then water can drain more readily.

When containers are located on a balcony, it is also necessary to ensure that all run-off water can escape freely. Regular clearing of leaves, spilled soil, etc. may be needed, so that catch-pits, channels or down-pipes don't become blocked. Blockages may result in damming up of water, which may overflow onto a balcony below, and possibly create an 'unfriendly' situation!

In any case the mess caused by poor drainage is unsightly and quickly gives an air of neglect. A possible solution would be to stand the containers on a layer of stone chip but beware of making this too thick as the additional weight could cause problems. The chips would also conceal any channels or catch-pit, so regular inspections are advised.

Soil mixtures
Garden soil is as unsuitable for outdoor planting as it is for indoor use. The amount of soil available to the roots of container plants is limited and they have no access to ground water, as they would have in nature, so are particularly vulnerable to drought and lack of nutrients.

The best way of counteracting these problems is to use a soil-mixture that is water retentive, but still fairly light, and won't consolidate into a hard mass when it dries. You could use similar potting mixtures as you would use for larger

houseplants possibly adding loam or compost to very peaty mixtures. Buying potting soil for several large containers can be an expensive business, but it is a false economy to use half garden soil, half potting compost. Garden soil is almost always too 'heavy' and hinders drainage. Well-matured compost would be better. You could also use older potting soil, or last year's grow-bag contents as a base for your planting mixture.

Potting mixtures are available in two main forms: peat-based composts, which are rather light, and John Innes Formula potting soil, which contain peat, loam and sand with some basic nutrients. Larger bags are more economical to buy than smaller ones. For larger shrubs and trees in larger containers more loam or compost should be added to the mixture to provide more 'body' and to allow the plants to anchor themselves more firmly. They are then less susceptible to wind damage and to drying out.

Making compost on a balcony
If you have a small balcony you can be forgiven for not having a compost heap! However, many people hate seeing 'useful' kitchen waste being thrown away. This waste vegetable matter can be turned into compost. First, you need to understand the basic principles of good compost making. The most important basic requirements,

Drainage is important and water must be able to run off quickly from a confined area.

Kitchen and garden refuse can be used on a compost heap. But don't use cooked 'left-overs', cheese or similar substances, as rats or mice could be attracted. Many preservatives are also fatal to the composting organisms. This should be remembered when choosing a preservative for a wooden compost bin. As a general rule, substances that are harmful to plants will also affect compost adversely.

over which you have some control, are air, water and shading. Compost is made from broken-down organic matter. Left-over leaves, salads or peelings from the kitchen can be used; thick stems should be cut into small pieces.

Now you need to start the 'heap'. Begin by spreading a layer of vegetable matter across the base of your heap or bin. Apply a sprinkling of either bone meal, fish meal or blood meal, to help the composting process. Cover this layer with a thin one of loam or clay. The heap is gradually built up by applying these materials systematically on top of each other.

Try not to establish the heap in a sunny spot as the outer layers will tend to dry out too quickly. If the heap becomes too hot cover it with some form of shading. Air must be allowed to penetrate to the centre of the heap and, for this reason, heaps should never be made too wide or too high.

The heap must be kept moist but not too wet. If it gets too wet, from watering or rain, not enough air will enter and instead of decomposing it will rot. Rotting material is smelly and cannot be used as compost.

To sum up: as long as the heap does not dry out, gets enough air, is kept moist and drains freely, you should end up with good compost.

There are as many ways of making compost as there are compost makers! There is no single method that has to be followed, but the basic principles will always apply. Given the general outline above you can now begin to construct a small 'composter'. This involves buying or making a container or 'bin'. There are

several makes of attractive compost bin available, some quite expensive, which you simply fit together and begin to use.

However, you can also make your own bin. If necessary it can then be tailor-made to fit a particular spot. It is better to choose materials that will not rot too quickly — the more durable the material, the less maintenance in the future. Steel sheets, timber, wire mesh, bricks or cement blocks could be used.

When making the container always bear two basic facts in mind: air and water. Air must reach all parts of the heap (or bin) and water must be able to drain easily.

A bin can be made from a wooden crate with slatted sides, so that air can penetrate at all levels. One side could be removed and adapted so that planks could be inserted into grooves as the compost level builds up. This same method can be applied to a structure made of mortared bricks or blocks, laid with air spaces between each brick. The fourth 'wall' consists of removable wooden boards, fitting into slots at either end. A thoroughly cleaned oil drum with plenty of holes knocked through the sides and base makes a useful bin. It is also clean and easy to move. You can increase mobility by constructing a frame, with castor-wheels, beneath the drum. During the week the bin can be positioned next to the door, and at week-ends, when you want to relax outside, the bin can be wheeled out of sight.

A big disadvantage of a bin that is too open around its sides (especially wire-mesh bins), is the rate at which it dries out. It is a good idea to use a plastic liner, with perforations for aeration and drainage.

It is useful to have a lid for your compost bin to keep rain and insects out and screen the contents from view.

An efficient compost bin.

Using both sills of the window

Plants on the inner and outer sill

A window usually has two sills, both of which can be used to good effect. The scope for colourful planting outdoors is wide. Once you get started, you may well find that what began as a simple window box, has suddenly become a major project involving the whole wall, rather than just the window sill! The possibilities are surprisingly varied. There are hanging baskets, for use both indoors and out, which can be hung from brackets attached to the wall. Increasing the width of window sills can provide space for many more plants. Flower boxes and troughs, in a variety of sizes and materials, may be built-in, stood on sills, or be supported on brackets (either suspended from railings, or bolted to the wall).

Don't overdo the decorating as it might become dangerous for you or pedestrians passing below. Make sure that all your plants and containers are properly secured, and that all are within reasonable reach for tending and watering. Plants in exposed situations will need regular watering; excess water, while draining away, may make dirty marks on walls, or annoy others below.

The upper-storey climate

Whoever chooses to make a garden on an outside window sill will, like any gardener, have to be aware of the micro-climate in their area. Conditions can vary in different buildings in the same district, or even within the same building.

One side of your home may have sunshine for virtually the whole day and be quite sheltered, while another side may be shady and very windy. Other changes can occur during the seasons. What was a sunny spot in May would possibly no longer be so in August, and wind directions can be totally unpredictable.

Before making a definite decision about

A curtain of hanging plants inside and a bright display outside provide a complete picture.

which plants to grow, make a careful study of the climatic conditions they will have to cope with. A windy situation would not be suitable for taller plants that could be blown over easily. A shady façade would be totally wrong for plants needing lots of sunshine for healthy growth. However, too much sunlight can also cause problems. It may reflect off the walls and windows and be far too bright for some plants. Keeping up watering, where everything is 'baking hot' can be tiresome. Excess sunlight can be reduced to some extent with a nylon shade cloth, an awning, or an umbrella. The best thing is to choose plants that will be able to withstand the conditions.

Campanula isophylla giving its best show to the outside.

Even common plants can be showy.

Tasteful and pretty displays

The choice of whether to plant flowers and ornamentals or vegetables in your window boxes depends entirely on your particular circumstances. A wide choice is available ranging from common to rare for either 'bloomers' or 'greens'. There are dozens of beautiful annual (bedding) plants to choose from, which can provide a wonderful show throughout the summer. Then there are more tender shrubs that have been kept indoors over winter, the many perennials such as Geranium, Ivy Geranium, Fuchsia, etc.

Amongst the wide range of vegetables to choose from are some of the newer mini-varieties. These have been specially developed for the home gardener to use in containers. Don't forget useful herbs, which can also be ornamental, and there is no reason why they cannot be combined very successfully with flowering annuals. Pots and troughs of 'tasty' plants are obvious choices for the kitchen window sill. It is so convenient to be able to pick a few fresh sprigs of a herb while you are busy preparing the meal.

As the kitchen is more of a work area, it doesn't matter too much if the plant containers aren't particularly ornate. Window boxes outside the lounge window should be as pretty and colourful as possible.

Many possible combinations

Beauty is in the eye of the beholder. One person will prefer blooms in a bright colourful mixture, while another will choose something more restful. There is also the question of whether to keep the window boxes green and growing all year round, or whether colourful annuals during the summer months is enough. These decisions will depend on your own preferences and circumstances. If a window box is to be used for winter decoration, dwarf and low evergreen shrubs should be used. These are among the few ornamental plants that can provide some colour even in winter. Examples include *Cotoneaster dammeri* 'Skogholm', *Hypericum calycinum, Aralia elata* and some *Erica* species. If you prefer a more restful scene, it is not a bad idea to find space for some smaller permanent shrubs in the troughs you use for annuals. They don't flower as well as the annuals but need much less attention. You must realise, however, that because of their shorter flowering period, many species are only decorative for a short while. So try to find shrubs that are still attractive and interesting when not in bloom, such as Iris, Lavender, Santolina and some succulents and conifers; plants with variegated foliage are always useful. The ideal solution is to combine the use of permanent shrubs with the seasonal planting of colourful annuals in between.

Tomatoes will grow both in and outdoors.

Common Thyme in flower.

Rosmarinus officinalis or Rosemary.

The exuberant annual

Annuals that will tolerate sun, wind and a certain degree of drying-out, are the best choice to provide a good 'show' in your window boxes. Modern annuals bloom well and for a long time and the choice of colours is almost limitless. What more could you want? Do be careful when choosing colour combinations, as a mixture of too many different colours can become a visual 'mess', rather than a harmonious blend. Troughs with two or three complementary colours will look far better than a mixture of more vivid tones.

Contrasting colours, especially grey and silver, planted amongst the annuals helps to highlight the displays. *Cineraria maritima, Helichrysum petiolatum* and several others are suitable.

Some vegetables and herbs can also look attractive and are well worth trying. A trough filled with a healthy crop of Iceberg lettuce can be as beautiful as any shrub. Mini-tomatoes, or strawberries, in full fruit, are very decorative as are healthy spinach or parsley plants.

A bright trough of summer annuals.

Getting used to the indoor climate

The transfer of a plant from a warm interior window sill to the fresher outside sill can be a major adjustment for a plant to make. To prevent damage or disease, the plants need time to get used to their new situation. You can help the plants by waiting until the night-time temperatures are more mild, or put them on the outer sill for a few hours each day, gradually increasing the time spent outside until, after a week or so, they can be left there all the time. Once outside, plants that are in full sunlight still stand the risk of having their leaves scorched, as the soft indoor light will leave them vulnerable for some weeks. So keep them shaded during the hottest part of the day.

Sowing or seedlings?

Nowadays things are made very easy for the gardener. In spring you can buy ready-grown seedlings, almost at the point of flowering from any garden centre. Reasonably sized vegetable and herb plants will soon have your flower boxes looking good. Buying seedlings eliminates all the inconvenience of sowing, pricking out, etc., but there is still a lot to be said for sowing your own seeds, and raising your own seedlings. Self-produced seedlings are more economical, and there is a vast selection of varieties to choose from.

Mint or Mentha.

81

Germinating seedlings under glass.

Outdoor plants from seed

It is quite easy to grow annuals, vegetables and herbs from seed. All you need are a few basic materials and a bit of patience. To start with you need some pots or trays, to sow the seed in. Install a good drainage layer of crushed stone chips and then fill the pot to within 1.5cm (½in) of the top with light, sifted potting soil. Soak the soil thoroughly, allow to drain, and then press it down lightly to provide a firm seed-bed. Scatter the seeds thinly and evenly over the seed-bed and cover with a very light layer of damp potting soil and again press this down lightly, to ensure that all the seeds are in contact with the soil.

For quicker results, and to conserve moisture and warmth, you can cover the container with a sheet of glass or plastic. Place the whole container in a warm, dark spot or simply cover the glass with some newspaper. You won't need to water the soil for a few days, but keep inspecting the trays and turn the glass over whenever it has collected condensation to prevent these droplets from splashing onto the seed-bed.

As soon as the little seedlings begin to appear through the soil they will need light.

Place the tray first of all in a light position in a warm room away from direct sunlight. By the time they have developed their second pair of leaves the seedlings should be able to tolerate full sunlight. Because seedlings have a tendency to grow towards light, it is not a bad idea to place a home-made reflector of aluminium foil behind the seed container. The light will then come from all sides and the seedlings will grow upright. Before long they will have reached the height of the edge of the tray and this is the time to raise the glass sheet higher above the pot. You can do this by using blocks or bricks to support the glass. Keep raising the height of the glass until, after about 10 days, the plants can do without protection altogether. By this stage they will be starting to crowd each other, and will need some thinning out. This is easily done by cutting off the unwanted plants at ground level using a small pair of scissors. Enough plants should be removed to allow those remaining to grow to a size of about 6 leaves without intruding too much on each other. When they have reached this size it is time for them to be planted out into their permanent positions. Keep in mind that, as they have been raised under relatively warm conditions, they will need to be 'hardened off' to full outdoor conditions. So give them protection from sun and wind for the first couple of weeks.

Decorating the balcony

Even a small balcony can be made bright and attractive.

around you? Perhaps you'd like an outdoor breakfast space for bright sunny mornings, or a bit of space for the children to play in the fresh air.

If you wish that all these alternatives were open to you, don't give up hope, as you will be amazed by what can be done with a small space.

Before you start to 'improve' your balcony, find out whether there are any regulations that have to be complied with, or if there are any restrictions on what you may do. For example, if you live in some houses or flats you may not be allowed to put flower-boxes on the walls. Finding out in advance can avoid disappointment or unpleasantness later on.

The way you arrange your balcony will be governed to a great extent by the direction it faces and the prevailing winds. Most plants dislike draughts and wind as much as people do. You can reduce the effect of the wind somewhat by providing screens. The various methods of wind screening are discussed later in this chapter.

If you are worried that nothing will grow on your north-facing balcony remember that some colourful annuals tolerate a degree of shade, as do some perennials such as Fuchsia and Ivy Geranium. Many smaller shrubs will also grow without sun but in all these cases the amount of light is important. It's a pity that colourful displays of flowers only appear during summer, whereas for the rest of the year there are only empty containers. Evergreen shrubs can give a winter balcony a less bleak look. What about a small fruit tree in a tub, or a bucket with tomato plants, or a large dish with culinary herbs?

A balcony, large or small, can be made into something more attractive by using any of a wide range of materials and devices. These include the use of timber cladding, tiles and other floor-coverings, and plants in pots of every description.

The possibilities are endless

Many older houses have balconies. They are usually small and not intended for sitting on, being a part of the façade of the building. Furthermore, they were not thought of as suitable places for plants. There was usually more than enough space 'downstairs' for plants. Yet for most people living in flats today the balcony is their only bit of outside space. Most modern balconies are small and uniform in style. It is difficult, therefore, to 'personalize' this space and make the best use of it.

Do you just want to look out onto something green and attractive, or do you want to sit in the sun with a few plants

Red-currants and strawberries in the corner of a balcony.

You can grow climbing plants over the balustrade, or a conifer in a pot with crocuses at its base. A shallow tub with water plants can also serve as an attractive pond, to which birds can come and drink.

Smartening up the balcony floor
Most balconies have a concrete floor. You can use this surface as it is to create your container garden, but it can be made more attractive by using a floor covering.

There are many floor covering materials available. Whichever one you decide to use, do make sure that it is tough and weatherproof, or you will find yourself having to re-lay the floor fairly soon. Weight is another factor to take into account. Before you start on your project, find out the carrying capacity of your balcony. After all, you don't want the building to fall down!

An instant way of decorating the floor is to paint it. For this you will need a special masonry paint, as a water-based paint would be unsuitable. Epoxy resin paints are the most hardwearing. Choose a colour that complements your plants

and furnishings. If your home is new, it is better to wait for a few months for the concrete to mature and dry-out completely, before applying any paint.

A wooden balcony floor has a pleasant, warm appearance. Different kinds of woods can be used. Pine would have to be treated all over with wood preservative. Hardwoods are more expensive, but wear better and don't need treating. Duckboards can be made from timber laths, and raised slightly above the floor, so that rainwater can drain away freely. Different types of floor tiles are very durable and attractive. Provided the balcony surface is level, tiles can be laid directly onto a glue or cement screed and the joints grouted with cement. Make sure that there is a slight slope for water to run off into the drainage system. Tiles and smaller mosaic tiles are available in such a wide variety of sizes, shapes and surface textures, that you can be sure of finding something to suit your needs.

Another weatherproof material that can be used is synthetic 'outdoor' carpeting. It comes in a roll, or as square tiles, which can be bought in many sizes and colours. Matting can be laid loose or glued down, if the surface is even.

The walls of the balcony

Another area that needs looking at is the balustrade of the balcony. This should be so designed to prevent small children from falling through or climbing up or over.

If the balustrade is made of open railings, it could be closed in, to provide more privacy, and act as a shelter and windscreen for plants. Many different materials are available that could be used for enclosing railings. Choose one that will be compatible with your plants and the building.

Canvas awning can be bought in various colours and widths. All that has to be done is to weave the canvas between the railings and tie it at each end. Don't forget to consider the colouring of the floor and plants when you choose the canvas.

Corrugated plastic sheets can be used effectively. Attach a light timber framework to the balustrade, then drill and screw the sheets to the timber with round-

headed screws or, better still, use rubber or plastic roofing washers with the screws.

Reed matting shows off your plants well and provides a natural background. Fasten it to an open balustrade with plastic-covered wire, and against a solid wall use masonry nails with washers.

Timber is a very versatile material and can be used in many ways. A screen can be made of vertical timber planks attached to horizontal strips at top and bottom. Spacing between the slats depends on how 'solid' the screen needs to be. Do not use planks horizontally, as they could enable children to climb up the balustrade. Sheets of waterproof plywood can be used instead of planking. When they are painted an attractive colour they provide a good background.

Smaller sections of ready-made timber fencing, in panels, may suit your balcony and can also be used as a good background against which to hang troughs and pots of trailing plants.

A pumpkin growing in a plastic bag.

A balcony for recreation

Sitting on a small balcony can be claustrophobic, especially if a few chairs are taking up all the available space. With a limited floor area, you will need all the space-saving ideas you can think of. You might be able to raise one section of the balcony with planking to form a platform. This can be used for seating with loose cushions and, if it is wide enough, then plants can be put on it as well. You can also make use of the space underneath by constructing a cupboard to store watering cans and other equipment. If you are lucky enough to have a balcony that gets morning sun, an outdoor breakfast corner can be created by attaching a simple folding table to the balustrade or inner wall. This can, of course, be folded away when not in use. Plain stools of plastic, cane or wood are light and will take up less space than chairs. These can be quite comfortable, particularly if they have cushions.

If your children love animals you can even have a cage built, for a rabbit or guinea pig, that would fit on a small balcony. It is best raised off the ground and faced away from the weather. They can also be used for displaying plants.

If you have young children then you can make them a sand-pit by laying an old car tyre flat and filling it with clean sand.

For summer meals why not a barbeque on the balcony? Modern barbeques come in a variety of sizes and are light, clean and easy to use. Many versions are on wheels and so can be removed easily when not needed. A shelf or work-top underneath could provide a home for the barbeque and some other large items.

Such features belong in a garden but can be as effective on a balcony or roof garden.

Water features on balconies

Something special for plant lovers with balconies is some form of water feature. Even a simple mini pond surrounded by plants is fun, but a series of mini ponds, linked to each other with flowing water, creates a more dramatic effect. Larger containers can be positioned at regular intervals or, as a complete contrast, you could create an informal arrangement, with different sized bowls at different levels.

Having saved space through good organisation, you now need to fill it with ornamental features. A small sculpture, correctly placed, can give much visual pleasure. Do make sure that the object is weatherproof. If you have large sea shells, or interesting rocks or pebbles, collected during your holidays, they could add 'personality' to the display.

You must always make sure that the bowls are quite steady and secured on bases of brick or cement block. You should also remember that water weighs 1 kilogram per litre (10lbs to the gallon). Don't overload the balcony without first finding out whether it will be safe. Full sunlight doesn't do ponds any good, as it results in a rapid growth of green algae. Putting water snails into each pond will, to an extent, control the algae.

Given the right facilities a balcony water feature can be used for growing various aquatic or semi-aquatic plants. You have to match the depths of container and soil with the particular water plants you want to grow, as their natural habitats will determine their requirements.

Some plants float, such as the Water Hyacinth, *(Eichhornia crassipes),* Duckweed *(Lemna),* Water Lettuce, and *Salvinia.* Others must root in submerged soil. The Yellow Flag *(Iris pseudacorus)* likes shallow water, while Water Lilies *(Nymphaea)* prefer deeper water. It is probably safest to choose from the floating and shallow water plants. If you already have a good collection of pots and bowls that could serve as ponds, arrange them and then select your plants according to the size of the containers. Aquatic plants must be kept permanently in water, so test your bowls to make sure that they do not leak.

Whilst rainwater is best for filling ponds, mains water is more convenient.

The plants you choose will each have their own soil preferences. Some will prefer a heavy, clay mixture, others peat, and some a light, sandy mix. Some plants are difficult to anchor into the soil. You can plant these in pots of suitable soil and cover this with a good layer of crushed stone, to keep both soil and plant in place. The pot can now be immersed in the pond.

A shallow bowl, filled only with water, can look good among a group of mini ponds

Garden peat can provide the base for a small peat-bog. A container, without drainage, and about 20cm (8ins) deep is filled with peat. Add water until the peat is saturated and a thin layer of water covers the surface. Shallow bog plants, such as Myosotis palustris *and* Caltha palustris, *should grow well.*

Myosotis palustris or Marsh Forget-me-not.

The Water Lily, Nymphaea alba, is not suitable for shallow ponds. You should choose varieties that tolerate shallow conditions.

Nymphoides peltata or Water Gentian.

Eichhornia crassipes, or Water Hyacinth, cannot be left outdoors in winter.

Nymphaea 'Charles de Meurville' will grow in depths from 40cm (18ins).

If your balcony is protected by corrugated plastic sheets, it is inadvisable for these to be left outdoors during freezing weather. Plastic becomes brittle and can crack or pieces may break off.

and bog gardens, and could serve as a reflective pond or a bird bath. Bowls or mini ponds that are to contain aquatic plants should be deep enough to contain a soil layer of 10–15cm (4–6ins), plus several centimetres or inches of water to cover it.

Never take wild plants from outdoor streams. There are enough garden centres and nurseries that can supply the whole range of aquatic plants and they will be able to advise on how to handle and grow them.

Try not to create only summer features on your balcony. A few bowls of bulbs in spring and some autumn-flowering shrubs will give a great deal of pleasure too.

Constructing a roof garden

Above:
Many houseplants can be displayed outdoors during summer.

Right:
Raised beds are ideal for vegetables, herbs and flowers.

Gardening at higher levels

We all like to think that our ideas are original and that the creation of roof gardens is relatively new. However, this is certainly not the case.

Recorded history has left us details of the times of Nebuchadnezar, in Babylon, nearly eight centuries ago, when the most fantastic and extensive roof gardens were established, which became known as one of the wonders of the ancient world.

These gardens were of an immense size, on a scale greater than anything that had ever been done before. For instance, the huge pillars that supported each tier of roofs were hollow, filled with soil and planted

with large trees. The floors under the roof gardens were well waterproofed. This consisted of layers of reed, covered with asphalt, then two layers of baked-clay tiles, and finished with a covering of sheet lead. The soil was then laid on top of all this, as the base for the gardens, and included underground irrigation systems. Nebuchadnezar needed a whole army of slaves to tend this vast garden.

In this day and age, when time is so valuable, we need to make sure that maintenance tasks are kept to a minimum. This is best done by careful planning beforehand.

A question of weight

When using plants to decorate a balcony or flat roof, there is a choice of basic setting-up methods.

One option is to confine yourself to arranging a limited number of plants, in containers, on certain parts of the roof area. The alternative is the establishment of a complete garden by covering the whole area with a growing medium, and planting wherever your plan dictates.

The term 'growing medium' is used instead of 'soil', as the mixture you should use is made up of the lightest possible components. The question of weight is obviously extremely important. Will your roof or balcony support the additional weight? You will have to find out what the carrying capacity of the roof is. The architect who designed the building is the best person to ask, but if it is not possible to ask him try the local council who will be able to advise you.

Cement paving slabs, railway sleepers, bricks and similar constructional materials are, in any quantity, extremely heavy.

Care must be taken with the choice of planting medium. Wet soil (after a shower of rain) will weigh nearly 2 tonnes per cubic metre (1.505 tons per cubic yard). Thus, if a layer of soil is spread to a depth of 30cm (12ins) across the surface of the roof, you will have a wet weight of soil of about 600kg for each square metre (or about 1105.95lbs per square yard). In winter you could have an additional weight of snow, of anything up to 75kg per square metre (138.24lbs per square yard). However, this is not the only additional weight, as there are also the plants and

containers, furniture, statues, screens, etc., and of course the people who will be using the area.

A water-tight base
Another important question to ask at the planning stage is: can the roof cope with all the additional moisture that will pour onto it?

In principle, drainage and waterproofing can be taken care of in new developments on existing buildings. Obviously, the best time to make provision for these factors is when the building is under construction. If this is not possible, how do you solve the problems of converting an existing roof into a garden, or cope with the extra weight?

The waterproofing on an existing flat roof was probably never meant to be a hard-wearing surface, so take care not to inflict any damage and cause leaking below. In more ambitious schemes, where contractors are involved, it is best if there is good co-operation between the landscape gardener and architect or structural engineer. The landscaper can advise on how the weight of the whole facility should be distributed and whether any parts will be more heavily loaded. Structural details can then be calculated by the architect.

Waterproofing of the roof surface needs to be particularly well thought out. Several efficient water barriers are available; some are painted on and others are in sheets or rolls. Aluminium foil sandwiched between bituminous or rubber compounds is very effective.

The big decision
Before you finally decide to go ahead with the creation of your roof garden think about the following things. A big disadvantage is the high initial cost. However, you will save on your fuel bills, as the roof garden insulates the rooms below, and the roof will certainly be well waterproofed.

The surface waterproofing of a flat roof usually needs re-doing every few years. This is due to the influence of weather, especially temperature fluctuations, and the ultra-violet rays from sunlight. A roof garden, if properly installed, provides good protection to the waterproofing and should extend its life considerably. Exact savings are difficult to calculate but they could add up to a fair proportion of the cost of the roof garden.

Plain or painted timber screens are attractive.

If you want plants to grow well on a roof you mustn't forget that you have removed them from their 'natural' environment. On a roof they will, for example, have to contend with a much thinner layer of growing medium than they are used to. In addition, many other factors are decidedly unfavourable — such as wind or the baking sun. It is therefore understandable that the growing medium must be of a good quality, and should be well manured at the time of installation. To maintain the plants in a healthy state, they will need regular feeding with both organic and inorganic nutrients.

Construction of a roof garden

Many of the materials that are used in the construction of a roof garden are better known by their specific brand-names. This can present problems, as products and names change or disappear from the market, and there is a constant stream of new products. The following descriptions of materials refer to the name they are generally known by, not their specific brand-names.

Before constructing your roof garden there are a number of points to consider:

1 root barriers
2 drainage layer
3 filter layer
4 growing medium

There are also problems associated with evaporation, rainfall, and anchoring difficulties with plants in the lighter soil type.

The extra waterproofing barrier that should be laid on top of the existing surface must be carefully protected during construction, as the slightest perforation can cause problems later. If extra weight is no problem then the casting of a layer of concrete over the waterproofing will achieve maximum protection.

If it is a problem, you can use one of the modern synthetic materials, such as sheets of polystyrene foam or heavy-gauge plastic sheeting. Together, these materials will provide protection and be a useful root barrier. It is essential that the roots of plants are contained in some way, so that

they cannot damage the roof structure or the waterproofing layer. Barriers can be porous, when drainage material is located below, or be impervious, as in the case of plastic sheeting or bituminous type sheets.

The drainage layer has two functions: it must allow the free escape of surplus moisture; and, at the same time, retain enough moisture for the plants to absorb. The most common lightweight drainage materials are the expanded clay granules, vermiculite and perlite. To prevent the drainage material from getting clogged up with particles of growing medium you need to insert a separating screen. Do not underestimate the importance of this filter layer. If the drainage layer loses its efficiency the whole project could be at risk. The filter can be made up of synthetic fibres — either woven or in the form of matting. Another possibility is artificial foam (urea-formaldehyde). It would have to be at least 5cm (2ins) thick, but 10cm (4ins) would be better. Water pipes and other facilities could be installed within this layer. It has the added advantage of being fairly water-retentive, so also benefits the plants.

Anchoring the roots

The substances mixed together as a growing medium for a roof garden cannot be called 'soil' as it will not, in most cases, contain any. When making up your mixture the first priority is to make it as light as possible. However, if it is too soft and light it will drain too quickly. You can give the growing medium some body by adding coarse sand.

It is important to balance the advantages and disadvantages associated with a lightweight growing medium. With strong winds and a light rooting medium that is either wet or dry, any unsecured plants will probably blow loose and topple over. A possible answer is to put coarse weave plastic mesh, with 'squares' of about 5 cm (2ins) into the rooting medium when it is first installed. Plants can then root down into and through this and become firmly anchored.

A herb corner near the kitchen.

For a roof garden, where many smaller plant types are used because of soil limitations, you can consider using · succulents, rock garden plants and smaller ornamental grasses.

Irrigating the roof garden

It is possible to water the plants on a roof garden in the conventional way, with a watering can or hosepipe. If the area is larger and there are lots of beds or containers this can become a tedious business. This applies particularly on the roof, as it will be necessary to water more regularly than in an ordinary garden. First, there is no underground water supply for the plants to draw on; second, because of the elevation and lack of protection from the elements, evaporation will be high and both plants and growing medium will dry out quickly.

This is a good reason for looking at other means of watering — systems that are easy to control and save time and effort.

You can choose between permanent watering systems laid on the surface or those buried within the growing medium. It is far easier to conceal the water pipes underground during construction than to attempt this after the garden is established. In most cases it would simply not be possible to bury the piping.

There are different types of irrigation systems. Drip-irrigation is one method and can be used by connecting 'drip-lines' to either underground or surface piping with quick couplings.

The easiest, but most expensive way of watering, is with an automatic overhead watering system, where different sized sprayers are strategically placed to apply a sprinkling of water to all parts of the garden. After some experimenting, you will discover the needs of your plants and can set the system to provide a specific amount at pre-set times each day (even when you are on holiday!). Some advanced systems are designed not to water if it has rained.

Automatic systems are not essential. You can just as easily decide for yourself when water is needed. By having to watch your garden more closely you will remain in better contact with your plants and be more likely to discover problems or pests before much harm is done.

Obviously, all matters relating to water on the roof need careful attention. A defective watering system, leaking pipe or blocked drainage system can have expensive consequences if they aren't discovered early.

A matter that seems obvious, but is frequently overlooked, is the care of water channels, gutters and downpipes. During adverse weather, a blocked downpipe could result in an overloaded roof. Avoid this by carrying out regular checks.

Various types of installation

Different materials and growing mediums can be used when making roof gardens. Below are outlines of some of the alternatives, showing the different materials and how to install them.

A flat roof garden system based on 'rockwool' is about 15 cm (6ins) thick. It consists of the necessary drainage layer over a protective barrier covering the roof's waterproofing. Above this is laid rolls of rockwool, enough to cover the whole surface (see Diagram A). This is not the same rockwool that is used in the building industry, but one that has been specially developed for horticultural use. This medium is unsuitable for larger plants and should only really be used for grass and ground-covers. You can still create a successful small garden using this base by putting groups of pots and troughs, containing taller plants, on wooden benches or staging.

The rockwool system will, without a load on it, but saturated with water, and with an allowance made for winter snow, have a weight in the region of 200kg per square metre (or 400lbs per square yard). This is about the maximum weight that the average balcony might be expected to carry.

Another system is shown in Diagram B. Here, polystyrene foam sheets laid across the roof surface serve as the drainage layer. This is covered by a permeable layer of weave which is fine enough to prevent particles of growing medium from washing into the drainage system. This is also the correct position in which to place a barrier to stop the advance of plant roots. A 10cm (4ins) layer of foam granules (or perlite) retains moisture for absorption by the roots. Cover the foam with a root-anchor net, and fill up the bed with at least 30cm (12ins) of growing medium. This can be composed of 50%−75% of potting compost, and the rest of plastic foam granules. The proportions will depend on the available depth. The compost component must be higher where the soil is shallower to provide enough substance to lower growing plants. For larger shrubs and smaller trees the depth of rooting medium must be

With the materials available there are few practical limitations on what can be built on a roof. You can create a normal garden with borders, pathways, paved areas and even water features. You can also consider less-common garden styles, such as the 'Japanese'. This style is a subject on its own, but has many possibilities.

In caring for plants on a balcony, much of the worry can be removed if some sort of screening can be installed, to enable you to temporarily close-off the adverse elements. With such a measure damage by strong winds, storms, rain or extremes of cold or heat can be averted. This protection will make conditions more pleasant for yourself as well.

greater (don't forget to increase the proportion of plastic foam).

Diagram C shows a different system, where a reservoir of water is created beneath the growing medium. The idea sounds hazardous but is quite simple in a well-constructed garden with good waterproofing. It is called a 'wet system'.

During construction a cement layer is laid, to protect the waterproofing, and is covered by a further impervious bituminous layer. This waterproofing must continue up the sides of the retaining structure to keep the water in the lower part of the first layer, which comprises expanded clay granules, across the entire surface to a depth of at least 10cm (4ins). The drainage system is so designed that all except the lowest 5cm (2ins) of water is able to escape freely. The water retained is made available to the plants by capillary action.

The growing medium is mainly potting compost to which you can add clay granules or foam pellets. This system is obviously very heavy.

Comparisons of weights per square metre of the three systems show that while the 'rockwool' method weighs 200kg (368.64lbs per sq. yd.), Diagram B, with its water-absorbent layer rates about 525kg (967.7lbs per sq. yd.), and the last 'wet system' could weigh upwards of 800kg per square metre (1474.63lbs per sq. yd.).

What depth of soil?

As has already been stated, the sizes of plants that you can put into your roof garden depend on the depth of growing medium you have to plant in. The following general rules can be borne in mind when selecting plants:

Low, spreading plants and ground-covers, and turf grasses prefer a minimum 20cm (8ins) depth of growing medium. This could be less, but then the plants become vulnerable to drying out.

Annuals (bedding plants) do well in a soil depth of 20–30cm (8–12ins).

Permanent shrubs and small trees will need at least 40cm (16ins), but preferably up to 70cm (30ins) for larger specimens.

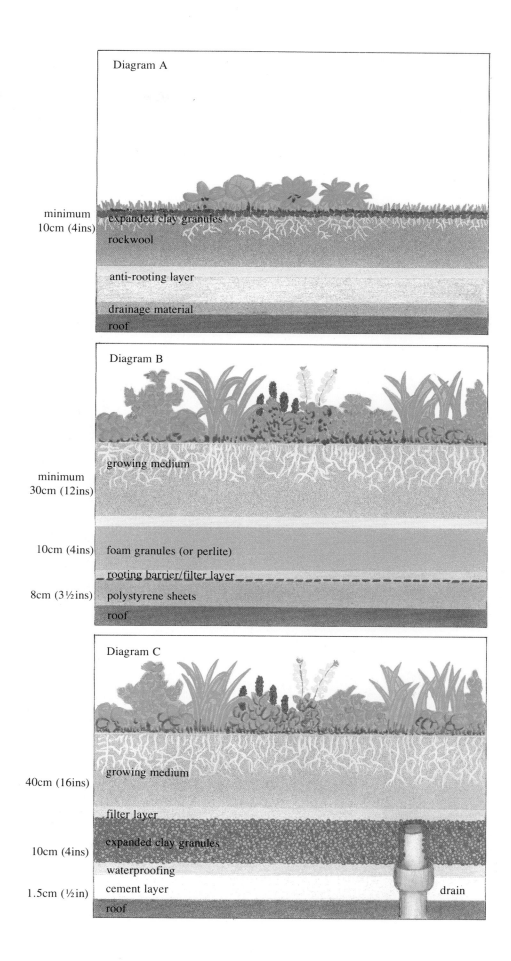

Diagram A

minimum 10cm (4ins)

expanded clay granules
rockwool
anti-rooting layer
drainage material
roof

Diagram B

minimum 30cm (12ins)

growing medium

10cm (4ins)

foam granules (or perlite)
rooting barrier/filter layer

8cm (3½ins)

polystyrene sheets
roof

Diagram C

40cm (16ins)

growing medium
filter layer
expanded clay granules

10cm (4ins)

waterproofing
cement layer   drain

1.5cm (½in)

roof

Placing of pots

'Classical' designs will always be appealing.

You can transform an entrance area with a little imagination.

To avoid an unsightly confusion when establishing a balcony or patio garden, try not to use too many different materials. This also applies to the pots and troughs and the display stands on which they are placed.

Practical and pretty

Gardening on balconies and roofs is, in most cases, confined to containers of some sort or other. These may consist of specially constructed flower boxes or beds, or individual (and portable) containers, such as pots, tubs, urns, etc. The great advantage of containers is in their diversity of size and shape, and in the ways in which they can be used. And of course, quite how easily you can move them. You can move pots according to the seasons, into or away from the sun or shade, and so you can change your arrangements at any stage. Pots with flowers can be moved out of sight when they have finished flowering, while ailing plants can be moved to a

'quarantine' area. Less attractive containers can be planted with trailing plants to hide the container. Plants treated in this way can also be placed in front of other containers, so as to eliminate that 'bareness' so often found in pot gardens.

Creating a view

Arranging groups of plants in pots may need more thought than you might first think. What you are in fact doing is creating a mini-landscape, and many of the basic rules still apply. The colours, sizes and shapes of the plants must be taken into account. The containers themselves are another important aesthetic factor. Too many pots, of different materials and sizes, cannot be regarded as a harmonious feature. You must have some degree of conformity. Try only to use one or two types of material for all the pots: terra cotta or cement are the most attractive, where space and weight permits. Fewer, larger pots will appear less cluttered than dozens of smaller pots, with their smaller plants. For the most luxuriant of effects, use the largest sized plants your space will permit. Even on a balcony, you can establish focal points, either with plants as the attraction,

*Second chance
for a wash
basin!*

or by using plants, perhaps to frame a view, or to enhance a piece of sculpture.

Working with vertical surfaces

Balconies and roof gardens are 'contained' by their surrounding walls and railings; it should not be left entirely to plants in pots at ground level to 'break up' the bareness of these surfaces. The logical solution to this problem is to utilize the surfaces as vertical gardens, by using plants, ornaments and statuary, and other architectural fixtures.

Flower boxes can be placed on racks, or on specially made brackets, suspended on either, or both sides of the railings. Brackets on other walls can also accommodate elongated troughs, and be used for bright summer annuals, or perhaps, permanent trailing greenery. A whole collection of plants, such as cacti, orchids, or bromeliads, could be grown in pots mounted to the wall. Creeping or climbing plants could be planted in pots on the ground, and be trained up a screen or trellis, again mounted to the wall. Self-clinging plants, like *Hedera* or Virginia Creeper are effective too, but they can become a nuisance.

Hanging baskets can be suspended from any overhead structure, or again, from brackets attached to the walls. There are many containers and ornaments made especially for mounting on walls; half-baskets can be screwed to the wall, and terra cotta and other ceramic half-round pots are most attractive with trailing plants cascading from them.

Many cement garden ornaments are suited to wall-hanging, or being built in, and can provide most acceptable focal points, especially when used in conjunction with plants.

Once a balcony has been refurbished and made more comfortable and attractive, it will be used more than before. That's the whole idea! You can save yourself more expense if you accept that the additional usage has some accompanying risks. Before you converted your balcony or patio perhaps it was hardly used, except for hanging out the washing. Improvements have now made the area pleasant so it will be used more often. Problems could arise exactly because of all the extra activity. For example, a pot could easily be knocked through the railings or a glass bumped off the balustrade. This is not so likely to be a problem if there is a garden below, but if there is a pedestrian way or another balcony, then the consequences could be more serious. Always be aware that accidents do happen, and take any obvious precautions. You might also consider obtaining Public Liability insurance cover.

Care and maintenance of plants in pots

The objective: healthy plants

An exceptionally lush and healthy plant in a pot will be eye-catching and a source of many compliments.

Neglected plants never look good, so to keep them in tip-top condition you should look after the containers, its contents and, of course, the plant itself.

The everyday maintenance of plants consists of watering, removal of broken shoots and dead leaves. Fading flowers should also be removed, unless they are to be followed by fruits or berries.

With good care and reasonable climatic conditions you can expect good results. In spite of all the careful attention some plants may still appear not to be doing well. Forgetting to water a moisture-loving plant even once could prove fatal. Drying out is probably the most common 'ailment' and you should remember that if moisture-loving plants start suffering they are more likely to be attacked by insect pests. Aphids, scale and white fly love to attack weakened plants.

Controlling the pests will not necessarily eliminate the cause. If after repeated treatments the pests come back again it would be better to replace the plant with another type. You should in time build up a good collection of plants that can tolerate your particular growing conditions, and still appear healthy. Don't be too critical. A plant in a container will always find it more difficult than the same type in the ground (there are a few exceptions, like *Sedum spurium).*

The chances of a plant growing healthily are increased by the quantity of soil it is growing in, so be as generous as possible. The bare soil surface under plants in larger containers can be covered by shallow-rooted ground-cover plants that will not take too much from the soil.

All pots and containers should have drainage holes in their bases to allow excess water to drain away. To prevent rotting, wooden barrels and troughs should be raised slightly above the ground, using hardwood strips or pieces of tile. In fact, all larger containers will benefit from being lifted slightly so that the underside of the container can remain reasonably dry and not rot or corrode too quickly. This also makes it easier for rainwater to drain away.

Occasionally you will need to move the container to clean up accumulated leaves, soil, etc. and remove any mossy growths from the shady sides.

Suitable plants for the balcony: a summary

A standard Buxus is a slow grower, so it is good where space is limited.

The right plant for the right place

Now that you know quite a bit about pots, troughs and other containers, you might think you are ready to plant them up. However, there is one more thing to consider, which is probably the most important of all: choosing the right plants. When planting in the garden the different needs of plants must be remembered; some like full sun, while others need some shade or shelter from the wind. This is often forgotten when putting plants into pots. And there are other problems, too!
The plants chosen must be able to withstand wind and be able to tolerate a bit of drying out occasionally if you forget to water them!

Watering is usually easier on a roof garden with a hose or irrigation system, but you still have to be careful, as the soil in containers or beds has no reserves of moisture (as garden soil does). Provided you supply your 'captive' plants with all the basic necessities, there is no reason why they should not have the same life-expectancy as the same types of plant in open ground.

Movable containers

Because containers can be moved you have more freedom with arranging plants than in a normal garden. You could plant up a trough with summer-flowering annuals, or another with only evergreen shrubs. The evergreen trough can be used as a background during the summer by placing it behind other containers. A trough of annuals that has finished flowering can also be quickly hidden behind other containers, or be removed entirely. Shrubs in pots can obviously be moved easily to change the appearance of your 'layout' whenever you like. So, with planning, a container garden can have advantages.

Later in this chapter you will find lists of plants that are, to varying degrees, suitable for the conditions discussed in this chapter.

Any list of plants, on whatever basis it is compiled, will have limitations. You must also realise that there will be many other plants available that could also be used under any specific set of conditions.

You will notice that some groups of plants are not included. Evergreens, for example, are not listed, but many evergreen species would be suitable for use in containers, especially the lower and slower growers. Even larger-growing types, such as holly, can be kept in check by pruning.

Annual plants are also not mentioned as, apart from the taller varieties, they are nearly all possible choices for container gardens.

Aquatic plants and rock garden plants behave in containers much as they do elsewhere so it is not really necessary to list them.

After the sections on small trees and shrubs, ground-covers, herbs, bulbs and seedlings, you will find listed selections of shade-loving plants, plants for northern aspects, hanging types and, lastly, 'specimens' suitable for keeping for many years in confined containers.

The term 'hanging plants' describes those that have a natural inclination to sprawl or drape, and can be used to 'spill' over the rim of a container and decorate or hide it.

In this way, hanging plants in suspended baskets, or in pots fixed to walls, can grow downwards to provide a curtain of green.

Berberis foliage and flowers are attractive.

Cornus mas

Smaller trees and shrubs for roof gardens and pots on balconies

Acer japonicum varieties
Japanese Maple. Leaves yellow or green. Slow, lower growing.

Acer palmatum varieties
Japanese Maple. Many dwarf varieties. Leaves green, yellow, purple, etc.

Aralia elata
Japanese Angelica Tree. Small tree. Deciduous. Good variegated types.

Amelanchier species
Deciduous. Good autumn colours. Small tree or shrub.

Aucuba japonica
Yellow-spotted evergreen, hardy. Slow and easily pruned. For berries, plant male and female plants.

Berberis species
Small and medium sizes very suitable. Various foliage colours, berries, flowers, deciduous or evergreen types.

Betula species
Birch. Deciduous. Need plenty of water. Discard when too large.

Buddleia species
Several species have silvery leaves. Fast growing shrubs. Various flower colours. Prune after blooming.

Buxus sempervirens
Boxwood. Evergreen. Slow. Can be clipped into shapes. Dislikes lime.

Callicarpa bodinieri giraldii
Deciduous, small shrub. Lilac flowers; purple berries. Prune after frost.

Calluna vulgaris varieties
Scotch Heather. Low, evergreen. Foliage ranges from green to yellow to bronze. Flowers of white, pink, purple shades.

Caryopteris clandonensis
Blue Mist. Low mound. Deciduous. Clusters of blue flowers.

Cercis siliquastrum
Judas Tree. Small tree. Purplish-rose flowers on old wood, before leaves.

Chaenomeles varieties
Flowering Quince. Deciduous, hardy. Many sizes and flower and fruit colours.

Cornus mas
Cornelian Cherry. Yellow flowers, before leaves, in early spring. Small tree.

Don't force too many different shrubs into a container. It is usually more attractive when the scheme is limited to one or very few species so that each can develop its own characteristic features and be appreciated for them. Colourful annuals can be mixed if a bright, warm display is wanted.

Hebe species do well in pots.

Erica gracilis.

Corylus avellena contorta
Corkscrew Hazel. Slow. Twisted branches.

Cotinus coggygria
Smoke Bush. Green or purple foliage. Deciduous. Up to 2m (6ft).

Cotoneaster species
Lower types, such as C. horizontalis and C. dammeri. Evergreen. White flowers, red berries.

Cytisus
Brooms. Various sizes, up to 1m (3ft) height. Blooms yellow, cream or red. Deciduous.

Daphne mezereum
Deciduous, small shrub. Fragrant, red-purple flowers, followed by red berries.

Deutzia
Smaller shrubs and trailers are best. Flowers white to rose. Deciduous.

Eleagnus
Green and variegated evergreens. Will need pruning to keep in trim.

Erica carnea
Heath and other species. Low-growing, in a variety of foliage and bloom colours. Most prefer acid soil.

Euonymus fortunei varieties
Hardy evergreens, some variegated, and of small size. Good in tubs.

Fuchsia magellanica
Taller growing, sprays up to 1m (3ft). Fairly hardy, but prune hard if frosted.

Gaultheria procumbens (and *G. shallon*)
First is low grower, up to 10cm (4ins). G. shallon will reach 45cm (18ins). Both have white blooms and red berries.

Genista sagittalis
Low, yellow-flowered Broom, up to 30cm (12ins).

Hamamelis species
Witch Hazel. Yellow flowers. Slow growers that will eventually become too large.

Hebe species
Evergreen shrubs, of many sizes and shapes. Several good smaller sorts. Green and variegated foliage.

Hydrangea species
Many species and varieties. Deciduous. Need plenty of water in summer.

Hypericum species
Yellow flowers. Sizes up to 1m (3ft). Generally evergreen.

Ilex crenata
Japanese Holly. Deciduous. Red berries. Requires pruning after a while.

Ligustrum
Privet. Several species suitable. Shrubs or small trees. Prune to shape. White flowers.

Lonicera nitida
Box Honeysuckle. Shrub up to 2m (6ft). White flowers.

Mahonia species
Hardy shrubs, up to 1.5m (5ft), with yellow flowers and black berries.

Malus species
Crabapples. Many good varieties. Some will eventually become too large. Blooms range from white to rose-red. Fruits from yellow to red. Prune to shape.

Pernettya mucronata
Evergreen shrubs, up to 60cm (24ins). Holds white, red or black berries for many months.

Potentilla fruticosa varieties
Range of forms, from 20–100cm (8ins–3ft). Flowers white, yellow, orange. Enjoy poorer, drier soil.

Prunus — flowering varieties
Flowering Almond, Cherry, Peach, Plum. Many flowering varieties will grow in tubs. Some will eventually become too large. Generally grafted onto a rootstock as a 'standard', or half-standard. Annual pruning will determine shape. Range of flower colours from white to rose-red (in single and double forms).

Pyracantha species
Firethorn. All species suitable. White flowers. Berries red to orange. Prunes well.

Rhus typhina
Sumac. Small deciduous tree. Good autumn foliage and fuzzy fruits on branch tips throughout winter.

Rosa
Rose family. All smaller types suitable, including standards and climbers.

Salix species
Willow. Smaller species, such as S. histata and S. repens. Flowers and catkins in spring.

Symphoricarpus species
Snowberry. All smaller types suitable. Flowers white to rose. Fruit usually white.

Spiraea species
Deciduous shrubs, with flowers ranging from white and pink to red. Smaller growers are good.

Viburnum farreri
Deciduous. Can become large. Flowers late autumn or early spring, with white-rose flower clusters.

Ground-covers

Acaena species
New Zealand Bur. Flat, creeping habit. Needs fair moisture.

Aquilegia
Columbine. 30–80cm (12–30ins) tall. Flowers white, rose, yellow and blue.

Armeria maritima
Sea Pink. Flowers pink to rose. Forms rounded hummocks. Slow.

Aubretia hybrids
Low, mat forming perennial. Flower shades from rose to deep red.

Bergenia species
Evergreen. Foliage plant for semi shade. Flowers white to rose and blue.

Campanula
Many species and varieties. Lower, trailing forms are best; taller types tend to be blown over. Flowers blue or white.

From top to bottom:

Rosa foetida 'Bicolor'.

Aubretia hybrid.

Campanula glomerata.

Acaena microphylla 'Kupferteppich'.

Cerastium species
Snow-in-Summer. Perennial, flat growing; silver-grey foliage; white flowers in spring.

Dianthus plumarius
Cottage pink. Spreads as grey mat. Flowering stems up to 30cm (12ins) tall; rose-white to red blooms.

Dicentra formosa
Bleeding Heart. 30cm (12ins). Blooms rose.

Doronicum formosa
Yellow, spring-flowering perennial.

Euphorbia species
Lower growing types suitable; yellow-green flowers. Milky sap is poisonous.

Galium odoratum
Low spreading perennial; white flowers.

Heuchera hybrids
Perennials, in compact, evergreen clumps. Flowers mostly white shades.

Hosta species.
Good foliage perennials, with range of foliage colours; flowers in spikes of white to blue.

Iberis sempervirens
Candytuft. Evergreen perennial, up to 30cm (12ins), with pure white flowers.

Lavendula angustifolia
English lavender. Usually 40–60cm (16–24ins), but dwarf types available.

Lychnis coronaria
Forms grey-leaved clumps; perennial. Deep-red flowers on 50cm (20ins) stems.

Lysimachia nummularia
Creeping Jenny. Flat growing or hanging. Yellow flowers and light-green foliage.

Mimulus species
Musk. Height 20–50cm (8–20ins). Flowers yellow, brown to red. Not fully hardy.

Phlox subulata
Mat forming evergreen perennial. Spring flowers of red, rose to white.

Polygonus affine
Creeping, up to 30cm (12ins) height. Rose-red flowers on erect spikes.

From top to bottom:

Lychnis coronaria.

Creeping Jenny (or Lysimachia nummularia).

Sedum 'Sunset Cloud'.

One of the many Houseleeks.

Primula elatior, veris, or *vulgaris*
Height 10–30cm (4–12ins). Yellow flowers.

Saxifraga species
Heights 5–50cm (2–20ins). Flowers white, rose, red and blue.

Sedum species
Stonecrop. Heights 2–50cm (½–20ins). All colours. Very wide choice.

Sempervivum species
Houseleek. Heights 5–20cm (2–8ins), including blooms. Flowers red or rose to white. Leaves in grey-green rosettes.

Solidago hybrids
Yellow-flowered perennials; lower types suitable.

Stachys olympica
Lamb's Ears. White, woolly-leafed perennial, low, with flowers (purple) on 40cm (16ins) spikes. Not frost hardy.

Thymus species
Thyme. All types suitable. Heights 2–40cm (½–16ins). Blooms rose, red and lilac. Good cover.

Tiarella cordifolia
Height to 30cm (12ins), including blooms. White flowers. Good ground cover.

Verbascum
All types suitable. Heights 40–200cm (16–80ins) (including flower spikes). Mostly yellow blooms; *V. phoeniceum* has purple flowers.

Verbena
All types suited. Height 15–150cm (6–60ins). Usually grown as annuals. Flowers purple, red, blue and white.

Vinca minor
Periwinkle. Height 40cm (16ins). Blue flowers. *V. major* also has blue flowers, and is useful in hanging baskets, with its long trailers. Both have variegated forms.

Shrubby Herbs

Hyssopus officinalis
Hyssop. Perennial, to 70cm (28ins). Dark blue flowers.
Use: leaves.

Lavendula
Lavender. height to 90cm (36ins), including blooms of violent colours.
Use: flowers.

Rosmarinus officinalis
Rosemary. height 1m (3ft). Blue flowers.
Use: leaves.

Ruta graveolens
Rue. Height to 80cm (30ins). Yellow flowers.
Use: leaves.

Salvia officinalis
Sage. Height 50cm (20ins). Blooms violet.
Use: leaves.

Satureja montana
Winter Savory. 35cm (14ins) height. Flowers white-lilac.
Use: leaves and tips.

Thymus vulgaris
Common thyme. Height to 40cm (16ins). Violet blooms.
Use: leaves.

Perennial herbs

Allium schoenoprasum
Chives. up to 40cm (10ins). Violet flowers.
Use: leaves.

Artemisia dracunculus
Tarragon. Height to 60cm (2ft). Flowers yellow-white.
Use: leaves and shoot-tips.

Levisticum officinalis
Lovage. Height to 2m (6ft). Yellow flowers.
Use: leaves.

Melissa officinalis
Lemon balm. 60cm (24ins) height. Flowers whitish.
Use: leaves.

Mentha
Mint, several species. some up to 1m (3ft). Flowers violet to white.
Use: leaves and tips.

Origanum vulgare
Marjoram. Height 50cm (20ins). Blooms rose to white.
Use: young shoots.

From top to bottom:
Allium ursinum.

Borago officinalis, or Borage.

Scilla hispanica hybrids.

Ajuga reptans, the Carpet Bugle.

Annual herbs

Anethum graveolens
Dill. Height 125cm (48ins). Yellow flowers. Use: leaves, young flowers and seed.

Apium graveolens
Celery. Height 80cm (30ins), including green-white blooms. Use: stalks, leaves.

Borago officinalis
Borage. Height 30—90cm (12—36ins). Light-blue flowers. Use: leaves and flowers. Flowers also for cake decorating.

Majorana hortensia
Sweet Marjoram. Height 50cm (20ins). Flowers rose, violet or white. Use: leaves and young tips.

Ocium
Basil. Several varieties. Height 30—60cm (12—24ins). Flowers white, violet to purple. Use: leaves.

Petroselinum
Parsley. Several varieties. Height up to 30cm (12ins). Use: leaves.

Satureja hortensis
Summer Savory. Height 50cm (20ins). Violet flowers. Use: young tips and leaves.

Bulbous and tuberous plants

Allium
Bulbous, onion-like. Height 20—150cm (8—60ins). Flowers white, yellow, pink, purple.

Anemone coronaria
Anemone. Height to 40cm (16ins). Flowers red, blue and white.

Begonia tuberhybrida
Tuberous Begonia. Many varieties; small or large flowering, hanging. Many colours. Tuber is frost hardy.

Canna hybrids
Tuberous, spreading roots. Flower heights up to 150cm (60ins). Colours rose, red, orange, yellow, in single or double forms. Leaves red, green or variegated.

Colchicum hybrids
Autumn Crocus. Height to 40cm (16ins). Flowers rose, purple, white, after leaves have disappeared.

Crocus hybrids
Height 10—15cm (4—6ins). Flowers yellow, mauve, blue and white.

Dahlia
Most suitable are Anemone-flowered, Mignon, Pompom and Top-mix groups. Variety of colours. Heights 30—100cm (12—36ins).

Calanthus species
Snowdrop. White flowers, to 20cm (8ins).

Hyacinthus varieties
Hyacinth. Height 30—40cm (12—16ins). Flowers: in many colours.

Ismene (Hymanocallis)
Height 40—60cm (16—24ins). White blooms. Protect in winter.

Lilium species and varieties
Select types that do not grow taller than about 1m (3ft). Many different colours.

Muscari species
Grape Hyacinth. Low, up to 15cm (6ins). Flowers white or blue. Hardy.

Narcissus
Daffodil, Narcissus. Many sizes and varieties. Best are those lower than 40cm (16ins).

Oxalis species
Heights 15—35cm (6—14ins). Flowers rose, yellow, pink, mauve and blue. Cover well in winter.

Scilla species
Heights 10—30cm (4—12ins). Flowers blue or white.

Tigrida pavonia
Mexican Tiger Flower. Height 60cm (24ins). Bright, mixed colour blooms. Protect bulbs in winter.

Tulipa hybrids
Select lower growing types, and botanical species. Many different colours.

Shade-loving plants
Most of these types prefer humus-rich soil.

Ajuga reptans
Carpet Bugle. Low ground-cover, with green, purple or variegated foliage; blooms on short spikes of blue.

Anaphalis triplinervis
Height 25cm (10ins). White flowers.

Arabis procurrens
Creeping habit; grows to 25cm (10ins) height. White flowers.

Asarum europaeum
Height 15cm (6ins). Brown-flowered creeper.

With shade-loving plants, you usually find that they prefer a light soil, rich in humus. Most species will have originated from forest environments, or similar shady situations, which are very often moist too.

Asperula odorata, the Woodruff.

Tiarella cordifolia.

Asperula odorata
Sweet Woodruff. Low, spreading perennial, up to 25cm (10ins). White flowers.

Astilbe chinensis pumila
Height to 30cm (12ins). Rose flowers. Creeping habit.

Bergenia species
Height to 40cm (16ins). Glossy, evergreen leaves; flowers white, rose, mauve and red.

Campanula species
Bellflower. Choose types with shorter flower stalks. Most prefer light shade. Flowers white, blue, mauve.

Convallaria majalis
Lily of the valley. Height 25cm (10ins). White flowers; creeping habit.

Coreopsis verticillata
Yellow daisy-like flowers, on stems up to 60cm (24ins) tall.

Doronicum orientale varieties
Leopards Bane. Spreading, lower growing, up to 50cm (20ins). Yellow flowers.

Epimedium species
Heights 15–50cm (6–20ins). Flowers yellow, brown, rose, red, white.

Geranium platypetalum (or G. ibericum)
Violet-blue flowers, on a lower, spreading plant of about 50cm (20ins) height.

Hosta species and varieties.
Deciduous foliage perennials, with flower spikes of shades of white to blue. Leaves in range of shapes and colours, from green to blue, to grey, and variegated.

Lamium species
Dead Nettle. Height 20–40cm (8–16ins). Leaves green or variegated. Flowers on trailing stems are white, yellow, rose, or mauve.

Lathyrus vernus
Non-climbing Sweet Pea, reaching 40cm (16ins). Flowers purple-blue.

Lysimachia nummularia
Creeping Jenny. Flat growing trailer; yellow flowers. Moisture loving.

Oenothera fruticosa 'Yellow River'
Height 30cm (12ins). Bright yellow flowers. Suitable for semi-shade.

Physalis franchetii
Chinese Lanterns. Height to 1m (3ft). Orange-coloured fruits; good for vase or drying.

Prunella species
Height to 25cm (10ins). Flowers usually violet, but also white or reddish. Enjoys shade.

Rodgersia aesculifolia
Good for deep shade. *R. pinnata* prefers better light. Height to 120cm (48ins). Flowers white or rose.

Rudbeckia fulgida 'Goldsturm'
Height 60cm (24ins). Yellow flowers. Will tolerate a certain amount of shade.

Saxifraga species
Height 10–60cm (4–24ins). Flower colours range from white and rose to red. Semi-shade, and some in full shade.

Tiarella cordifolia
Height to 30cm (12ins). Creeping habit, with white flowers.

Tellima grandiflora
Height 40cm (16ins). Flowers green-white.

Vinca minor
Height 40cm (16ins). Blue flowers. Tolerates full shade. Green and variegated foliage, on trailing stems.

Waldsteinia ternata
Height to 25cm (10ins). Yellow flowers. Evergreen with creeping habit.

Plants suited to hanging containers

Arabis caucasica
Mats of grey foliage; carpets of white flowers in spring.

Begonia
Hanging varieties. Colours mostly reds, rose and yellows.

Cerastium species
Flat, mat forming, with silvery foliage and white flowers.

Fuchsia Mrs W. Rundle.

Fuchsia varieties
Some types have 'hanging' habit, in many flower shapes and colours. Most have to be protected in winter.

Glechoma hederacea
Ground Ivy. Ground-covering trailer, with green and variegated foliage, and blue flowers.

Hedera helix varieties
Common Ivy. Widely used evergreen trailers and climbers, in a variety of leaf shapes, sizes and colours.

Iberis species
Candytuft. White, mauve or rose flowers. Annual and perennial types.

Lobelia erinus varieties
Annual trailers. Flowers in shades of white, blue and red.

Lobularia maritima
Annual. Flowers white and violet.

Lysimachia nummularia
Slender, trailing stems. Yellow flowers.

Pelargonium peltatum
Ivy geranium. Trailing habit, with single and double blooms, in white, pink, red, and many shades (and bi-colours). Not winter hardy.

Tropaeolum majus, or Nasturtium.

Citrus microcarpa.

Petunia varieties
Annual, in a variety of colours; 'cascade' types are best for baskets.

Sedum sieboldii
Rose-red flowers; leaves green, bluish, or cream.

Tropaeolum majus
Nasturtium. Annual, spreading and hanging, in many colours and shades.

With a little imagination, and with careful handling, you can try many other plants in troughs or baskets. Just remember that your choice must be wind tolerant, and not be too drought sensitive. Understandably, taller-growing plants should not be amongst your selection, as they either blow over or need extra staking and support.

Tub plants

If you want to keep larger 'specimen' plants in tubs, as 'orangery-type' plants, you'll need a suitable overwintering place for them. You cannot simply 'put them in the garage' for the winter.

The following species are the easiest to handle amongst the more permanent tub plants:

Agapanthus praecox
Light-blue blooms on stalks of 60cm (24ins) height. A perennial that will die back in winter, if not protected. Can be kept in a frost free space, or heated garage during winter. During a mild winter they can be left outdoors with some covering.

Agave americana
This is the largest growing agave, whose leaves can reach a length of 150cm (60ins). When an agave reaches flowering age (after many years), it can produce a flower stalk of 2–4m (6–12ft) in height. The leaves have very sharp tips so either cut the ends off or push corks onto them to prevent injury.

Citrus species
Citrus trees can develop into magnificent display plants. They need cool winters of at least 5°C (40°F).

Fatsia japonica
Well suited to tub culture, especially with light shade. Needs to be slightly warmer than citrus during winter.

Laurus nobilis
Laurel. A traditional tub plant, usually seen with a clipped, round head, or other shapes. Will not tolerate any frost.

Yucca filamentosa and *Y. flaccida*
Both species can produce flower stalks of up to 2m (6ft) in length. They are relatively hardy, but will only tolerate a light frost.

Apart from the above exotic species, there are many more popular types of shrub and perennial that are extremely attractive when displayed on their own in tubs. A good example is *Hydrangea macophylla* and amongst the perennials, the many *Hosta* varieties can be very decorative. Both of these examples can be left outdoors during winter.

Bonsai: starting with a young pine tree.

Bonsai pots must be relatively small, and should not draw attention away from the tree.

Choice of pot depends on shape of root system.

108

Adventures with plants

Bonsai

Special bonsai pot, with enlarged drainage holes, for threading tie-wires.

Experimenting with plants

For adventurous plant-lovers who enjoy experimenting, the indoor garden offers many opportunities. Among the pots and containers of 'ordinary' houseplants, you can always find space for a miniature tree, a few colourful bulbs, or for a plant in a glass container. You might even find space for a children's garden where they can grow their own plants. It is wonderful for a child to see a new plant developing from a pineapple top or to grow a tree from an apple seed.

By experimenting with plants you get to know them better which helps to strengthen the bonds between man and nature. For young and old, the value of this relationship should not be underestimated.

Of course there is always the possibility that an experiment will not work. When doing anything new and unusual with plants, know-how and experience tend to come with practice. Of course you are bound to make some mistakes on the way! So you will find several 'green' experiments described in this chapter to improve your own chances of success.

Mini-trees in pots

'Bonsai' is the art of growing dwarfed trees in pots. Although the word 'Bonsai' is Japanese (literally 'plant in a pot'), it is generally accepted that the art originated in China. Miniature trees were already being grown in containers as far back as the T'ang Dynasty (618 – 907) and the culture was called P'en tsai. A few centuries later Bonsai culture was being practised in India and Japan, where the art was further developed.

During the last 100 years there has been a renewal of interest in Bonsai in Japan and since the beginning of this century these miniature trees have become known and grown in the West. Nowadays there are Bonsai societies in most large towns that spread knowledge and provide encouragement for this satisfying pastime.

To grow or buy your trees?

Bonsai trees can be bought 'ready-grown' at any of the better stocked nurseries or garden centres. However, they are certainly not cheap. Don't let yourself be put off by this though, as it does not mean that the growing of Bonsai trees is an expensive hobby. It is quite possible to grow your own trees from seed. Seeds are available from seed specialists, but you can collect your own seed just as easily if the right species grow in your area. If the tree you choose is difficult to grow from seed you can always try other methods of propagating, such as taking cuttings, layering or laying-in. Grafting is not recommended as this type of propagation tends to leave ugly scars on the stems. This is undesirable in a work of art, which is, after all, what these trees are.

Pots and materials for Bonsai

To propagate trees from seed you will need seed trays, and all the items needed for any seed sowing. For Bonsai growing you should not need more than one or two plants of each species, so you can sow seed of more than one type in the same seed tray. Later, when the seedlings are established they will be ready for transplanting into pots or dishes.

When selecting a suitable pot, bear in mind that the pot should never detract from the tree. For this reason it is best to choose a neutral colour or a colour that is reflected in the shades of the stems, foliage or flowers. Glazed pots are better than unglazed, as they do not dry out as rapidly and have a better appearance.

The size of the pot depends on the size of the tree. Choose the smallest one possible as the root growth must be restricted to keep the Bonsai small. It is possible to

obtain a genuine Japanese Bonsai pot.
Bonsai trees must have well drained
containers, so make sure that the pots have
adequate holes in the bottom.

Aids and tools for Bonsai
Wire is essential for the shaping and
training of branches. Pipe cleaners are
useful for training young, tender branches,
as the fluffy material covering the wire
prevents damage. Wiring of older branches
is best done with stiffer copper wire or
plastic-coated florists wire.

For the pruning of Bonsai use a strong pair
of scissors with sharp points, and a really
sharp knife. A stiff brush comes in handy
for loosening soil from roots before root
pruning. A planting trowel is useful when
re-potting, while a teaspoon or stick can be
used to keep the potting soil loose.

Soil mixtures for Bonsai
A mixture of 50% clay, 10% leaf mould,
10% sharp sand and 30% peat would be
suitable for most Bonsai trees. This basic
mixture can be adapted to suit the needs of
particular species. Trees that grow
naturally in acid soil will benefit from
having extra peat in the mixture, while
those that grow on chalk benefit from
having the leaf mould content increased.
Obviously the soil mixture you prepare
must be based on what the tree would
naturally prefer. Don't get the soil for your
mixture from natural sources, as it could
contain organisms carrying disease.

Keeping records
The cultivation of Bonsai trees is a precise
art. It is therefore sensible to keep a record
of the dates when they were topped,
pruned, fed or re-potted. The origin and
life span of the tree can also be of
importance. You can keep track of when
the tree is going to need any particular
treatment by the records you keep. You
can, in addition, make comparisons. In this
way you will undoubtedly discover that
even trees of the same species will react
differently to the same treatment.

Keeping Bonsais small
Trees have a natural tendency to grow
large, and fairly quickly. To retain the
characteristic shape of a tree in miniature,
its uncontrolled growth must be restricted.
This can be achieved by regular pruning of
the roots, pruning the growing tips, and

Bonsai is an art, and the result a work of art.

Tools and accessories of a Bonsai grower.

clipping the leaves. A tree maintains a
balanced relationship between the extent of
its root system and its crown. An extensive
root system can take up plenty of water and
nutrients, and this has a direct influence on
the growth of the parts that are above
ground. It follows that reducing the root
system will result in slower development of
stems and leaves. Bonsai culture makes use
of this basic principle. Trees that have been
grown from seed usually develop a tap

110

Top:
Bonsai must be removed from their pots for root pruning.

Middle:
Root pruning helps keep the tree small.

Lower:
Bonsai look best in a simple setting.

This Bonsai has a balance between blooms and foliage.

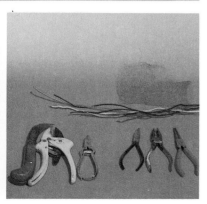

The pruning of the root system must be done with care. Remove the tree from its pot and shake off as much soil as possible from the roots. A stiff brush can be of assistance here. Trim away older roots, or those interfering with others and cut back other roots to one third of their former length. The uppermost three or four roots should not be removed as, at a later stage, it may be desirable to expose them on the surface of the soil, as a feature, which would be spoiled by premature pruning. Bonsai trees usually need to be re-potted and root pruned every two to three years. The best time for this is between February and March. If the tree shows earlier signs of over vigorous root development, then an intermediate re-potting and pruning might be necessary. The signs are easy to recognise: the roots reach the sides of the pot and push up to the surface, or begin growing out through the drainage holes underneath.

Leaf pruning of Bonsai trees
There are two main reasons for leaf pruning Bonsai trees. In the first place, growth is stimulated, and in this process,

root. During its first year, this must be reduced to about a third of its original length. To do this, the Bonsai must be removed from the seed tray, pruned and then planted into a normal plant pot. At two years old, the rest of the tap root should be removed. It may be necessary to remove or cut back some of the other roots at the same time. This process will have to be repeated at regular intervals.

111

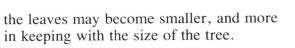

From top to bottom:
Good drainage is essential.

Berried Bonsai at its best in autumn.

Shaping and pruning is precise work.

Spring beauty of a young Bonsai.

the leaves may become smaller, and more in keeping with the size of the tree.

In specific cases, leaf pruning can help give the tree a better, or a particular shape.

You may only need to remove excess leaves, or leaves that overlap each other, or are too close together. If you want smaller foliage, then you must remove some of the leaves, by cutting them off close to the stem. A new shoot, of reduced size, can then develop from the bud in the axil of the removed leaf.

Leaf pruning is a disturbing experience for a plant, and it is not surprising that only healthy and stronger plants can survive it. You can begin leaf pruning when the tree is about four years old. Prior to this, only light pruning should be undertaken. In Maples and a few other species, the response to leaf pruning is rapid. It is possible to prune these species twice in one year. In most other species, once a year is

enough. Where leaf pruning is done twice a year, the first clipping must be done as soon as the leaves have fully developed in spring. They then produce new leaves which can be trimmed later in the summer. Trees that are to be leaf pruned only once a year, should be done in mid-summer, and the process is then repeated the following summer, if the first pruning was not effective.

Pruning and topping of Bonsais

The raising of a Bonsai tree involves the forming and shaping of its features, and this cannot be achieved without pruning (as is also the case with normal outdoor trees).

Heavier branches that spoil the shape of the tree can be removed between autumn and the end of the winter. Smaller twigs can be cut in June, while buds may be nipped from spring through until the end of summer. Pruning of branches and twigs is

A true copy of its 'big brother'.

The shaping of a Bonsai will depend on the preference of the grower, on the type of plant, and on its present shape. When you are still learning the art, it is easiest to let younger trees develop more natural forms. Shaping and styling can be applied as experience is gained. An alternative is to train the tree according to traditional Japanese rules (which are also applied to the floral art of Ikebana). According to these principles, the stem represents 'heaven', with 'man' on the left side and 'earth' on the right. Other Japanese styles are: the Hankan, where the tree is made to look like an ancient, wind-swept specimen; the Ikadi-Buki, where a small forest is created from a horizontal stem, growing on the soil, and the Kengai, where a weeping habit is developed. Joining a Bonsai society is probably the best way of learning the basics of this art.

done according to the same rules that apply to pruning in the garden. You will need to pick out the buds if the tree threatens to produce too many leaves. Terminal buds of main stems and branches are removed once the limb has reached the desired length.

After pinching out of buds, or topping, the tree should be misted with a fine spray, preferably with rain water, or soft tap water.

Conifers need a slightly different treatment. In spring they develop pale green 'candles' in the tips of their branches. These are new shoots, and cannot simply be clipped off as this would result in dead, brown coloured needles on the tips. You must clip them carefully between two bunches of needles.

The wiring of Bonsais
Pruning on its own will not be enough to shape a Bonsai tree into a less rigid, upright form. Also, despite careful

A Bonsai collection involves much time, so would not suit everyone.

113

After topping and disbudding, spray with a fine mist.

Years of hard work to develop this shape?

bottom of the pot, before the plant is installed. On the underside, the wire can be held in place with a small stick, and its upper end can protrude about 1.5cm (½in) above the soil surface. Later on any wiring that needs a firm anchor can be attached to this end.

Bending or cutting-in

The wire must be wound evenly and firmly around the trunk or branch to be bent. It should not be too tight, as the branch will still need a little space to expand its diameter as it develops. If the trunk or branch seems too stiff or too brittle to be bent into the shape you want, a small incision can be made at the place where the 'bow' is wanted, and then continue with the wiring.

Special bending clamps and other devices for more difficult subjects can be obtained if necessary. Finally, always twist the wire in the direction in which the stem or branch is to be bent, and for the first few days after wiring, spray frequently and keep the plant out of direct sunlight.

handling, you may find that a bend appears in a stem where it was not wanted, or the branches grow too upright. If this happens, you can encourage changes by bending the stems and twigs to the desired shapes, and using wires to maintain these new forms. After several years of being held in a new shape with wires, the tree would have 'grown' into this shape and will retain it once the wires are removed. With deciduous trees, wiring should be done some time between April and June. For conifers, October to January is most effective.

It is a good idea to make provision for wiring when you are re-potting. Wires can then be pushed through the holes in the

Maintenance of established Bonsai trees

The only regular maintenance that a fully grown Bonsai tree needs is daily syringing in summer, regular watering, and occasional feeding. It may also need to be topped now and then. During the first few years it is necessary to re-pot and root prune every second or third year. Even if the tree has been correctly pruned at an early age, it will still need to be done now and again.

Trees that have reached an age of ten years can remain in the same pot for a further five years, with careful management. Blood and bone meal can be used as fertilizer for Bonsai trees. Ordinary houseplant feeds are also suitable, but only in very diluted form.

Special devices are used for bending stems.

'Tree on rock' in Japanese style.

Bulbs in the home

Daffodils, hyacinths, tulips, grape-hyacinths and snowdrops will all grow indoors.

Bulbs for inside

During the dark months of winter, the indoor garden tends to be somewhat colourless. Very few plants choose this time to produce flowers. There is much to be said for using bulbs to produce colour — such as tulips, hyacinths, narcissus and crocus. They can provide a very colourful display on your window sill at a time when there is little else, i.e. between December and April.

Methods of forcing bulbs

Bulbs can be induced to start producing their blooms in different ways.

The special glass pots filled with water and containing a hyacinth bulb are well known. Most bulbs are grown in soil, or in a fibrous peaty mixture, but it is also possible to use gravel in water-filled pots, troughs or bowls. With all the methods, water is essential. During the previous growing season each bulb has been developing and storing enough nourishment to produce a flowering stalk. The best blooms come from the largest and healthiest bulbs. These are relatively more expensive but they do give the best blooms. For the best results unpack the bulbs as soon as they arrive and store them in a cool, dry and dark spot.

Potting up of bulbs

The potting up of bulbs should be done between the end of September and the end of December. You can start by planting those which would flower first in the garden. If these are planted late, they will also flower later. Hyacinths and tulips planted at the end of September, usually flower in December. If they have been planted after the middle of October, flowers can be expected in February or March.

Bulbs can be planted in an ordinary potting mixture. The pots or bowls should be unglazed. First, half fill the pots with soil,

then place the bulbs onto this, 1.5cm (½in) apart. See that the tops of the bulbs are level with the rim of the pot. Then fill the pot with soil, and press down lightly without damaging the bulbs. After firming down, the potting soil should be about 1.5cm (½in) below the rim of the pot. This makes it easier to water without making a mess.

Cool, dark storage for bulbs

Before the bulbs can be induced to start flowering, they need to be stored in a cool, dark place. The best results are achieved by burying the bulbs (in their containers) about 15cm (6ins) deep in the garden. The ground above them should be covered with reeds or straw to protect them from frost. If this is not a method that is convenient to you, then you could store the bulb pots in a cool, moist and dark spot in your home. A cellar is ideal for this purpose or a cupboard that is dark and unheated. Centrally heated homes are less suitable for forcing bulbs as the atmosphere is usually too warm and dry. Kitchen cupboards are often suitable or the garage, provided it doesn't get too cold.

Into the light

When the bulb shoots have grown to about 7.5–10cms (3–4ins) in length, then the containers with their bulbs can be brought into the light. If after their stay in the dark, the flower shoots do not develop, but

While it is still winter outdoors, bulbs can provide indoor colour.

remain stunted in the heart of the plant, this is a sure sign that their stay in the dark was too short. If there is any doubt about when to bring them out, it is always safer to leave them in darkness for longer than to bring them out too soon. In general, the longest stored bulbs will provide the best blooms. Forcing early flowering bulbs is the most difficult. Some of the problems can be overcome by placing paper caps over the shoots after they are brought into the light for the first time, and leaving them covered for a week. Later flowering bulbs can be brought directly into the light without further attention. Best results are achieved at a temperature of about 20°C (68°F).

Bulbs in gravel and water

Another popular method of growing bulbs is achieved by using pots and bowls (without drainage holes) filled with gravel and water. Only heavy bulbs of top quality will give good results with this system.

Set about potting up in this way. Wash the gravel thoroughly, and half fill the pots with it. Place the bulbs onto this gravel and fill up to three-quarters of the height of the bulbs with pebbles or grit to hold the bulbs firmly upright. Lastly, add water up to the level of the bases of the bulbs. The bottoms of the bulbs must not stand in water, or they may rot. The water level must be regularly checked and topped up.

Special glasses for hyacinths

Special glasses or vases have been developed for forcing hyacinths. For these glasses you must obtain prepared bulbs, preferably of top quality, which have been refrigerated to prepare them for blooming.

Remove any dirt or loose scales and then place the bulb on the glass. This should be filled with water to within 1–2mm (about 1/16in) of the base of the bulb. The glass is then placed in a dark position, in a cellar or cupboard. Water must be checked and topped up at weekly intervals. After 6 to 8 weeks the shoot should be about 7.5cm (3ins) long and the flower bud should be easily felt. Usually at this stage the long, white roots will have reached the bottom of the glass. Now you bring the glass into the light and, within a week, it should start blooming.

Forced bulbs do not keep

Generally, it is not worth keeping treated or forced bulbs after they have bloomed for a second year's blooming. This is because the bulbs will not have had the chance to build up sufficient reserves of nourishment and, being in a 'spent' state, are in no condition to produce a further flower crop. This is especially true of the early bloomers.

If you do not want to waste the bulbs, cut off the flower heads as soon as they have faded and place the bowl or pot in a cooler place. Later, the bulbs can be planted out in the garden — but do not expect too much in the way of blooms.

Some general remarks, tips and advice for the growing of some of the better known bulbs.

Bulb	Remarks
Hyacinth	*Hyacinths are potted up in soil from the beginning of October to the end of November. For the earliest blooming you need prepared bulbs. For flowering in January and February unforced bulbs can be used, but all need the 'darkness' treatment. Place bulbs 1.5cm (½in) apart in bowls or pots. When shoots are 8cm (3½ins) long and the buds can be felt, the bowls can be brought out of the dark. Miniature hyacinths can be forced in pots with gravel and water. When the shoots are 5–6cm (2½ins) long, they can come into the light.*
Tulips	*Tulips are potted up in potting soil at the same times as hyacinths and placed in darkness. When early shoots are 6–8cm (2–3ins) long, and those of the latter type 8–9cm (3–4ins), they can be brought into the light.*
Narcissus	*Narcissus varieties must be planted in soil from the beginning of October to the middle of November. The bulbs should not be completely buried so leave the top third showing above ground. When the shoots are about 10cm (4ins), at the end of January, then the containers can be brought into the light. It is also possible to force certain varieties in bowls of gravel and water. If this method is used the bulbs must be planted between the middle of October and the end of December. The pots can be brought directly into full light.*
Crocus	*Crocuses are forced by*

Spring indoors. Bulbs are blooming, and cress is ready for picking.

placing them close together in a dish on a layer of gravel. Cover them lightly with gravel to keep them upright. Add just enough water to reach the undersides of the bulbs. After a short time in the dark, the dish can come into a light room which is not too warm.

It is possible to grow crocuses in specially designed glasses. Yellow crocus varieties are difficult to force.

Plants from fruit and vegetables

Fun for the children

The cut-off top of a carrot or pineapple conceals a complete plant, and a potato or bean can develop into a plant inside your home. With a bit of effort it is possible to turn your kitchen into a complete 'vegetable garden'. The plants may not be quite as beautiful as houseplants but a great deal of pleasure can be gained from creating something from discarded fruit or vegetables. Younger children can have great fun if they are given the opportunity to experiment with off-cuts and have a section of window sill to put them on. They will also learn more about the 'wonders of nature' in an enjoyable way.

Plants from kitchen refuse

It is very easy to grow a plant from a carrot top. Simply cut off the top 1.5cm (½in) of a largish carrot and place this piece, cut side down, in a shallow dish of water. It will soon develop fine feathery leaves from the top, and roots from the base. For the best results, the water level should just cover the base of the carrot, and the dish should stand in a good light.

A beetroot can be grown in the same way. This is particularly good as the beetroot has colourful leaves which would not look out of place amongst decorative houseplants. If you look around the kitchen you are sure to find more root vegetables that could be grown into new plants.

How about salsify, or parsnips, or turnips?

New potato plants

It will come as no surprise to learn that potato tubers will grow into new plants! Anyone who has stored potatoes for a while knows how they

Endive 'offcuts' can provide attractive kitchen greenery.

develop 'sprouts'. These sprouts are nothing more than young leaves and roots. Choose a potato tuber which is not too large with several developing 'eyes', and balance it in the neck of a jar which is filled with water to just below the level of the tuber. It will soon start growing. Place it in a cool, shady position, and for the best shape, remove all but two or three of the sprouts. They can grow quite tall and may need support. Sprouting potatoes can also be planted in pots. Apart from the foliage display they would ultimately form tiny new potatoes on their roots.

A pineapple plant

Pineapple plants are very attractive and are sold in nurseries as houseplants. With a bit of care it is possible to grow your own from the discarded top from your next pineapple. This is how to do it. Cut off the green top with about 2.5cm (1in) of flesh attached to it. Scrape out the fleshy part, and then allow the whole piece to dry in the air for two to three days. Then place the top onto the surface of a pot containing a light, sandy potting mixture, with soil just covering the base of the crown. The potting soil must not be kept too damp. In most cases the pineapple crown will develop roots and the new plant will start growing. This plant will be slightly different from the ornamental species sold in nurseries but will be just as decorative.

Beans, pips and other seeds

Apples, peaches, melons, cucumbers, tomatoes and a host of other fruits can be grown from seed. Suitable seed can be found in ripe or, even better, over-ripe fruits.

Wash the collected seed under running water then lay them on a sheet of absorbent paper and let them dry in the sun. After a few days sow the seed in a pot containing a light potting mix and put it in a warm, dark place. As soon as the germinating seedlings appear above the ground the pot should be brought into the light.

Beans, peas and other legumes all contain seeds and each can be sown to produce a new plant. Do remember that most legumes are picked young so they are soft and tender, but their seeds will be too immature for sowing. It is better to use the dried 'pulses' that are used in soups. These dried beans, peas or lentils should first be soaked in water for a few hours before sowing. As with most other seeds, it is best to place the seed tray in a warm, dark spot until they start germinating.

Onions and garlic

Onions and garlic are bulbs like crocuses and hyacinths. It is therefore very easy to produce new plants from these. An onion can be planted in a hyacinth glass or in a pot filled with potting soil. The garlic bulb contains more than one plant. If you remove the outer skin you will see that it is made up of several segments. Each of these can produce a plant if placed in a pot with a light potting mix and kept moist. An onion

will produce a stalk and flower-head during the course of the summer if it is placed on a bright, sunny window sill. You will hardly ever have the same success in blooming with a garlic plant, but as compensation for the lack of flower each segment will form a whole new bulb. At the end of summer you will be able to use your own home grown garlic.

A forest at home

Once children have developed a taste for producing plants from kitchen 'waste', they will probably not want to stop there. There are many other plants that have a complete plant inside them just waiting for a chance to grow.

It is a whole new experience for children to create a forest in the home. This can be done by sowing acorns, chestnuts, horse chestnuts and other tree seeds found in the garden or park. When planted in a pot and placed in a cool, light place these will eventually germinate and start growing into trees. Regular pruning will keep the trees down to a manageable size. They can grow for years on a window sill and once they get too big they can be planted outside.

Stimulating a child's imagination

Children are curious and always on the look-out for new ways of exercising their imaginations. A house garden can present a number of possibilities. A trough with cacti, succulents and sand can set the mind thinking of cowboys! A trough with water plants is another example.

Then of course there are the more dramatic plant types, such as the carnivorous species, and the mobile types (Venus Flytrap and Sensitive Plant are examples of these).

The Sunflower, that develops in one season from a tiny seed to a giant plant with huge flowers, is always a favourite.

You can even get a cabbage to flower indoors.

Centre: A red cabbage can still manage a second leaf display.

A tiny pumpkin pip will result in a giant plant.

Potted vegetables and herbs

A 'vegetable plot' in pots, buckets and bags.

French beans have few roots so only need a small pot.

A modern trend

More and more people are discovering that certain vegetables are not only tasty, but can also be good to look at. Growing your own vegetables and herbs on a window sill is extremely satisfying.

Some plant breeders and seed producers anticipated this trend and have developed many varieties of mini vegetable specifically for growing in the home garden. Of course, it is possible to use any of the old favourite varieties. Those who have allocated a space on their window sill for garden herbs can get seed for virtually every useful variety.

When developing a vegetable garden indoors, it is best to start early in the spring.

The climate indoors

Vegetables and herbs are normally grown outdoors, and the indoor gardener must always keep this in mind. You will need to reproduce outdoor conditions as closely as possible. The first problem you'll have to contend with is light intensity as inside will be somewhat darker than outdoors. Most vegetables would do well on a south-facing sill. In other situations, the lack of light will need supplementing with artificial 'grow-lamps'.

The temperature indoors can also give rise to problems. Behind glass, the temperature can rise to a level higher than is healthy for vegetables and herbs. In the summer when the sun is high, you may have to provide some form of shading. The majority of vegetables and herbs flourish at temperatures between 18°C/66°F and 22°C/72°F. At night the temperature should not fall below 15°C/60°F. Root vegetables are the exception. For them the normal room temperature is rather too warm. Find them a place in a cooler room which can be slightly darker than a south-facing window sill.

Finally, ventilation is important for the mini vegetable garden but keep in mind that the plants will not respond well to draughts.

Pots, soil mixtures and fertilizer

Vegetables and herbs have the same basic needs regarding pots and soils as the average houseplant. You can use the ordinary commercial potting soils, and any good glazed or plastic pot or trough will be perfectly adequate.

Naturally, the pot or trough must suit the particular 'crop' to be grown in it. If you are growing carrots a deeper pot is needed, whilst lettuce, with its shallow and smaller root system, only needs a shallow dish.

The care of vegetables and herbs is similar to, and just as important, as with houseplants. They will have to be watered and sprayed regularly and most important, the fertilizer programme must be kept up to date. When choosing fertilizers, remember that leaf vegetables need a high nitrogen feed, potassium is beneficial to root vegetables, and ripening fruits need enough phosphorus. So for each group of vegetables you will need to find the appropriate fertilizer.

Vegetables and herbs from seed

Sowing vegetable and herb seed is not difficult but must be done with care. Fill well-drained pots or trays with light potting soil to within 1.5cm (½in) of the rim, and dampen it. When the soil has been firmed down it is ready for sowing. Larger seeds, such as beans, can be sown by making holes with a stick and inserting a seed in each hole. The whole tray should then be covered with a thin layer of soil. With finer seeds it is simply a matter of evenly scattering the seed, as thinly as possible, over the damp soil and covering with a very thin layer of compost or fine sand, which

should be firmly pressed down with a plank. The seeds — both large and small — will germinate more quickly if they are covered with a pane of glass and placed in a warm, dark place. To prevent condensation causing rotting of the seed or seedlings, turn the glass over each day.

Care of vegetables and herbs
As soon as the seedlings begin to appear above the soil they will need some light. Place the trays in a light spot, but not in direct sunlight. Once they have formed their second pair of leaves the plants can be moved to their permanent position. The removal of the pane of glass should be done in stages. When the plants start growing above the rim of the tray or pot the glass should be raised on blocks. Fresh air can then get to the plants. Each day raise the glass slightly higher until, after about a week, you can remove it altogether. At this stage it is time to thin out the surplus seedlings. On the backs of seed packets there are usually instructions as to how far apart the plants should be.

The excess plants can be removed carefully from the seed tray and planted in another pot. Most herbs and vegetables will respond well to this treatment but it will not work with root vegetables.

Vegetables for the house garden

The best known vegetables suitable for growing indoors are listed below, with notes on their growth habits and other important features.

Vegetable	Remarks
Aubergine (Egg plant)	Grows well in a light spot in grow-bags or in a 20cm (8ins) pot. Must be helped with pollenation by tapping the stems during flowering to distribute the pollen.
Beetroot	Beetroot will do well in a trough in a cooler position. Dwarf strains are available. Sow direct and thin out where too close.
Carrots	For pots and troughs on a sill use the newer, short varieties. They prefer a light, sandy soil and cooler situation.
Cucumber	Baby cucumbers will grow in a larger size pot. Their taste is somewhat sweeter than the normal varieties.
French Beans	Sow 6 seeds in a 20cm (8ins) pot. If all grow, thin out to 4 plants. Spray the plants daily whilst in flower to aid pollenation.
Green Peas	The dwarf varieties do very well in a 30cm (12ins) pot. Provide some support by way of twiggy branches.
Lettuce	Lettuce do well in grow-bags but also in troughs or 10cm (4ins) deep pots. For healthy development they need regular, good watering and fresh air. They prefer a cool spot, with good light.
Peppers	Peppers will grow well in a south-facing window. The smaller varieties will need a 15cm (6ins) pot, and plenty of feeding. Spray leaves and flowers to aid pollenation.
Radishes	Apart from needing plenty of water, radishes are quite the easiest vegetable to grow. Their demands are few and they can be cropped in a short time.
Tomatoes	Tomatoes need good light and warmth to grow well. They can be planted in grow-bags, larger pots, or even hanging baskets (if miniature, or trailing type). There are several good miniature varieties. Tomatoes respond to regular feeding and must never be allowed to dry out.

A lightly shaded spot is fine for chives.

Sage prefers full sunlight.

Dwarf peas are specially adapted for home culture.

Herbs

This list includes the best known herbs and some notes on their growth and care.

Herb	Remarks
Basil	*Basil likes a warm, sheltered position and well drained soil. Pinch out flowers to promote shoots.*
Chives	*Needs semi-shade, and well drained soil but must be watered frequently.*
Garlic	*Garlic likes a sunny position and a light soil to which well rotted manure has been added.*
Marjoram	*Give marjoram a sunny spot and good, well drained soil. It is inclined to spread and become leggy, so needs clipping back now and then to keep in shape.*
Mint	*Mint likes a cool, shady spot and ample water. There are many interesting varieties and flavours of mint, besides the usual spearmint and peppermint.*
Parsley	*Likes semi-shade and a fertile, but well drained soil. Cut back in September to encourage new leaf formation.*
Rosemary	*Buy a young plant from a nursery and pot up in well drained soil. Prefers a sunny situation.*
Sage	*Likes full sun and ordinary, well drained soil. Plants are inclined to become leggy, so need regular trimming.*
Tarragon	*Likes a sunny position. Must have sharp, well drained soil. To encourage leaves pinch out flower buds as soon as they appear.*
Thyme	*Thyme forms an attractive little bush and there are several interesting varieties. It needs sunshine and well drained soil.*

Parsley (left) and mint (above) are both much-used herbs. They do well on a cool window sill.

Bottle gardens

A carefully prepared bottle garden can grow for many years with little maintenance.

Bottle gardens

Growing plants in bottles is a relatively new hobby. At the beginning of the last century an English researcher discovered by chance that it was possible to grow plants in a sealed bottle. He became so fascinated by the discovery that he went on to test over a hundred different plant types in this controlled environment.

He found that plants, unable to cope with the polluted air of London, thrived in a bottle. He also observed that a carefully prepared bottle with plants could be kept for years without needing any attention.

This was particularly important for plant dealers who, needing to import their wares from distant countries, started shipping their cargoes in sealed, portable crates. With the arrival of air transport this method of transporting plants declined.

Within the protected enclosure of a bottle the moisture content is captive, there are no great or sudden temperature fluctuations, and there are no draughts. For sensitive plants that are badly affected by the dry climate in centrally heated rooms, enclosure in glass can be a great advantage.

It is often worth the trouble of cultivating delicate and rarer species in bottles if it is not possible to provide their needs in other ways. Plants in glass provide a fascinating display and require virtually no attention..

Different types of bottle

In principle any bottle that can be easily opened and closed, and has an opening large enough to allow plants and materials to be inserted, can be used to create a bottle garden. The colour of the glass can, however, affect the result.

Coloured glass absorbs a certain amount of the light rays, and the reduced light reaching the plants inside could cause growth problems. Plants growing in a red-coloured bottle are likely to be stretched and spindly. Clear glass bottles remain the best choice, but if you really want to use a coloured bottle, then choose a light-green one. Shade-loving plants will do well under these circumstances.

Plants for the bottle garden

Plants that naturally prefer a humid climate could grow for years unattended in a closed bottle garden.

Cacti and many succulents are, on the other hand, better in an open bowl that has a dry climate.

Each plant variety makes its own demands and you will have to take these into account. It follows that plants that have similar climatic needs are likely to be suitable companions in a bowl or bottle.

Different bottle gardens can be created for different 'climates'. You can, for example, put one in a cool room and another in a warmer spot. You could make a bottle garden for plants that need good light, and another for shade-lovers. Obviously, the eventual size that the plants can reach will depend on the size bottle they are growing in.

Soil mixtures for bottle gardens

A bottle garden has no holes in the bottom of the container to provide drainage. The soil mixture must therefore have a loose, open texture to allow air and moisture to penetrate easily. It must also contain a certain amount of nutrients. General potting mixtures are frequently based on sedge peat. To improve porosity, perlite, fibrous peat and coarse, washed sand are added to it. This will be suitable for most of the houseplants that can tolerate the closed atmosphere of a bottle.

Moisture-loving plants may need a bit more peat in their mixture. Cacti and succulents will do well in a mixture of 3 parts potting soil, 2 parts compost, 1 part perlite and 1 part fine gravel.

Drainage in the bottle garden

To collect any excess water, some sort of drainage layer is necessary. Depending on the size of the bottle this layer should be between 1.5cm–5cm (½in–2ins) thick. A functional drainage layer could be made of washed grit, to which about 20% of charcoal chips have been added (this helps to keep the soil sweet).

To prevent the potting soil from washing down into the drainage material, install a 'filter' layer, of fibreglass mat or sections of nylon stocking.

Preparing the bottle

Before you can start planting up the bottle garden, the bottle must be cleaned carefully. The inside is best done with a soft cloth and some window cleaning fluid. Persistent stains can be removed with bleach. After this treatment, rinse the bottle thoroughly to make sure that no trace of the cleaning substances remains. Once you have made sure that the inside is completely dry, you can start the garden off by installing the drainage layer. Moisten the materials slightly to lessen the chances of dust which is not always easy to clean off afterwards. In a bottle with a narrow neck, pour the drainage gravel in with the aid of a funnel and level it off with a long, thin stick. The filter layer can then be put in place and soil carefully poured in on top of it. Soil depth will depend on the size of the container but is usually about an eighth of the depth of the container.

When the soil is levelled it should be lightly tamped down. This can be done with the aid of a 'tamper' which can be made by sticking a cork onto a knitting needle.

Planting up the bottle garden

Planting up a bottle garden with a reasonably wide opening is relatively easy. Starting with the largest plants, remove them carefully from their pots, and shake off surplus soil from below the root ball. Tease the roots out a bit and then plant in the usual way.

Once all the plants are in place in the bottle, firm the soil carefully around them and level or shape the surface. An attractive effect is achieved by covering the bare soil with a thin layer of gravel or crushed stone. You can now water the plants, but not too much as any excess cannot be removed easily. After spraying the leaves with a fine mist, the opening can be closed off with a piece of glass or a stopper.

When planting bottles with narrow necks the first thing to do is make the planting holes in the potting soil. This can be done with a teaspoon attached to a thin cane.

Remove the soil from the roots by washing under a tap. The plant can be lowered into position with the aid of a length of wire with a suitable bent hook on its end. Hold the plant in place and use a second stick to cover the roots. When all the plants are firmly in place, the foliage and inside of the glass can be cleaned with a soft brush attached to a cane. The easiest method of watering is by syringing with a fine mist until foliage and bottle are quite damp. Within a day or two you will be able to see the plants require more moisture.

Maintaining a bottle garden

Bottle gardens standing in full sun will need a regular exchange of fresh air by removing the stopper or covering at frequent intervals. During excessively hot weather it will be necessary to provide some shading. These warmer gardens, and those that are not completely closed, will need to be watered lightly now and then.

In general, the soil colour turns lighter when watering is needed, and that lack of moisture condensing on the inside of the bottle is a sure sign of low humidity. It can also become too damp in a bottle. The cure is to remove the stopper or cover, and keep the bottle in a warm spot until surplus moisture has evaporated.

Then there is the question of feeding. Even plants in a so-called 'closed system' will eventually need nourishment. Always use a very diluted pot plant fertilizer (use about one-quarter of the recommended dilution). Apply feeds only half as often as you would for normal houseplants. Wait until the bottle needs water, or let it dry out a bit, and apply the feed as part of the watering.

If you start a bottle garden in an old aquarium, make sure that its base is waterproof. The top opening must be covered with a pane of glass.
When a bottle or other container with a small entrance is used, then you can either leave the top open or only partially closed.

The propagation of plants

The plant reproduces itself

Seeds come in all shapes and sizes.

Propagate your own plants
When you have developed a taste for indoor gardening you will want to do more than simply look after your houseplants. Sooner or later you will decide to produce your own. This can be done by means of seed sowing, cuttings, division and several other methods.

Plants can also reproduce in different ways. Firstly, there is reproduction by seed. Because this form of increasing its numbers involves the reproductive organs of the plant (stamens and pistil of the flower), it is called sexual reproduction. All the other forms of reproduction, such as cuttings, division, layering or laying in, are undertaken without involving the flower and are known as asexual reproduction (or more commonly vegetative propagation).

The nature of the particular plant dictates which reproductive method should be used. Some plants are not easily grown from seed, or else produce little or no seed, while others are not easily increased vegetatively.

The new plants propagated vegetatively from a parent plant will have exactly the same characteristics as their parent.

If you take cuttings from an attractive, healthy houseplant you can be certain that the new plants are not going to differ from the parent in any way. This applies to any form of asexual reproduction.

Plants that are grown from seed can differ from their parents. Most differences are usually so small that they are unnoticeable, but they can also be quite distinct. This results from cross-pollination between different plants of the same species.

Seed from a variegated plant will usually produce normal, green leafed offspring, whereas cuttings would retain the variegated character. Plant breeders always select seed from healthy parent plants, which have well developed 'typical'

characteristics of that species, as the seed is then more likely to reproduce those features.

Soil for sowing
To germinate, seeds need adequate moisture and fresh air. A suitable medium for sowing must be able to retain moisture, should be light, and must also be free of harmful organisms (especially fungus types). The amount of nutrient in the soil is of little importance as the young seedlings obtain nourishment from food reserves stored in the seed itself.

An airy, moisture retaining soil can be obtained by using a potting mixture based on garden peat or leaf mould, sieved and mixed with fine, sharp sand.

For most houseplants one part sand to seven parts potting soil will be suitable.

Seed sowing
You can now obtain seed of many of the popular flowering houseplants, and should be able to grow them without much difficulty. A few pots, or a propagating case, filled with a seed mixture is all that is needed. Moisten the soil, press it down and scatter the seed evenly over the soil. With very fine seed it may be easier to put the seed in the palm of your hand, take a pinch of seed at a time, and sprinkle by rubbing your finger and thumb. Cover the seeds with a thin layer of sharp sand.

To prevent the spread of disease, disinfect your seed trays between use. Use sterilised soil and use fungicides at the first sign of infection.

New pots and seed trays do not need disinfecting. New clay pots should be soaked in water until they have fully absorbed all the moisture they can. If this is not done they can absorb too much moisture from the seed or potting mixture, and could cause problems.

The first stage: warmth, humidity and darkness

With careful preparation of the seed bed and the provision of correct conditions, you can expect a good proportion of the seeds to germinate. To obtain good results the seed must be kept warm and moist and kept in darkness until germination starts. As an alternative, you could cover the pot or tray with a sheet of glass and place a newspaper on the pane to exclude all light. Turn the glass pane over every day to prevent the condensation drops that form on it from dripping onto the seedlings. The droplets can sometimes cause rotting of seeds or seedlings.

Once seedlings start to appear above the soil remove the newspaper. The young plants will be too sensitive to withstand bright sunlight and will need some shading.

As the plants grow larger, you will need to raise the glass sheet slightly higher each day until, after about a week, it can be removed altogether.

Watering is very important. Check regularly as seedlings can die quickly without it.

Pricking out and bud nipping

If all goes well with the seedlings they develop rapidly and soon begin to crowd each other. At this stage they will need to be transplanted. Nurserymen call this first transplanting 'pricking out'. This needs to be done to provide more space for each plant and encourage the development of a better root system. During this transplanting the root system is damaged and disturbed. This encourages it to branch out more and form a more compact root ball. The increased branching helps the development of the plant.

The seedlings can either be transplanted into another tray spaced further apart or better still, transplanted into individual small pots — trays with small individual compartments are ideal for first transplants.

To prevent tall, spindly growth you will often need to encourage early branching of the parts of the plant that are above the ground. This can be done by nipping out the growing tip of the plant. Buds of side branches are then encouraged to shoot and will produce a bushier, well branched plant.

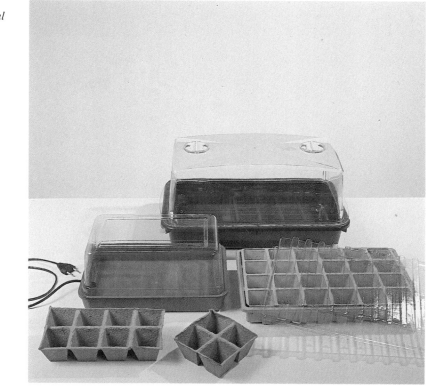

Propagating units are useful aids to seed sowing. Some are heated underneath.

A seed tray with raised glass covering.

Cuttings and division

Asexual reproduction

Many species of houseplant cannot be multiplied from seed. Some will not flower and others will not set seed or will form non-viable seed. There are even some plants which will not grow 'true to form' from seed. Asexual or vegetative propagation is based on the plant's ability to develop into a new plant, which has the same properties as the parent, from pieces removed from the parent plant. Some people might think that this way of reproducing is less natural than reproduction by seed. This is not so. In nature it frequently happens that pieces of a plant become detached and go on to develop as new individuals. Vegetative propagation is simply an extension of this natural ability.

Cuttings in water

Plants such as *Coleus, Tradescantia* and *Impatiens* have soft, watery stems and grow very easily from cuttings. Simply insert a piece of stem from one of these plants into water in a jar. After a while roots appear and the piece grows into a new plant once it is planted into potting soil. If you add some diluted nutrient to the water every fortnight, the cutting can stay in the water for several weeks and you can watch the roots developing. It is advisable to change the water now and then. If you don't there is the chance of the plant suffering from a build up of salts in the water. This simple method is not typical and for most plants the taking and growing of cuttings is a little more complex. Instead of using water you will need to prepare a special mixture for the cuttings.

Soil for cuttings

A good soil for cuttings can be prepared by mixing equal quantities of moss peat and coarse, washed river sand. The river sand encourages the cut part of the cutting to develop callus, and then roots. As an

A tiny begonia grown from a leaf cutting.

alternative, you could use sedge peat and sand as your basic medium.

If the cuttings in the soil form callus growth on the cut portion but don't start rooting, there is probably too much sand in the mixture and you should add more peat. A lack of river sand can lead to rotting as excessive moisture is then retained. Lack of or bad root development can have another cause. A number of houseplants have woody stems which do not root easily even in the best rooting medium. In these cases, a root promoting substance can help. These are chemicals based on plant hormones that stimulate root development.

Woody cuttings should have their cut ends dipped into the rooting powder before they are inserted into the soil.

Keep cuttings small

It is very tempting to take large cuttings. A large piece already looks like a plant, after all, and should speed up the process. But it isn't that simple! A large cutting with many leaves continues to lose water through transpiration via the leaves, while it is unable to absorb water until it has developed roots. Consequently a large cutting is more likely to wilt and die than a smaller piece with less leaf area. It is advisable to remove the lower leaves from a cutting, especially from the part that will be placed in the soil and would rot off.

The length of a cutting will depend on the size of the parent plant and the health of its branches and twigs. A geranium cutting can be 10–15cm (4–6ins) long, but a *Ficus elastica* (Rubber Plant) could be up to 30cm (12ins) in length. In most cases, a length of 6–10cm (2–4ins) is recommended. For the best results the stem should be cut just below a leaf or leaf axil. This should be done with a sharp knife or blade to prevent bruising or tearing of the stem tissue.

Propagating needs slim fingers, or a tapered sucker-stick.

A Steptocarpus leaf cutting.

Tips, stem and leaf cuttings

Different types of cutting are taken from different parts of a plant. Usually it is the upper portion of a branch or twig that is used to make a cutting. This is called a tip cutting.

A stem cutting is a section of stem, without the tip, usually with at least one leaf attached. After a tip cutting has been removed from a stem additional lengths can often be cut as stem cuttings.

Certain plants, such as *Saintpaulia* and *Streptocarpus* can produce new plants from single leaves. These are leaf cuttings. You need healthy, well matured leaves for best results.

Stem cuttings

Setting stem cuttings into the soil in pots or propagating trays is easy. Water the soil mixture well and simply use a pencil or sharpened stick to make a hole for each cutting.

Cuttings are quite often attacked by mildew so it is sensible not to space the cuttings too closely, and not to put all the cuttings in the same container.

Cuttings root quickest in a warm, moist environment. You can improve conditions for your cuttings by bending some wire and pushing the ends into the pot or tray to create a frame. Place a clear plastic bag over the entire container and fasten it around the pot with string or an elastic band. If you can find a place on a warm window sill for these mini cases the cuttings will soon develop into independent plants.

As soon as roots have formed and the plants start growing, remove the plastic bag.

Making leaf cuttings

Making cuttings from leaves is very similar to taking stem cuttings. The leaf stalk of the leaf must be put into the soil up to the leaf blade and the whole pot placed in a plastic bag, using bent wires to support the plastic. This creates a humid, warm environment and within a little while young plants should start appearing at the base of the leaf blade. When the new plant is growing on its own the parent leaf can be severed and used again.

Rex Begonias are so easy to propagate, that even pieces of leaf can be used to produce new plants. Cut the leaf into squares of about 3cm (1½ins) and lay pieces that have a section of vein running across them onto the soil surface. Small pebbles can be used to hold them down. After a while, small plants should start growing from the undersides.

Sansevierias can be propagated by cutting a leaf into lengths of approximately 5cm/2ins, and pushing them into the soil to half their length. They can be kept drier than most cuttings. Remember though that even pieces from a variegated plant will only produce green plants.

Exceptions

Leaf cuttings of *Peperomia* and *Crassula* type plants need different handling. They tend to rot in a humid atmosphere so, in this case, do not use a plastic bag.

The Umbrella Plant *(Cyperus alternifolius)* needs a completely different type of treatment. Place a leaf with a piece of stem about 10cm (4ins) long in a glass of water after trimming off up to two-thirds of the 'umbrella'. The underside of the leaf should remain on the water surface and new plants grow from here after a few days.

Stem or tip cuttings of plants that contain a milky sap should not be placed directly in the soil. You must first let the cut surface dry off. You can speed this process up by dipping the cut ends into rooting powder or cigar ash.

The seed of certain houseplants can take a long while to germinate. This tries the patience of the home gardener and increases the chances of problems arising from fungus infection. There is much to be said for speeding up the germination process. Before sowing, it can be advantageous to soak the seed of difficult species in lukewarm water for a day or two; hard coated seeds are the most likely to benefit. But do not leave seeds under water for longer than two days, or they stand the chance of rotting after suffering oxygen starvation.

134

African Violet with its parent leaf.

Plantlets on the leaf edge of one of the many Kalanchoë varieties.

Self-propagating plants

There are some houseplants that have the ability to reproduce themselves asexually. The Spider Plant *(Chlorophytum)*, *Kalanchoë tubiflora* and Mother-of-thousands *(Saxifraga stolonifera)* are common examples of plants with this ability. Hence the term 'self-propagating' plants.

On the long, supple stems of the Spider Plant, new young plants form, complete with roots, and have only to be cut off.

The young plants that form along the leaves of Kalanchoë tubiflora can be propagated in the same way — if they don't fall off and root themselves before you get there!

Mother-of-thousands, like the ornamental strawberry, forms new plants at the ends of trailing runners which root as soon as they touch soil.

Propagation by division

The rapid growth of a houseplant is usually desirable but it can lead to problems if you don't have the space for enormous bushes.

Many plants can be pruned and cut back but plants with rhizomes, or those that keep sending new shoots up from their bases, expand laterally and soon outgrow their pots. *Aspidistra, Clivia,* and most ferns, are examples. The best time to remove some of the surplus growth, by dividing the plant, is in spring at the time of re-potting. Knock the plant out of its pot, shake off loose soil and look carefully at where the plant can be divided naturally, with sound sections of stem with some leaf and root on the part to be cut off. Use a sharp knife or secateurs to divide the plant into two or more pieces and pot each portion separately.

Layering

As they grow taller some plants tend to lose the lower leaves on their stems and don't grow new ones to replace them. This bare stem can completely spoil the appearance of the plant. *Ficus elastica, Dieffenbachia, Schefflera* and *Monstera* are typical examples of plants that do this.

One way of dealing with this problem is to try to induce the upper portion to root, while it is still attached to the main stem; this process is called layering. Directly below the lowest healthy leaves of the plant, make a longitudinal cut in the stem, reaching about a quarter of the way through the stem. Insert a sliver of wood, or matchstick, to keep the wound slightly open. Push some sphagnum moss into the cut, and wrap a ball of moistened moss around the cut portion which is tied in place with string. The whole ball must now be enclosed in a sheet of plastic, to exclude all air. Place the sheet around the moss ball, and tie it firmly, starting below the ball first. Dampen the moss thoroughly from the top before tightly securing this upper opening.

No further watering is needed. If the method is successful, roots should appear after a few weeks. Once they have developed sufficiently, cut off the upper stem, just below the new roots, and plant the 'new' plant in potting soil. It will require regular watering and misting for a while.

The parent plant's stem can be cut back to about 10–20cm (4–8ins) above the soil, and should shoot out again, as a rejuvenated specimen.

Laying-in
Laying-in is one of the oldest methods of vegetative propagation and is more generally used for outdoor trees and shrubs. There are some houseplants that can be increased in this way, especially those with long trailing stems, such as *Hedera* or *Columnia*. These plants tend to root easily from cuttings anyway. To root a stem which is still attached to its parent, make a scratch or small cut on the underside of the stem where you want it to root. Lay this damaged part onto the soil surface of a separate pot. Make sure that good contact is made with the soil by pinning the stem down with pieces of bent wire. Once the section has rooted firmly into the new pot it can be severed from the parent plant.

Ferns are asexual plants, and reproduce themselves by way of spores. These are usually borne on the undersides of the mature fronds. The spores are released into the air when ripe and if they land on a moist spot they begin to germinate into a small, flat plantlet. Later, this will develop male and female parts, fertilisation will occur, and a new fern grows out from this 'sexual' stage growth.
Ferns can be increased by sowing spores. This is best done by partly filling sterilised trays or pots with sifted leaf mould, peat and sand mixture, also sterilised. Scatter the spores onto this layer, and cover the tray with a pane of glass. In time, new plants will be produced.

Ficus elastica *and many other houseplants have leathery leaves, that remain attached to the plant for a long time. In such cases, it is not advisable to remove leaves from a cutting, except for the portion that will be inserted into the soil. It is better to roll the leaves into a cylinder around the stem, and restrain them with an elastic band. Once the cutting has rooted, the leaves can again be unrolled. By using this method transpiration is reduced, but the maximum amount of foliage is retained.*

Making your own plants is a wonderful experience.

Chlorophytum propagates easily. Simply cut off plantlets as needed.

Reduce the leaf area of tip cuttings to lessen transpiration.

Make tip cuttings of Hypocyrta.

Clivia is easily divided.

Tip and stem cuttings

Aeschynanthus ceropegia
Cissus antarctica (Kangaroo vine)
Columnea varieties
Fatshedera lizei (use hormone powder)
Gynura aurantiaca (purple velvet plant)
Hedera helix (Ivy)
Hoya species (Wax Plants)
Nerium oleander (Oleander)
Philodendron wendlandii
Phyllocactus varieties
Sedum sieboldii
Stephanotis floribunda (use hormone powder)

Tip cuttings

Abutilon varieties (Chinese Lantern)
Acalypha hispida
Ampelopsis brevipedunculata variegata
Aucuba japonica (with hormone powder)
Begonia in variety
Beloperone guttata (Shrimp Plant)
Brunsfelsia calycina (use hormone powder)
Callisia elegans (Wandering Jew)
Campanula isophylla 'Alba' (Italian Bell Flower)
Chamaecereus silvestri (Peanut Cactus)
Codiaeum variegatum (Croton) (use hormone powder)
Coleus blumei
Crossandra infundibuliformis
Cytisus racemosus (Broom)
Dipladenia sanderi
Euonymus varieties (Spindle Tree)
Euphorbia splendens (Christ Thorn)
Fatsia japonica 'Variegata'
Ficus repens (Creeping Fig)
Fittonia argyroneura
Fuchsia hybrids
Grevillea robusta (Silky Oak)
Hibiscus rosa-sinensis (Hibiscus)
Hypocyrta glabra (Clog Plant)
Hypoestes taeniata (Polka-dot)
Impatiens hybrids (Busy-Lizzie)
Jasminium polyanthum (Jasmine)
Kalanchoë blossfeldiana
Lampranthus blandus (Ice Plant)
Lantana camara
Monstera deliciosa (Swiss Cheese Plant)
Opuntia microdasys 'Rufida'
Passiflora coerulea (Passion Flower)
Pereskia aculeata 'Godseffiana'
Pelargonium in variety
Pellionia pulchra
Pernettya mucronata (use hormone powder)
Pilea cadierei (Aluminium Plant)
Plumbago auriculata
Punica granatum (Pomegranate)

Rhoicissus rhombifolia (Evergreen Vine)
Rochea coccinea (Crassula)
Ruellia in variety
Sanchezia nobilis
Setcreasia purpurea (Purple Heart)
Solanum pseudocapsicum (Jerusalem Cherry)
Sparmannia africana (House Lime)
Syngonium vellozianum
Tradescantia albiflora 'Albovittata'
Vinca rosea

Leaf cuttings
Begonia rex hybrids
Epiphyllum ackermannii (Orchid Cactus)
Saintpaulia ionantha (African Violet)
Streptocarpus hybrids (Cape Primrose)

Division
Adiantum tenerum (Maidenhair Fern)
Agaonema robelinii
Anthurium species and varieties
Asparagus sprengeri
Aspidistra elatior
Calathea makoyana (Maranta)
Crassula lycopodioides
Helleborus abchasicus
Maranta species
Nephrolepis cordifolia 'Plumosa' (Sword Fern)
Nertera granadensis (Bead Plant)
Pellaea rotundifolia (Button Fern)
Platycerium bifurcatum (Stag's horn Fern)
Pyrrheimia fuscata
Spathiphyllum wallisii
Zantedeschia aethiopica (Arum Lily)

Aerial layering
Dieffenbachia varieties (Dumb Cane)
Dizygotheca elegantissima (False Aralia)
Dracaena in variety
Fatsia japonica
Ficus species and varieties. (Various Fig Trees)
Monstera deliciosa
Philodendron species
Schefflera actinophylla

Streptocarpus are increased from leaf cuttings.

Any easy way of inserting tip cuttings into water.

Piggyback plant (Tolmiea menziesii) forms rooted plantlets on its leaves.

Leaf cuttings of Rex Begonia.

Flower arranging

A popular hobby

Modern, informal decoration in a church.

Knowledge is necessary

The number of professional florists is small compared to the vast number of people who arrange flowers as a hobby. In a great many homes you will find a vase of flowers in the centre of the dining-room table. When they begin to fade they are replaced. Another bunch is bought from a florist, or the market; the bunch is untied, a little is cut off the stems, and the whole bunch is put into the vase and then back on the table.

The art of flower arranging (for an art it is), involves a great deal more than this. With flowers and other plant material you can decorate and enhance your home with an endless and ever-changing display. As Europeans, we are likely to find the Japanese principles of floristry somewhat strange as they are an extension of religious and philosophical symbolism. However, Japanese styles have had a great influence on Western floral techniques.

Learning more about flower arranging will enhance your pleasure. You need to know what you could use on a shallow water surface. Which flowers keep well? And which wilt quickly?

You don't only use blooms in a floral piece. Leaves, twigs, fruits and many other materials can play a part. The knowledge that can be gained about natural materials is limitless. And then there are the containers: vases, jugs, urns and so on, and the properties and problems associated with them. Then there are all the aids and accessories which become indispensable when you are a serious 'arranger'.

Floristry is a satisfying hobby as with so many possibilities and variations you should never be bored.

A bit of history

Flowers seem to have been an important part of our lives for very many years. Even in prehistoric graves traces of pollen have been found, indicating that flowers had been buried with the body.

Decorative vases which contained ornamental displays have been recovered from ancient Egyptian sources. From their early monuments and tombs, carvings and inscriptions reveal the widespread use of greenery and flowers in religious, as well as everyday life (although it is not possible to identify most of the species used). What is known is that the Lotus flower had great value in religious symbolism, where it represented fertility and immortality. Acanthus leaves, palm fronds, papyrus and Lotus motifs were frequently used on columns and capitals, for decorative and symbolic effect.

The Persians were great lovers of nature and developed parks and gardens. Records indicate their use of roses in general cultivation. Many symbolic references to flowers and plants are woven into the tapestry of their carpets, even those from earliest times.

The early Israelites used garlands of palm fronds, vine leaves and citrus, and there are many biblical references to gardens. King Solomon is said to have had a magnificent

A derivative of the Roman form of laurel wreath is seen in wreaths of gilded or silvered leaves.

garden. More is known of the Greeks and Romans. The Greeks are well known for their use of wreaths of oak and laurel to decorate their victors and heroes, whereas smaller wreaths of olive leaves and roses were worn as headpieces.

The Romans used flowers extensively in their religious ceremonies, and laurel wreaths were generally used as headpieces. They were responsible for the introduction of many plants and flowers to different parts of Europe and the Middle East. They were also good at 'adopting' plants, used for seasoning or medicine, from the peoples they conquered.

After the fall of the Romans, we have the monks in monasteries all over Europe to thank for conserving and cultivating within their walled gardens many of the herbs and flowers we know today. As time passed these plants were used more and more in cottage and farm gardens, until the start of the Renaissance with its upsurge and spread of knowledge of all the art forms. Together with the demand for country mansions, palaces and newer developments in the cities, came the demand for services of landscape designers, horticulturalists, gardeners and so on, to develop the new gardens and parks. Botany and plant breeding were to proceed apace as new and important sciences.

Botanical gardens were established at many centres, and botanists travelled widely in their search for new specimens.

Artists began to use flowers increasingly in their paintings and still-life creations. Eighteenth-century art is particularly interesting in that it provides insight into the varieties grown at that time. The roses seen in these paintings were very different from todays blooms. They were full, vigorous botanical species, including *Rosa gallica, Rosa damascena, Rosa rubignosa, Rosa foetida* and other well-scented, 'old-fashioned' types.

Flowers that frequently appeared in paintings were the Peony *(Paeonia officinalis)*, various poppies *(Papaver somniferum, P. orientale* and *P. rhoeas)*, Syringa *(Syringa vulgaris)*, Honeysuckle *(Leonicera periclymenum)*, Water Forget-me-not *(Myosotis scopioides)*,

and many other types still being used today. Fruits, birds, butterflies and other insects often found their way onto these painted arrangements.

At the beginning of this century it became fashionable at weddings and jubilees to use baskets of blooms with plenty of ribbons as fillers. They were made for the occasion and, being without water, wilted soon afterwards.

European floral art

As interest in and demand for flowers increased so the plant breeders hybridised flowering plants, to develop more desirable blooms on longer stems. These changes were reflected in the different shapes of bowls and vases.

Floral art had several main 'periods', which more or less coincided with the prevailing architectural, cultural and economic conditions of the time.

Even today when an arrangement has to be made for an older building or church, of a particular architectural style, the floral style and choice of blooms should be appropriate. The styles mentioned below relate to their historic periods.

The *Renaissance* style is really a forerunner to the exuberant styles of the eighteenth century. Vases were mostly tall, with narrow openings, and arrangements were vertical and slim. An

English bouquets are well known. A variety of flower types in many harmonious shades is typical of this style. Experts and enthusiasts regularly compete in competitions and shows and standards are very high.

A simple arrangement that complements its surroundings.

144

Empire bouquet was elaborately made up from 'old-fashioned' blooms which were all very full.

This was followed by the *Biedermeier* bouquet, round in shape, and usually tightly fitted into a 'cornet'.

At the start of this century with the great interest in things Japanese it is not surprising that Japanese floral art also had its followers. Soft shades, trailing and hanging blooms in matching fragile vases, and a basic simplicity characterised this style.

Each country has its own typical floral styles. A bouquet made in America, England or France, at the same time would certainly reflect its country of origin. Yet it is the Japanese influence that has affected Western floral art most profoundly. Japanese floral art is not only a form of decoration but part of a wider philosophy which is even taught in their schools.

Western adaptations of the Japanese art tend to overlook all symbolism and simply follow the simple guidelines of aesthetic form.

Japanese floral art

Japanese floral art, known as *ikebana*, encompasses different styles. What makes it distinctive is its simplicity. The bare minimum of materials are used. All originate from nature and each item, whether flower or twig, is carefully and deliberately chosen. Branches are bent and twisted until they take on the exact shape that is wanted. Each flower is given its own space in order to be looked at individually. These arrangements are not something that are quickly put together in a spare half hour! They need hours of thought and endless patience to imitate nature. The symbolism, which is an underlying principle, represents earth, sky and man, and is reflected in the materials and their arrangement.

As well as flowers, such as the much used Chrysanthemum, stones, stumps, branches and pieces of moss are amongst the natural items used. The arrangements are created in special vases or bowls, with significance placed on colour and shape for different purposes or seasons. In the traditional Japanese home there is usually a special niche or corner for the display of the ikebana piece.

Special arrangements are prepared for feast days. The following combination, for example, is used for a New Years' floral arrangement: conifer branches (symbolic of a long life) are combined with bamboo (symbolic of patience) and plum blossom (the symbol of courage).

The making of the ikebana piece gives more satisfaction than the finished article. However, there are many exhibitions of floral art and tremendous interest is always shown by the public.

Japanese floral art has traditions which go back hundreds of years. The art was practised exclusively by men until the end of the last century. Flower arranging still has great significance through its reflection of religious and philosophical ideals. It is still taught in schools where students are able to practise under the supervision of experts.

It is a pity that in the attempts to produce larger and better blooms their scents are so often lost.

A simple posy of chives and hosta leaves.

Just as our flower arranging patterns have been influenced by the Japanese, with the use of less material and simple lines, so the opposite has happened. Japanese floral styles have been 'softened' and 'westernised'. But there is no question that their styles have lost any individuality.

145

Flowers that do well in water

What are cut flowers?

When you pick a flower and put it in a vase of water it becomes a cut flower. If, in a while it starts hanging its head and despite all treatment cannot be revived, this is clearly not a good cut flower! So a primary requirement for a good cut flower is that it should last in water for a reasonable period of time.

Various and differing demands are made on cut flowers. A florist who sells bunches of flowers would want them to last for at least a week. The last thing he wants is for a customer to return with a bunch of wilted blooms after two days! Florists also prefer flowers with the longest possible stems, as they are the easiest to work with.

If you pick flowers from your own garden and they only last for a few days in water, then they are probably not true cut flowers. But this does not prevent their having given pleasure for those few days. Because of the transient nature of cut flowers, replacing faded blooms with new ones provides an ever-changing scene.

Don't throw blooms away too soon. Even flowers that are past their best are often still useful. A posy may dry out on its own and still look good enough to keep. It all depends on the type of flower. A bowl of roses that has finished blooming can still provide a pleasing effect.

Care of cut flowers

When buying cut flowers make sure that they really are fresh. Blooms that are already wide open won't last all that long in water. Carry the flowers home in a wrapping of some sort to prevent unnecessary drying out.

Don't put the flowers in a warm room when you get home. First cut off a short piece of each stem and place the bunch in a deep bucket of water (not too cold) to draw up as much water as they can. After a few hours, when they have freshened up, you can begin arranging. Remove the lower leaves from the stem and any thorns that will be below the water level in the vase.

If you have picked the flowers from your garden there is another point to remember. Don't pick flowers in the heat of the day but rather cut them early in the morning when the stems are stiff and erect. Further handling is the same as for bought flowers, i.e. stand them in lukewarm water, in a cool place, to take up as much water as they can.

If you pick flowers while out walking — only ones that are not protected or rare species — be sure to get them into water as soon as possible, especially if it is a hot day, otherwise you may find that they have lost so much water that you end up with a wilted bunch that you simply cannot revive. In such cases it would have been better to have left them where they were.

If you are travelling further afield, it is a good idea to take along some sort of container to put flowers in before they dry out too much.

Flowers are not all picked at the same stage of growth. Roses, tulips and narcissi do well picked at bud stage and will open in a vase. On the other hand, if you pick dahlias, sunflowers or carnations as buds, they will not open any further in water. The best stage for cutting many blooms is given in the list at the end of this

Cape species can be equally effective dried or in water.

chapter. If you are unsure about when to pick a particular flower, experiment with a single bloom and watch what happens.

Although research has been done into prolonging the life of cut blooms, the fact remains that flowers are fairly short-lived, and once cut, the flower's lifespan is reduced even further. The process of decay can be put off for as long as possible by keeping the water fresh and clean, by changing it regularly, or by adding a bacteriolytic substance to kill decay organisms. Besides delaying the decay process, natural growth processes can be stimulated by adding sugars to the water. These are taken up by the stalks. There are also commercially prepared life extenders for cut flowers. When diluted in the correct proportions and added to the water, they are claimed to extend the life of the blooms dramatically.

Remember, when picking flowers in the garden or in the wild, they may not always be suitable as cut flowers. It's simply a matter of experimenting to see which will last. When the flowers are arranged in the vase do remember to check the water level regularly and do not stand the vase in direct sunlight or near a heating source.

List of suitable varieties
It is possible to list all the cut flower types that are available from a florist, but this can be done easily by looking through the nearest florist's window. It is more beneficial to provide a list of the less common species which you could try growing in your own garden.

The annual cut flower
The following is a list of annual cut flowers (raised from seed) that grow, bloom and die all in the same season:

Narcissi form the basis for many late winter arrangements.

Various substances are available that can prolong the lives of certain cut flowers. There are specific remedies for carnations, mimosa, tulips and woody stems.

147

A field posy with spring annuals.

Althaea (Hollyhock): there are several species, some annual, some biennial. Flowers both single and double, on spikes up to 2m (6ft) tall. Use in large arrangements.

Amaranthus has several forms grown for foliage of tassel-like flowers. Love-lies-bleeding has long, red tassels that can be dried.

Antirrhinum (Snapdragon), has a wide and colourful range of varieties, from low to tall. Seed is available for mixed or separate colours.

Calendula officinalis or Pot Marigold, has bright yellow or orange flowers. Useful for bedding and cutting, lasts well in water which must be changed often or it may smell.

Callistephus (China Aster): half-hardy annuals, in a wide range of colours. Well worth growing as cut flowers but don't plant for two years running as they tend to suffer from wilt. Single and double blooms are available and grow easily from seed.

Centaurea or *Cornflower*. Besides the well known blue these come in shades of purple, pink and white. Very attractive in informal arrangements in summer.

Chrysanthemum segetum: grown in borders and for cutting, is yellow with brown centre on 60cm (2ft) stems.

Cosmea or Cosmos, lasts well in water and is free flowering right up to the first frosts. Colours range from white to rose and pink.

Delphinium (Larkspur) is a tall annual up to 1m (3ft 3ins) in height, with colours from purple to blue and pink. They are amongst the most useful of garden flowers for cutting. Can also be dried for use in winter.

Eschscholtzia (Californian Poppy). Picked at bud stage, the many colours are useful in small displays; plants are tender.

Gaillardia: a hardy annual that makes a good cut flower. Has bright, daisy-like orange or yellow flowers.

Gypsophila: the annual variety of this large family has a mass of tiny white flowers on delicate stems (sometimes called 'Baby's Breath'). Very useful for backgrounds and can be dried.

Helianthus, the Sunflower. Pick when fully opened then place the stems in a few centimetres of hot water for half an hour before using. Dramatic, large arrangements can be made with these giant blooms but smaller varieties are available.

Lavatera or Mallow, has tall spikes of open pink or white blooms which are very pretty and for taller displays.

Matriarca: a bushy, hardy perennial usually grown from seed as an annual. It flowers in the first year with creamy-white or yellow flowers. Pick when fully open. Has the typical smell of chamomile.

Matthiola (Stock): the heavy scent and pastel shades make these very desirable cut flowers. They are not too easy from seed and need heat for germination. Can be grown under glass for winter flowering.

Nicotiana is a half-hardy annual, which has been hybridised to produce a good pastel colour range. The trumpet-shaped blooms on upright stems give a delicate touch to an arrangement.

Nigella or Love-in-the-mist, has pale blue flowers surrounded by a crown of fine bracts. An excellent cut flower which must only be picked when fully open. It also develops decorative seed pods to use in dried arrangements.

Rudbeckia: bright yellow to orange blooms in late summer, with some shaggy heads and all with distinctive brown or black centres, are excellent for arrangements. Can have single or double blooms.

Tagetes the Marigold, is available in an enormous range of sizes and shapes, of both plant and bloom, from a few centimetres to nearly 60cm (2ft) tall. Single or double, the cheerful yellow or orange blooms are a favourite for garden and vase. Change water frequently to avoid smell.

Tropaeolum the Nasturtium, a bright, sun-loving annual, does well in pots and borders. A cheerful cut flower that lasts well in water. Round leaves are also useful.

Zinnia: these daisy-like flowers borne on stiff, upright stems in a range of sizes, colours and flower forms, make good blooms for arranging. Handle carefully, as stems are brittle.

The colourful Nasturtium is edible too!

Calendula is a useful cut flower.

149

Herbs as cut flowers

You are probably so used to picking herbs to put into food, that you have overlooked their possibilities as additions to a bouquet. Allow some parsley and celery plants to flower; their white, umbrella-shaped blooms look most attractive amongst mixed summer flowers. These plants will flower during their second year, but if sown early enough might bloom at the end of the first summer.

The yellow flower heads of dill rival the brightness of the Calendula, and an interesting blue bouquet can be put together with flowers from borage, sage, hyssop and winter savory.

Biennial cut flowers

During its first year after sowing, a biennial grows in size and forms roots and leaves. In the second year it flowers, sets seed and then dies down. Among the biennials there are many good cut flowers: Hollyhock *(Althaea)*, the wonderfully perfumed brown, orange and yellow Wallflower *(Cheiranthus)*, the blue Forget-me-not *(Myosotis)*, the papery Iceland Poppy *(Papaver nudicaule)* and, not to be forgotten, the many different varieties of Violet.

Cut flowers from perennials

Perennial plants producing flowers suitable for cutting are best obtained from a nursery. Don't just buy one of each sort, get at least three, better still five, because when you only have a few flower stems it is a pity to remove them (and there wouldn't be enough for an arrangement). In spring, you could pick the bright yellow flowers of Leopard's Bane *(Doronicum)*, from clumps in your own garden. The Primrose *(Primula)* also flowers at this time — you have a choice of many colours and varieties. And the bright yellow, buttercup-like flowers of *Trollius* wouldn't look amiss in your bouquet.

Further into the summer you can enjoy the Columbine *(Aquilegia)*, together with Larkspur, *(Delphinium)*, Lupin, Iris, Peony, Phlox, and Cat-mint *(Nepeta)*. These all make excellent cut flowers from which to make your summer arrangements.

In July and August, the delicate Baby's Breath, *(Gypsophila)* is in bloom; used fresh or dried, it adds a light touch to an arrangement. *Helenium*, with its yellow and brown flowered varieties seems to offer a foretaste of autumn.

Chrysanthemums and Asters, however, are true autumn flowers. A lesser-known autumn bloom is the beautiful Windflower *(Anemone japonica)*; it can grow to 1 metre (3ft tall), and is found in both white or pink varieties. They bloom until late in the autumn.

Always try to pick flowers early in the morning and store them in a cool spot, plunged into deep water, so that they can absorb as much as possible. Many home grown flowers will not last as long as bought blooms, but will give just as much satisfaction.

An added advantage of these perennial flowers is that you are not very likely to come across them in florists' shops.

Cut flowers from shrubs

Old-fashioned shrubs, such as Lilac *(Syringa)*, and Mock Orange *(Philadelphus coronarius)*, are not only most attractive in the garden, but also provide sprays of perfumed beauty for the vase. Be sure that the lilac flowers are fully open before picking, and remove most of the leaves as they tend to wilt. *Rhododendron* varieties, and the related *Azalea mollis*, are also suitable for cutting. The Hydrangea is a very popular garden shrub, especially the varieties with large, rounded flower-heads, which are very effective in larger arrangements.

Two flowers that can be used both fresh and dried are the Achillea *(Yarrow), with its white or yellow umbrellas, and* Anaphalis *with its velvety foliage and white blooms in winter.*

Top:
Primula veris in natural surroundings.

Centre:
Strawberry basket filled with Primula vulgaris.

Roadside collection of ground ivy and grasses.

Roses are in a class on their own in that they are not used together with other blooms to any extent. It is so easy to buy roses from the florist, either singly or by the dozen, that one can almost forget that they can be easily grown in the garden.

It is not necessary to provide a list of good cutting roses, as most will do well in water. Both climbing and shrub roses can be picked at any stage; the best stage for cutting, to give the longest cut life, is when the buds are just starting to open. If the bud is still too tight when picked it may not open at all; if it does the colour may be spoiled. The wild, botanical roses have a wide variety of flower shapes and colours, growth habits, and sizes. In general, their blooms don't last as long in water as the more modern varieties. Nonetheless, their perfumed fragrance, and interesting flower shapes make them well worth using; besides which, they produce colourful hips in autumn which are also most attractive in a vase.

Picking from the countryside

If you limit your picking of wild flowers to those that are so common that they are regarded as weeds, then no-one is going to mind if you collect a small bunch now and again. But you must not start picking the scarcer sorts on either private or public land or you're likely, rightly, to land yourself in trouble. So it would be advisable to find out which wild flowers are protected in your area.

A flower that most people mistake for a dandelion is the Coltsfoot *(Tussilago farfara)*. Their buds appear above the ground as early as February. You can pick these 'harbingers of spring' either as buds, or fully open. They will remain fresh in water until they develop their fluffy seed heads.

Another 'weed' that flowers nearly all year round, and looks pretty in a small vase (although most lawn owners would disagree) is the little daisy, *Bellis perennis.* The Cuckoo Flower *(Cardamine pratensis)*, another spring flower, appears before the Cuckoo, from which bird it gets its name. It grows in marshy fields, being a moisture-loving species, and doesn't like being out of water for long. In early spring Cow Parsley *(Anthriscus sylvestris)*, with its white, umbrella-shaped flowers, and growing anything up to 1m (3ft) tall, fills the roadsides. When picking for the vase, do remember that they fade very quickly if left out of water.

Wild flowers look best together. You can emphasize this in an arrangement by using a collection of wild flowers from a particular area. They will look better together than when mixed with cultivated blooms.

Field Poppies *(Papaver rhoeas)* evokes different images in different minds: for some, it's the flower of Flanders fields, and still used symbolically on Remembrance Days. Other old-timers will remember the fire red of poppies and the brilliant blur of cornflowers mixed amongst golden corn, in arable fields in the days before weedkillers. Although poppies don't last long in water a vaseful brighten up any room. Pick them in the early morning, when they start to open, for the best effect.

True Camomile, *(Matricaria chamomilla)*, likes freshly turned soil; masses can often be seen growing on building sites. The flowers can be picked and used fresh, or dried and used as a medicinal herb. It flowers in May and June. Another plant of the ploughed field is the Corn Marigold *(Chrysanthemum segetum)*, which is a useful addition to an informal arrangement.

A plant that may, at first glance, put you off, is the white Dead Nettle *(Lamium album)*. (The 'dead' refers to its inability to sting). It appears early in spring, and has a characteristic whorl of white, tubular flowers. It is found in forests and waste land and lasts very well in water. Red Clover *(Trifolium pratense)*, and White Clover *(Trifolium repens)* decorate meadowlands through summer to autumn; the red clover, especially, makes a pretty little cut flower. The white can be used but its stems are much shorter. One of the reasons for getting out into the country in August and September is to see the hillsides and moorlands purple with heather. Most wild heathers *(Calluna)* are shades of purple with occasional whites. Their woody branches can be used fresh or dried.

Using accessories: leaves, branches and fruits

Leaves, branches and fruits

Arrangements need not only be made of flowers. Accessories and other materials have an equally important part to play. Amongst the main non-floral plant material that we can use with flowers, or on their own, are leaves, branches and twigs and fruits.

Leaves in flower arrangements

In early pictures of flower arrangements, foliage appears to have played no part at all, leaves were shown rarely and then only when attached to a flower stalk.

Nowadays, foliage is very often used to outline the basic shape of the arrangement before any flowers are inserted; they certainly can add body and contrast to displays and can help to accentuate the blooms.

The difficulty with using foliage is frequently due to our lack of knowledge as to whether a particular leaf or stem will last in water. One rule is to only use leaves that are fully mature. Young leaves tend to wilt quickly and may not revive in water. Remember that leaves continue losing water, through transpiration, so can use up all the water in a vase. The more foliage you use, the more frequently the vase will have to be topped-up.

Leaves of perennial plants that can be used in vases include *Hosta* (various types), *Bergenia* and *Alchemilla*. The last mentioned, Ladies Mantle, has delicate flowers, similar to *Gypsophila*, and can also be used to 'lighten' a bouquet. Fern fronds are, of course, ever popular in summer arrangements; but here too, make sure that the fronds are fully mature before you pick them.

There are many shrubs with foliage suitable for use in vases. It is well worth the effort of planting some of them in your garden,

Not only flowers are used in flower arrangements.

You may not think of using foliage from trees; but oak and beech are much used; try both green and brown varieties of beech.

so that you have a supply of foliage close at hand. To ensure a continuous and adequate supply of cutting material, consider planting more than one plant of each species. But do not cut too much while the plants are still small as you may spoil both their vigour and their future shape. *Pieris* and *Leucothoe* have firm, leathery leaves, as does *Eleagnus*, with both green and variegated varieties. They last well in water. *Forsythia* has upright spikes, while *Camelia* branches can be persuaded to bend or curve. For hanging greenery, varieties of *Hedera* (Ivy) are most useful at any time of year. Do try Honeysuckle (*Lonicera*).

Fruits in arrangements

Mahonia and *Berberis* (Barberry) are related; some species from each family have attractive but differently coloured berries. These berried branches look good in coarser or more informal arrangements. Another very useful berry bearing family is the *Cotoneaster*, whose species bear yellow, red or orange fruits; these may also be appreciated for their distinctive foliage. The best known berry is probably the Holly (*Ilex aquifolium*). Christmas decorations would seem strange without its red berries. If you have a holly tree in your garden, which doesn't produce fruits, the chances are you have a male tree; consequently, you need a female tree to bear fruits.

The berries of the Guelder Rose *(Viburnum opulus)* are most attractive in autumn arrangements, as are berried sprays of both the Fire Thorn *(Pyracantha)*, and the Hawthorn *(Crataegus)*.

The hips from the various rose species are to be found in abundance in autumn hedgerows. They are not only useful for making jelly but look very appealing in a jug.

Branches and twigs

During winter, when you are missing the cheering colours of your garden, try making an arrangement with the bare, twisted branches of the Corkscrew Hazel *(Corylus contorta)*. It can be rewarding to plant a winter flowering Jasmine, *(Jasminun nudiflorum)*, against a wall. From December to March the bare stems bear yellow blooms which can be used as pre-spring blossom.

The intermittent, winter flowering plum, *Prunus subhirtella* 'Autumnalis', has semi double white blossoms which flower between November and March. A more prolific flowerer is the Japanese Flowering Cherry, *Prunus serrulata*. This has many varieties, flowering mostly in April and May. They, too, can be cut for the vase while still in bud but, remember, not too young.

Some other early flowering shrubs are *Cornus mas* (the Cornelian Cherry), the Witch Hazel *(Hamemelis)*, the Japanese Quince *(Chaenomeles)*, and *Forsythia*. All these species can be picked while in bud. Alder *(Alnus)*, and varieties of Willow *(Salix)*, produce catkins in spring, and are much sought after by flower arrangers.

These pages should have given you some idea of the very many different plants, their foliage and fruits, that can be used for indoor displays.

Autumn display with fruits and berries.

Be careful with berried arrangements. Some fallen fruits can cause serious staining of furniture or floors. Berries of Sambucus, *although attractive, tend to drop all too easily.*

Arrangements in bowl or vase

Vases and other materials

An important question is, what are you going to put your flower arrangement in? Briefly, into anything that is water-tight! Obviously, the container must suit the materials to be arranged.

Vases in the widest sense of the word

Formal floral styles are arranged in the more formal type vases, and do follow certain rules and guide-lines such as the number of blooms, the shape of the arrangement and correct proportions, the colours, and how and where they are to be used. The style of the vase must suit the style of the arrangement. Its colour should be in harmony with the colour it is to contain; if the vase colour is too striking, or of a totally unrelated colour, it will detract from the display.

To get back to the style of vase: a copper kettle, pewter tankard or measuring jug can be used to make elaborate arrangements. You can use an excess of flowers, allowing your imagination to run free. Japanese and Chinese vases, which tend to be avoided by most modern florists, lend themselves to 18th-century arrangements. Examine the still life paintings of their period for inspiration. Ceramic vases that take the form of fish, flowers, angels, and suchlike can be used for the type of arrangements that were popular at the beginning of this century. The problem of their smaller water capacity can be overcome through the use of some of the more modern technical aids now available.

For modern arrangements, naturally, modern vases are best. They are usually lower, simpler, and more stylized in form. If you want to create a 'rustic' arrangement, use a container in keeping with the country image; for example, earthenware pots, milk-cans or storage jars. Plastic containers are available everywhere nowadays as vases and as containers for oasis foam. Purists do not regard these as vases, but still they can be used most effectively provided the container is hidden by the arrangement. Materials that are natural always seem to suit the floral art best. Many potteries produce hand-made vases and it is worth investing in a few for your flower arranging. Earthenware ones must be glazed if they are to be used as vases — if they are not, you can always place another waterproof receptacle inside them to hold the water. If the vase leaks use it instead for dried arrangements. Vases that are plain, well made and of subtle colour, should always be your first choice.

Flowers to be used in an earthenware vase can, for the most part, be coarser, more down to earth, than those intended for a sophisticated glass vase. The character of glass will impress itself on the arrangement. Glass is hard, cold but transparent. This last point must always be borne in mind; you don't only see the part of the arrangement above the vase but also that part which would be hidden in an earthenware vase. Special care must be taken in keeping a glass vase *and* its water clean.

Baskets have been used in flower arranging for a very long time. At the beginning of this century baskets made of wire-mesh, lined with sphagnum moss were used; flowers were inserted into the moss and attached to create a 'ball' of colour. Although these creations don't last long, they do form an effective short-term decoration. The present basket arrangement can be made to last longer. Baskets may be made of cane, reed, willow, split timber or bamboo; some are made without handles. The size and shape of handle should be in proportion to the basket size, and should be strong enough to enable the whole to be moved when full of water and blooms. Once you have become enthusiastic about the floral arts, you will soon find that you have acquired yet another hobby — that of collecting vases!

Ceramic vases are often rough underneath, and can scratch furniture. Glue some felt patches to the underside to solve this problem.

Containers other than vases can be used for flower arrangements. An old soup tureen, teapot or gravy dish can be most effectively used for original displays.

*Baskets come in all
shapes and sizes.*

Tools and materials

Many aids have come onto the market in the past few years, making floral work far easier. You only have to peep into the back of a florist's shop to see this. There may be floral art classes in your area. It is always surprising to see how different people can use the same type of flower in quite diverse ways.

Knife and secateurs

A good knife can prolong the life of your cut flowers. Florists use a small, folding, but easily held knife; this would usually be a grafting or budding knife. There are various types and sizes to choose from. Once you've made your choice be sure to sharpen it to a good edge, and always keep it sharp. A clean cut stem, that has not been bruised, can absorb water freely and can consequently live longer.

A pair of secateurs is useful for cutting branches and tougher stems. Never use your secateurs for cutting wire as you will damage its blade; instead use wire-cutters which are designed for the task.

Aids for floral art

There are also other tools and materials that are quite invaluable. The florist is well versed in the use of these aids, but in the ordinary way the enthusiast wouldn't have them in his or her home, at least to start with. Look upon these aids as a necessary evil. You should use them as little as possible. They should never be visible. For, with all the natural materials you are using, you will want the whole apearance of the arrangement as a whole to be natural, with no wires or other artificial aids visible.

If you want to make an airy arrangement in a shallower bowl you will need to use a *pin-holder*. These 'little beds of nails' have a base of lead, providing stability, and the spines are best made of copper, as it prevents rust which can leave ugly marks on glassware or ceramics. Even though pin-holders are fairly heavy, it is always safest to 'stick' them down in the vase with plastic putty or plasticine to eliminate any chance of the arrangement collapsing. Both vase and pin-holder must be completely dry when the attaching is done — with the slightest moisture it won't hold. Some pin-holders are fitted with suction-caps, but

Some stems won't remain upright in a pin-holder. Thin stems can first be inserted into cut off sections of thicker, hollow stems. Several thin stems could also be bound together, and then pushed into the holder. Fill hollow stems with thinner solid stems. Stems that split easily can first be bound with tape.

these do not always hold, or else they become loose after some hours, with possible disastrous consequences.

When buying a pin-holder, always check the spacing of the pins — if they are too close together you may have difficulty getting thick or hard stems into them; if pins are too far apart, thin stems cannot be supported.

Some vases have a *flower holder*, which fits inside the container; they are usually dome-shaped ceramic or glass pieces, with holes in them. They don't work very well as they give very little choice or flexibility of directions. It is probably more useful to discard the holder, and use a piece of wire mesh, shaped to fit the vase (but not, of course, if you are using a glass vase!).

Wire mesh, or chicken wire, as it is often called, can be used in vases with wide openings or deep interiors. Mesh is usually galvanised or plastic-coated — either can be used, but do make sure that the plastic-coated mesh is 'woven', in the same manner as chicken wire, and is not the collapsible type.

The advantage of using wire mesh is that the stems can all be completely submerged. It is available in various gauges and mesh-sizes, so you can choose the one that suits the sizes of flower stem you are using. Use a mesh with larger holes for your larger arrangements where probably you will be using plants with thicker stems. Cut the piece of mesh quite a bit larger than the width of the vase, remembering that it must be folded down to reach the bottom of the vase, so that it cannot be pushed down when you push the stems in. Crumple the mesh a bit so that it fits snugly in the vase, then form its top into the shape of a dome.

Lead strip is sometimes used to hold a few branches of the taller flowers in place. A thin lead sheet is cut into strips of 1–2cm (½in) in width, and up to 30cm (12in) lengths. A strip is then wrapped around a stem and its ends folded over the edge of the vase, thereby holding the stem upright.

Clay is still used sometimes, but it does nothing whatever to prolong the life of the blooms. It is suitable for the smaller Christmas arrangements. When the piece is completed and the blooms and foliage have been pushed into the ball of clay, make a few holes in the top of the clay to hold a bit of extra moisture.

Green filler, comprising short sections of conifer shoots and stems loosely inserted upside-down into the vase is used to support flower stems. The disadvantage of this practice is that the water quickly becomes polluted and will smell awful! The advantage, though, is that it can be simply collected from the garden, and it does work well.

Glass tubes with rubber stoppers are sometimes used in florist's arrangements. They are used for flowers with very short stems and must be refilled regularly as their capacity is small.

Without *Oasis* (a water-retaining foam) a great many flower arrangements would just not be possible. This man-made product is available in different shapes (bricks, rounds or cylinders), and also in different densities, from hard to soft, and so can be selected according to the types of stem the flowers have.

Oasis is intensely hygroscopic, and will become totally saturated with water, when allowed to soak — this must be done before you start an arrangement. Do not force it under the surface; gentle pushing, with a flat hand is quite enough. Handle the foam carefully, since dents and holes cannot be repaired and, in any case, it has a limited usage period.

Oasis can be held in place in the vase with special prongs or clips. You can allow it to protrude up above the level of the neck of the vase, and so it is excellent for horizontal work.

When the arrangement is completed, the oasis foam must be kept moist, as the water evaporates from it fairly quickly. Oasis is usually a grey-green colour so do make sure that it is well-hidden by your arrangement.

Before oasis was developed, both *sphagnum* and *peat moss* were used to do this job. But it is far more difficult to make a good sphagnum ball than to simply cut off a piece of oasis.

Peat moss retains a lot of moisture, and used to be used for funeral wreaths and table decorations. After the coarser part of the material has been removed, the peat was formed into a moist ball, held in place with string and wire.

Sphagnum moss is still used, both to conceal oasis, and to help reduce evaporation; it thus can provide a background that still appears to be of a natural material.

Cushion moss is used decoratively in plant bowls, and can be held in place with wire staples. Do not collect this moss from forests and woods; you may well find some growing in the shady areas of your garden, or perhaps on a shaded part of the roof.

Iceland or *Reindeer moss* is imported from Scandinavia, and is used in Christmas decorations. it is very dry when bought, and must be soaked for several hours before using.

Florist's wire is used in corsages and bridal bouquets. It is usually coloured green; the paint reduces rust, and the colour makes it almost invisible. It is available in a range of thicknesses. Florist's wire has the great advantage that it holds any shape into which it is bent.

Wire staples are used to attach moss to various backgrounds.

Copper *corsage pins* are needed for attaching the corsages to clothing.

Florist's tape is used to camouflage corsage stems or wire, and to pad them out when and where necessary. Tape is sold in rolls and is slightly stretchy and so should not be stored in a warm place.

Plastic sheet can be used to line and waterproof baskets. String, in various thicknesses is always useful for all manner of tasks, including the binding of hand-held posies.

Flowers for festive occasions

*Plain and
simple use of
colour.*

*Colours of flowers can
look quite different at
night under artificial
light; some are
particularly badly
affected, notably blue
and violet shades.*

Decorating with flowers

When making up a floral arrangement, you
should take into consideration the fact that
it will not be standing entirely alone. It will
be placed in a specific room or location,
and must be regarded as being part of that
decor. It is important that you should know
beforehand which space an arrangement
must fill. If it is for your own home, have a
good look around the room, note its
predominant colours; could the
arrangement be made to harmonize or
contrast with these colours? It is usually
rather better to try to make it harmonize
with its surroundings.

Form and colour

It is always better if you can make the
arrangement in the place where it is going
to stand. You can then gauge exactly what
form it should take, and which colour
combinations suit. Also, if the arrangement
is large, it will not then need carrying.

Judgment is obviously something that takes
a while to learn. When you have more
experience it will become easier to judge in
advance, or away from the site, how a
piece will fit into a particular situation.

Colour plays an important part in all our
daily lives. Without our realising it, we are
influenced by the colours and tones around
us. This fact is used widely in the
decoration of larger institutions, offices and
hospitals, for instance. Colour can disturb,
calm or stimulate. Yellow, red and orange
are stimulating, lively and warm colours.
Blue is a passive, cool colour.

When making an arrangement for a large
room or space, use bright colours, as this
will make it stand out more. These same
bright colours could be unsettling in a more
confined space. It would be better to use
more restful colours in this case.

The colours used within an arrangement
can be made to harmonize, or contrast,
with each other. An arrangement of
larkspurs, in various blue shades with grey
foliage, gives a completely different feel to
that of a mixed arrangement of red
carnations and blue forget-me-nots.

There is also an accepted practice of using
certain colours for certain occasions or
celebrations. Thus different shades are used
for a funeral than would be used for a
wedding or christening. These customs and
traditions can vary from country to
country. There is also a colour code for
church festivals. For example, at Easter,
colours would be white and gold; red and
gold for Whitsun. These schemes are not
strictly followed. Whatever the colours or
rules, the flowers must form a composite
whole with their vase, bowl or basket.

159

Spring bouquet, where twigs and young leaves have not been forgotten.

Seasonal aspects of floral arrangements

In spite of their form and colour some combinations of flowers simply do not go together. For example, if wild flowers were to be combined with exotic blooms, neither would receive the attention they deserve.

Different types of bouquet can be made. A bouquet of different types of flower, arranged well, and blending with their surroundings, has a decorative value. But the individual blooms in such an arrangement lose their identity, to the extent that at a later date you will probably not be able to remember what types of flower were used in its make-up.

When making an arrangement you have to keep to the individual character of the flowers and foliage you are using. With these as the focal point, you find that they more or less decide for you what type of treatment will be needed.

Sometimes you may use a small vase with only a few blooms. On another occasion it may be a bouquet collected while out for a walk in the country. This could include not only flowers, but leaves, twigs, grasses or fruits. The prettiest example is the poppy. When you place a bunch of red poppies in a vase by themselves, you have isolated them from their natural surroundings. But if instead you were to make up an arrangement of poppies, cornflowers, wheat-ears and other grasses, you would see immediately how much better the poppies appear.

Arrangements can also be made that reflect the rhythm of the changing seasons. Nowadays there are so many different flowers for sale coming from all over the world (and all the year round), that one cannot always tell which season it is by merely looking at an arrangement. In the autumn beautiful displays can be made from coloured leaves and branches bearing

fruits and berries. Most plants will have finished flowering but have seed-heads or fruits that are also very decorative.

Winter's touch can be brought indoors with an arrangement of gnarled, bare branches, pebbles, stumps and weathered seed pods.

Spring again brings the tender buds and shoots onto bare branches and, of course, the early bulbs. And summer, with its luxurious colours overflowing, when large, bright and cheerful arrangements can again fill the home.

Arrangements in vases

Most arrangements are made in vases. This is not surprising, as a vase is specifically intended to provide the elements needed by cut flowers. It provides support, and supplies water, but can be selected just for its own appeal as well.

You can select your vase to be the centre-piece of your display and use only a few flowers or foliage stems to enhance the

By reflecting the year's changing seasons in flower arrangements, you become a little closer to nature. During the sombreness of winter, you can begin to look forward to the first buds and blossoms of spring. But if you maintain a profusion of bought blooms throughout the year the appearance of the first snowdrop will have little meaning.

Bulb bouquet.

161

All stems to be inserted into oasis foam must first be cleaned up and cut cleanly at an angle. If any thorns or leaves are left on the lower part of the stems, they will make unnecessarily large holes and then will not stand securely. When removed, the hole will be hard to fill.

beauty or form of the vase. Normally, you would start off with the flowers as the prime element and choose a vase that will suit. It is a great advantage to have a good selection of vases at your disposal so that with each arrangement you would be able to make the appropriate choice.

Flowers in a vase *should* represent something much more than simply some flowers and a vase that just happen to have been used together. A glass vase needs a different type of treatment to a ceramic vase. Vases made from synthetic materials could be said to be far-removed from the natural materials that are being used, and which do not always have an affinity to them. The technical aids used will depend largely on the particular vase in question. When using glass vases, you have to be especially careful, as anything you put into them will be clearly visible, and so should not detract in any way. A posy of flowers in a small glass vase can be supported by partly filling the vase with selected gravel or river-bed pebbles; these will, of course, have to be washed first to prevent muddying of the water.

When you require some lengths of flowering branch or foliage to stay upright in a slim glass vase, the answer may be to use some narrow lead strips to help secure them (and these would hardly be noticed). The solution to the problem of supporting stems in a wide glass vase is to cut a piece of pre-soaked oasis, a little smaller than the

vase, and fill the space between vase and oasis with gravel.

Working with ceramic vases
A ceramic vase will provide few problems if it has a wide enough neck. It can be filled with chicken wire, oasis or 'green filler'. To use a deep vase for flowers with shorter stems, and without using vast quantities of oasis, place a smaller vase or jar upside down within the deep vase and fit oasis on top of this.

To quite an extent, the shape of the vase will dictate the form your arrangement should take. Shallower dish or urn-type vases probably offer more scope for the imagination than more upright types, but they also need constant replenishing of water. However, with modern materials and aids you can become more adventurous and try new forms for yourself. Whatever the form or style you are creating you should always fill the vase with water first. When using oasis, allow a few centimetres to stick up above the rim of the vase; this allows you also to work horizontally, and even get the stems to 'hang' down. Don't forget that you can use foliage as well as blooms; they provide a more restful effect in a floral display. Foliage can also be used to form the primary 'lines' or shape of the arrangement. In addition, you can use foliage on its own, with very satisfying results. For example, in early spring, try an arrangement of Guelder Rose *(Viburnum*

Building up an arrangement.

opulus), Eleagnus, Skimmia, Hedera and some bare branches of Witch Hazel *(Hamemelis)*. The easiest and most common type of one-sided arrangement is the triangle. Begin with the tallest point (with either bloom or foliage), and then the two base points of the triangle, which should be close to the level of the rim of the vase.

Apart from the ultra modern pieces it is usual to create displays where all the stems and foliage 'radiate' from one point, the 'heart' of the arrangement which is obviously just above the lip of the vase. This point is often accentuated with a large or darker bloom.

Try using a shallow bowl for a floating arrangement by floating flowers on the water in the manner of a water-lily (Nymphaea).

Arrangements in bowls

Dishes or bowls are more generally used for containing fruit or placing under pot plants. It is not usual to think of them in terms of containers for a flower arrangement. It doesn't seem practical to place blooms in so shallow a container. However, with modern aids, the main problems can be overcome. A not too deep bowl is more of a presentation tray where the blooms and the tray form an entity as arranged.

When arranging flowers in a dish without a rim, you'll find that it's hard to know where to end the arrangement; the flowers seem to overflow the space and go their own way. A dish with a rim has more clearly defined limits. Don't use too many

flowers in a dish arrangement. The use of a pin-holder is desirable in most cases. It can be easily hidden with the minimum of material — a few leaves, and a few pebbles alongside, and the holder is out of sight. If the dish is too shallow for a pin-holder then use oasis. Use as little as possible to make it easier to conceal — there are special fasteners available to hold it in place. Any good florist should stock them.

Arrangements in baskets

Arrangements in baskets are entirely different from those in vases or bowls. With most arrangements you can get away with using the minimum of blooms or foliage, but with a basket this would not be feasible. Whether a basket is large or small, it needs to be literally filled to overflowing to be effective. Of course, baskets are not watertight, so either you must find a container that fits inside it, or line it with a thick plastic sheet and fill this with oasis. If the basket is fairly deep, you could use a bucket or vase with a wide neck inside it. As you will seldom find a perfect fit, and you need the inner container to be stable, fill the space between vase and basket with crumpled newsprint. If the basket has a handle use it as a feature, and don't let it become too lost amongst the foliage.

A basket in its natural colour looks better than one that has been painted. Earlier basket arrangements used plenty of coloured ribbons as added decoration. This is a nice touch, and can appear very romantic with the ribbons toning in with the colours of the blooms.

Arranging with short-stemmed flowers

An idea to try if you find that you have a fair quantity of flowers and foliage with stems that are too short for the usual type of arrangement, is to create a column or pyramid of colour, using oasis foam as the foundation. Oasis comes ready-shaped, as bricks, cylinders, etc. If you can't buy the shape you want, then you can easily shape your own from the normal bricks. After allowing the oasis to soak up water, place it in a shallow dish, and cover it with the flowers and foliage with their stems cut short so that the material conforms with the outline you are creating.

This type of decoration is particularly effective at Christmas when conifer foliage

and cones can be used. Many variations on this theme are possible.

A decorated table

A graciously decorated table without flowers, for some special occasion, would be hard to imagine. The possibilities for table decoration are almost limitless provided that certain simple rules are observed.

When a florist is making-up table decorations in a hotel you may well encounter a conflict between the head waiter, who regards his table settings as being of greater importance, and the florist, who is equally keen to make the floral pieces the highlight of the table. Fortunately, at home when a dinner party is being organised both tasks will probably be undertaken by the same person so no clash of interests occurs.

The table setting should be looked at as a whole, and the floral arrangement should not detract from other aspects of decorating. In particular, ensure that they do not hinder conversation by blocking the view across the table. A table arrangement should never exceed 25–30cm (10–12ins) in height.

The shape and size of the table more or less determines what shape and size the decorative piece must be. A circular table definitely needs a round arrangement placed exactly at its centre. An oblong table could have a low, elongated display, that can be viewed from both sides.

The colours of the blooms must blend or contrast with the rest of the table setting: it is best not to use over bright or overly striking colours. Also, your workmanship will really be put to the test as no floral arrangement is so closely scrutinised as a table decoration, which is literally 'under your nose' for a good part of the evening. The best test is, once you have completed the arrangement, to sit down and critically view your work as your guests will certainly do. Be certain that none of the 'workings' shows at all.

Table arrangements can be made in dishes, vases, soup tureens, or other pieces of your dinner service. Filled with oasis, they can provide some continuity to the general display.

A dinner party may take place under artificial or candle light. Beware then, of blue or lilac shades. A centre-piece that looks fine in daylight, can look sickly and washed out under artificial light.

When entertaining friends by laying the table as a buffet, you will find that you will be far less restricted with regard to height or width of your flower display. Apart from flowers, vegetables, fruits or even herbs can be used effectively. A pyramid oasis, covered with chicken wire and attached to a board, will provide a sound base.

Table arrangement in matching colours.

165

A decorated gift.

Christmas wreath.

Vase and arrangement: a double gift!

On a long table, you can place more than one arrangement, so long as the symmetry of the table is observed.

The rest of the table decoration must be as carefully set out as the flowers. Decorative candle holders or glasses, a few scattered individual blooms, all add to the festive feel. (If you are using loose flowers, ensure they are only put out at the last moment.) You could place a small button-hole or corsage at each place, perhaps matching the flower arrangement, or a single bloom on each napkin. The possibilities are endless, especially if there is enough space. Don't, however, make the decorations too fussy or elaborate. Leave room for the dishes, too! It is, after all, the dinner that is important and the flowers merely decoration.

Decorating a gift

When someone receives a wrapped package with a posy of flowers arranged on it, it appears doubly decorative. The stems of such a mini-bouquet should be made long enough that they can be placed in a small vase. Another way of presenting a gift is not to wrap it up at all, but to decorate it with flowers. Some objects, such as glasses or cups, present no problems: simply use a piece of damp oasis inside the object, with a small posy arranged in the normal way. Remember that the gift is the important item, so allow the flowers to show it off, but not smother it.

Other objects are not quite as easy to decorate, but with a bit of florist's wire, oasis and tape, most obstacles can be overcome. Remember to harmonize the colours of the flowers with the gift. Ribbon often provides the best way of adding a 'finishing touch'.

Festive floral art

People who don't normally attempt flower-arranging will often try their hand at some form of decoration at Christmas time. It is certainly a pleasurable pastime to decorate the home with evergreen branches, pine cones, holly, and all of the other traditional bits and pieces. Provide a greeting at the door with a Christmas garland. Make this in the same way as a dry flower wreath, but use greenery, small pine cones, conifer twigs, dates, Eucalyptus, oranges or peppers. Make sure that the materials you use are evenly distributed around the wreath; use a bright red ribbon to form a bow, and hang it on the front door. It should remain fresh for some time.

Similar but smaller wreaths can be used as table decoration for your Christmas dinner. Naturally, this will have to be done in 'Christmas' style, not forgetting to use bright coloured candles. A sophisticated colour scheme could use white candles to contrast with the greens and browns that abound in nature at this time of the year. Cheerful decorations can be made using red candles; repeat the appearance of red with holly berries (and add some red peppers, for good measure). Golden yellow candles combine well with the branches of golden conifers, with oranges, lemons and yellow peppers for added brightness. A Christmas decoration for a wall can be made by using a soup ladle and decorating its deep bowl with greenery. Attach a shaped piece of damp oasis to the bowl with tape and fix the ladle to the wall. Stick pieces of conifer, holly berries and leaves, pine

Christmas display.

cones, ribbon, etc. into the oasis. Push some twigs in at an angle to hide the foam and its binding. Pine cones will need wires attached to their stalk ends. Red ribbon can both finish off and highlight the decoration.

A table can be decorated for Easter in much the same way as is done for Christmas, except that the decorative material available at Easter is entirely different. All sorts of spring bulbs will be out, and many spring flowers; Primula, Crocus, Daffodil, Tulip, Violet, Forget-me-not, and dozens more. Many of these early blooms have rather short stems and need to be made into smaller posies rather than trying to create a larger display in a vase. The posies can be grouped in a shallower bowl or glass dish. Branches that are beginning to send out their spring foliage and blossom can also be used in these arrangements. Coloured eggs are, of course, a part of traditional Easter decoration, and these can be either included in an arrangement or grouped at its base.

Because flowers from the garden are rather scarce at Easter, it might be an idea to spread them around by placing a few at each person's place, in an egg cup or, even better, in a coloured, empty egg shell. You need slightly more than half of the egg shell, glued onto a large, flat button, to permit it to stand firmly. Fill it with damp oasis foam and decorate with small flowers and leaves. First make a hole with a

167

needle for stems that are fragile. Children usually love making this type of decoration and are often better at it than adults. Avoid making these mini-bouquets too large.

St. Valentine's Day, on the 14th February, named after St. Valentine who lived during the 3rd century. He was a priest who gave advice and assistance to all who asked. Although there is little evidence that he had anything to do with romance, this day has become symbolic of lovers declaring their affections. Flowers, of course, play an important part in this ritual. If you wish to present someone special with a 'Valentine' then what better than a 'heart' full of flowers. Cut a flattened heart shape from damp oasis foam and fill it with flowers and foliage. If you don't have enough small blooms, then first cover the whole area with Icelandic Moss, held in place with coloured beads on pins, then fill the rest with flowers.

When visiting a patient in hospital it is nice to take a bunch of flowers. It is even better if you have already arranged them in a small vase or container and take this along. This avoids the bunch having to lie around until after visiting hours, and then possibly

being dropped into the nearest receptacle, be it a drinking glass or a jam jar. Don't take strong-smelling flowers to someone who is ill. The heavy scent of hyacinth or jasmine can be overpowering indoors. And don't make the bouquet too large as the night table may be the only place to put it on. The flowers are the important part of this gift and the container of little importance. Save better-looking jars for this purpose; mustard jars or yoghurt cups can be camouflaged by careful draping with bits of greenery. They can then be discarded after the flowers have faded. Choose flowers in cheerful colours and try to avoid white as the patient probably sees enough of this.

When out visiting you might take your hostess a bunch of flowers. Most will enjoy receiving flowers, but a busy hostess will have to find a vase, and arrange them at a time when she has her guests to see to. If you are a close friend you can, of course, offer to do this for her. It is possibly more thoughtful to take along a bouquet which can be simply placed in a vase without even untying the string. It doesn't take any great skill to put together such a bouquet. The 'arrangement' is made between thumb and fore-finger; start with a background of taller greenery or conifer stems; onto this, arrange the blooms, one by one in order of stem length, and starting with the tallest. Pretend that the circle made by your finger and thumb is the neck of the vase. In this way all the stem ends will be long enough to reach the water. Bind the finished bouquet firmly, at hand level, and cut off all the stems at the same level so that they will stand evenly in a vase. A matching ribbon and cellophane wrapping will just 'finish' the arrangement off, and it can now be placed in a vase.

When gathering flowers in the fields or garden, you can gather them together, in your hand, as a posy that can be placed

directly into a vase. With a bit of practice this becomes quite an easy task. Either a modern or an old-fashioned bridal bouquet can be made up in this same manner. This follows the *Biedermeier* style, with flowers packed closely together. Larger, or coarser flowers are not used, and stems need not be very long as the bouquet is intended to be held in the hand. The portion that is to be held must never be made too thick or it may be a nuisance to the bride. You can thin it down by wrapping the stems tightly with tape shortly before the occasion. This type of bouquet has the advantage of not looking as stiff and artificial as a wired bouquet. Furthermore, it can be made up far earlier — even the previous evening. Select blooms not only for colour, shape and size, but also for their ability to remain out of water for the few hours of the wedding and yet still look good. Another advantage of this type of bouquet is that it

Bridesmaid's bouquet.

A corsage fit for a queen.

Corsage and button-hole.

A very bright, colourful jacket only needs a simple but restful corsage, whereas a plainer top can take a busier display of brighter colours. But don't make a corsage so large that the wearer is hidden! Or so small that it simply can't be seen.

could be made by the bride, groom, member of the family or a friend, which cannot be said about a wired bouquet, which needs a considerable amount of expertise to achieve good results.

In the next chapter on dried flowers, there is a description of how to make up a bouquet for the birth of a baby (cradle bouquet). Precise instructions are given on how to wire the dried flowers. With fresh flowers the process is exactly the same, except that where the stem is cut a piece of damp cotton wool is applied to help prolong the life of the flowers; this is held in place by the wire. The whole wired stem is then bound with florist's tape to conceal wire and cotton wool.

The 'held' part of a wired bridal bouquet is all wire. Because the wires are covered with florist's tape they can easily be wound together into a 'stem'; the arrangement should hide all of these parts.

The bouquet can be either elongated or round in shape. An oblong one should be formed as a slender, triangular shape.

Colour is of great importance in a bridal bouquet. It must reflect the colour of the dress, and suit the features of the bride; thus, a tall, slim and blonde girl would need a different bouquet to a shorter, dark-haired girl. If there are bridesmaids, they usually carry smaller bouquets made of different flowers from those being carried by the bride.

Traditionally, the bridegroom should have a flower in the button-hole of his jacket of the same sort as the bride has in her bouquet. Carnations, with a sprig of greenery, are most commonly used as button-holes. It is more original to wear something different. Wire a few very small flowers and leaves together to form a miniature corsage. All the parts must be wired and twisted into a 'stem' which is then taped. The button-hole is pinned, stem down, on the left-hand lapel of the jacket.

Corsages for women are also worn on the left side of the jacket or dress, with stalk ends facing upwards. Corsages are usually far more elaborate than button-holes. You can use many different types of flower and foliage, provided they are not too large, and can survive for some time without water. All the flowers and leaves must be wired separately. To gauge the correct lengths you can lay the corsage out on the table. It is, in fact, like a bridal bouquet, but in miniature. Thus, all stems are cut to predetermined lengths, so that when they are eventually bound together all the cut ends are at the same level. The longest stem will belong to the bloom furthest from the centre of the corsage, while the central blooms will have virtually no stem. The florist's wire, or silver wire that is used for smaller work, is very fine and soft so as not to damage slender stems. Florist's tape should hide all signs of wire and bind the individual wires into a single 'stem'.

Corsages can be made to reflect the different seasons, and it is surprising what can be done with only a small amount of material. A few rose hips, hop fruits and ivy leaves will provide the makings of an autumn corsage. Spring corsages can be made with Snowdrops, forget-me-nots, a few florets from a hyacinth, and a few leaves or fern-tips.

Flowers for sympathy

Flowers are present throughout one's life. Even a final farewell to the departed is traditionally expressed with flowers. Why not make the last tribute to a dear friend or loved one yourself? You will probably know which flowers were their favourites, and so could try to include these. Flowers from the immediate family and closer friends are placed on the coffin, and others alongside.

Such arrangements need to have a particular shape; in most cases they will need to lie flat and be viewed from above. They should have a flat back,

A final tribute.

and be designed as if the main viewing would be from overhead.

They could be in the form of a bouquet, made-up and bound in the hand, and with stems cut very short.

Oasis foam could also be used as the foundation for an arrangement. It will need to stand in a shallow, waterproof container or tray that will not be visible. Start by installing greenery to hide the base and provide a background. Imagine that all the stems are radiating out from the centre of the foam.

A self-made floral tribute is certainly the most personal of farewells.

Working with dried flowers

Bouquets and displays using dried flowers and fruit

About pollen and anthers

The flower is often the most conspicuous part of a plant. Its existence was never intended for the enjoyment of man — that is purely incidental — but none the less a pleasurable 'by-product'. So if the attractive colours (and also the heavenly scents) of flowers are not really meant for us, why were they created?

The colours and scents have the vital function of attracting passing insects who are enticed to gather the nectar from the flowers and, unwittingly, in return they carry off pollen grains on their bodies. When the next flower of the same species is visited, and again without the insect knowing it, some of the pollen grains may be rubbed off onto the sticky stigma of this bloom. The majority of flowers are pollenated in this way, and this leads ultimately to the formation of fruits and seeds. It is not only insects that pollenate flowers. Some are aided by the wind and others are self-pollenating.

Thus, the flower is not created for humans at all but is only concerned with its reproduction and the continued existence of that species.

Flowers have fascinated people for centuries

People have always tried to extend the short lives of blooms through paintings, embroidery and by drying them. Fifteenth-century painters enlivened their biblical subjects by including in their paintings miniature representations of medicinal herbs. These more elaborate examples made the diagrams in Middle Age herbals look quite plain by comparison. During the Renaissance, the practice of collecting specimens of plants and preserving them in herberia was one of the many methods of 'rediscovering' nature, as was studying botany. Collections of plants were dried and kept in books for reference. At this time the first botanical gardens were also being established where plants could be grown as living collections. In both botanic garden and herbarium, the whole basis of plant naming and classification was being introduced.

The preservation of plant material in some or other form is not a new idea. Generations ago the drying of plants was widely practised, more for learning than for pleasure. Today, flowers are dried mainly for decorative purposes.

Flowers drying in a loft.

Symbolism of plants

You can see, by studying old paintings, that there is a symbolism in the representation of flowers and plants. The artist would not only include them for decorative effect, but wanted to use them to convey a specific message. In 15th and 16th Century biblical paintings, plants are not prominent in the foreground; they provide background for the figures. In this way Alpine strawberries (*Fragaria vesca*) with their bright red fruits became the heavenly fruit to feed the starving children.

A legend tells of how Jesus used the Ground Ivy (*Glechoma hederacea*) to cure the Apostle Peter of toothache. There are paintings of Jesus as a child holding branches of Black Nightshade (*Solanum nigra*). People believed that this poisonous little plant could ward off evil spirits. Lilies also feature prominently in early paintings, and were regarded as the symbol of purity and love.

By studying plants in old paintings we

Plant symbolism is not always the same in different countries. Shepherd's Purse, Capsella bursa-pastoris, or rather its fruits, closely resembles the purses of the early herders of England or Holland. The French, however, have a less friendly name, calling it a 'Judas Purse'.

Vase full of dried flowers.

sometimes come across some peculiar surprises. Certain blooms painted without petals, or flowers or plants shown in completely wrong situations are amongst many examples. These anomalies can probably be explained away as ignorance or artistic licence.

Flower paintings

At the end of the 16th Century, different types of flower started appearing in paintings. Earlier depictions of wild flowers and herbs, with their symbolism, were of growing plants or simply pieces of plant. Now, for the first time, flowers in many shades and tones started appearing

intentionally cut and placed in vases as decoration.

The artists, with commissions from the Church to paint religious subjects, started placing emphasis on more worldly matters. There were also increasing requests from wealthier citizens for paintings of more interesting subjects to decorate their homes.

At first, quite a few wild flowers appeared in these still life paintings, but they gradually made way for cultivated, garden flowers, such as peonies, hyacinths, tulips, carnations and iris.

The paintings were not always drawn from life but from the artists' imagination, as flowers from different seasons were often

*Book ends of
early 'timber
books'.*

put together in the same arrangement.
Probably preliminary sketches were made
of different blooms, and these were put
together later to form a composition.

By examining the paintings of still life
subjects down the ages, one can follow the
development of different styles of flower
arranging.

Now, in the second half of this century, the
trend has again turned towards nature and
this is reflected in paintings and drawings
of plants and flowers. It's not the large
garden-hybrids that draw attention, but the
simpler wild species. This new recognition
can only increase as more people become
aware of the great beauty of flowers.

The herbarium

If you have an interest in the flowers of the
countryside it can be rewarding to start
your own herbarium. Many pleasant hours
can be spent tramping field and lane in
search of new specimens.

A herbarium is not just a collection of
compressed and dried plant material. The
original meaning was herb book. A herb
book from the 16th Century, for example,
was no mere collection of dried plants but
also an index of herbs, with details and
recipes for their medicinal and other uses.
These early herbals contained dried
specimens, but also had wood-cut etchings
of the plants along with the pages of
descriptive text.

It was only much later that the term
herbarium was broadened to include the
collections of botanical specimens, to be
used for reference and research.

Why a herbarium?

The herbariums of the 16th and 17th
Centuries were collections of medicinal
herbs, used by apothecaries (who were
forerunners of doctors). The books
provided the means of identifying and
testing whether he had the right herb or

not. From the pure herbs he concocted his
medicines. These books of samples and
specimens were kept in special cases, and
formed the basis of medical knowledge.
Even today, herbaria are used to compare
plants with one another, to identify them
and clear up difficulties in their naming.

In earlier times, and even today, long
expeditions were embarked upon by men
such as Leonhart Fuchs, Sir Joseph Banks
and William Forsythe. Many plants are
named after these early collectors who
described, drew and pressed vast amounts
of plant material and brought them back to
Britain and Europe. One of the greatest
plant collectors was undoubtedly Carl
Linnaeus (18th Century) who also did a
great deal of work on the classification of
plants into families. In fact he started the
whole system which is still used today. As
early as the 16th Century a German
physician, Leonhart Rauwolff, had made
up a herbarium of medicinal herbs brought
back from his travels in the Far East.

The early herbaria were relatively simple;
they became far more complex and detailed
in the 17th and especially the 18th
Centuries. Gradually, herbariums became
the province of the botanist, who studied
plants for their own sake, rather than for
their practical application in medicine,
foods, etc. Great herbariums were started
at many universities and are still in use.
Kew Gardens, with its great tradition of
plant collection, identification and research,
is still a world leader in this.

Timber books

As a parallel to early herbariums the
identification of trees was sometimes
undertaken through the use of special
'books' that were in fact cases containing
samples of the individual tree, and made up
from the wood of that species. Pieces of
bark, dried leaves and fruits were all
included. An accompanying text would

Arranging your herbarium sheet.

provide further details. Tree or timber identification was not of great interest to many, so these 'books' were not often seen.

Collecting and drying flowers

You can dry any flowers that you have collected, and you can extend your collecting to fruits and seeds. Fruits and seeds are designed by nature to survive all manner of difficult circumstances so they are likely to dry quite well too.

There are four methods usually used to dry flowers: in a vase, in a box with sand, hanging or by pressing.

Before you start drying flowers there are a few points to remember. If you intend going off into the wilds to collect flowers you must realise that some species have unfortunately become so scarce that they are protected by law and so must not be picked. This does not necessarily mean that they need be missing from your collection. You will simply have to use another way of including them: by making pen drawings or photographing them, for example. In this way rare plants can be prevented from becoming even more scarce.

You will find that after spending some time with wild plants you will want to know more about them and their habits. The obvious solution is to obtain one of the many good specialist books on wild flowers.

Drying flowers

To start the drying . . .

with a small flower-press,

or with a brick weight.

The correct picking time

Choosing the right time to pick flowers is very important when you want to dry the blooms. Some need to be picked at bud stage and others just as they open fully.

If you want to make them into a bouquet, then the durability of the blooms is closely related to the stage at which they are picked. In the later descriptions of flowers suitable for drying, the correct times to pick are given. Flowers that are going to be pressed should be picked as soon as is possible after they have opened fully to preserve their best colours.

In all cases flowers for drying should be picked on a dry day.

Make you own herbarium

If you want to make your own herbarium you will need to dry the flowers and foliage flat, i.e. pressed between sheets of paper. Such a collection of plants, if it is to be done scientifically, must be collected and labelled according to a system where each plant type is provided with its correct scientific and family name, common name and the location where it was found. The specimen, with its details is then stored in appropriate 'books'.

If you enjoy collecting plants even when on holiday, try to obtain the correct names of your specimens before leaving for home. Later, at home, you can arrange and label everything at leisure.

Use white mounting paper or board and attach the dried specimens with thin strips of linen tape. You can also cover the whole sheet with self-clinging plastic sheet (clingfilm), and use small labels to identify each plant. Of course it is not necessary to wait for a holiday to do all this! You could make up a card of flowers to remind you of a particular walk in the country, or have cards that reflect the different blooms of the changing seasons.

How to press flowers

If the time between picking and pressing is likely to be more than an hour or so, it would be sensible to place the stems in water, to keep the material as fresh as possible. Almost any type of flower is suitable for drying; but for pressing, those that are too thick, large or fleshy (and contain a high proportion of water) are not likely to give good results. Some flowers lose nearly all of their colour when dried, and so are not worth preserving. As you become more proficient and experienced, you will get to know what can and can't be done and what practical problems are likely. For instance the poppy (*Papaver rhoeas*), can lose all of its petals during drying; but the same poppy if picked at the crack of dawn will give no such trouble.

Besides drying flowers you can, of course, dry leaves equally well. There are many fascinating colours and shapes to work with. Finally, the actual pressing . . .

Firstly, don't attempt pressing between sheets of newspaper as the ink often comes off and won't enhance more delicate specimens. Absorbent white paper, especially blotting paper, is best. Take a large sheet and fold it in two. Place the plants to be pressed carefully between the sheets, spacing them so that they do not touch each other. The next doubled sheet with its load of plants is laid on top of the first sheet. You can continue in this way until you have a pile of folded sheets. On top of this pile you can place a flat board, and weigh it down with some bricks.

The most effective way of pressing flowers is with a book press, but not everyone is lucky enough to possess one. Small flower-presses are available, suitable for tiny blooms and leaves.

Make your own flower-press

You can make your own flower-press without much difficulty, and choose a size that will suit the amount of material you wish to press. A large press does not always work better than a smaller size, as drying problems are more likely to occur with the former.

Get two sheets of rigid plywood, of about 20 x 25cm (8ins x 10ins) or 30 x 30cm (12ins x 12ins) in size. While holding the two sheets together, drill a hole close to each corner, to accomodate a threaded bolt with a butterfly nut. By tightening the nuts, the two boards are pressed together and this is the principle behind the flower-press. Between the boards insert sheets of corrugated cardboard and blotting paper, cut to the same size as the press. All is now ready for the first batch of flowers.

When are the flowers dry?

There is no simple answer to the question of how long it will take for flowers to dry. An average time would be a few weeks, but some blooms dry quicker than others, and the prevailing climate and time of year and many other factors will all influence this rate. Small leaves and flowers need not be inspected or disturbed during drying, but the larger, more fleshy types will probably need the blotting paper changed if it is damp, as this moisture could encourage mould to develop, or else retard the drying process.

Once the plants are dry, they are ready to be handled. If you are creating a herbarium, then you can go ahead and paste the specimens in, and label them.

If you intend to make up arrangements at a later stage, then you will need to store the dried blooms until they are needed. Carefully remove them from the blotting paper (this can be re-used, after drying) and place them between soft paper in portfolios or file covers. You can make your own out of display card. Organise them into some sort of filing system, so that you can find various items without having to disturb too many other pieces that are not needed — dried plants are very brittle. It is not a good idea to keep your stock of dried flowers together in a box or drawer as they will certainly become damaged.

While you are busy placing or removing plants from blotting paper, always remember to replace the weighted plank on the stack; also make sure that the weight is evenly distributed.

Air dried flowers

If you wish your dried flowers to retain their natural shape, obviously you should not use a press to dry them. The most convenient and simple method is to hang them, upside-down, to dry. Make the blooms up into small bunches — too many blooms per bunch can result in the middle

Dried flowers need careful handling. Store them somewhere that is not too dry, to avoid excess drying out of their stems. Don't store the bunches together in a carton. It is better to leave them hanging until needed.

ones not drying properly. Tie the bunches with elastic bands; as the flowers dry they lose moisture and volume, so that shrinking stems could fall out of bunches tied with string.

Choose the site for hanging your flower bunches with care. It needs to be fairly dry, otherwise you might find the flowers suffering from mildew instead of drying.

Don't put them in direct sunlight, as this will fade most blooms. Lofts or attics are the most likely situations in many homes, provided they are dry and well-ventilated. If you don't have a loft then a spacious, dark, dry cupboard would do. After a few days you should be able to feel that the flowers are starting to dry. In three to four weeks they should be completely dry.

Drying flowers in a vase

A less well-known method of drying flowers is to place them upright in a vase to dry. Many people will have discovered this method by accident when a bunch of flowers has not been thrown out and, instead of withering, has dried into an acceptable 'dried' arrangement. Naturally, this treatment is not suitable for all types of flower. You would probably have a reasonable success with many types of

roadside wild flower and grass. Don't put too much water into the vase or the plants will stay moist for too long.

Hydrangeas, when picked at the correct stage, will react favourably to this method of drying. With those flowers that do not respond well to drying, and for many foliage types, better results can be obtained by using the *glycerine method.* This is, in fact, a variation of the vase method. Instead of plain water, a mixture of glycerine and water is used. The plants absorb this mixture, and it preserves them. The leaves on the branches must be mature, but still green, with perhaps slight tinges of autumn colouring. Once a leaf has its full autumn colour it is no longer able to take up any liquid. This method doesn't dry out the leaves or blooms in the conventional way. They change colour and become 'greasy' but the stems remain supple. You can often buy brown beech stems prepared in this way.

The recipe for this treatment is: add to 1 part glycerine (obtainable at chemists) 2 parts boiling water. Insert into this mixture, stems that have been freshly cut (at an angle, for maximum absorption) or else crushed. They need to be about 10–15cm (4–6ins) deep in the solution. The length of time they need to remain in the solution will depend on the type of plant. Feel the leaves now and then, and when they feel greasy they are ready to be removed. Hydrangeas will do well with this treatment.

Drying flowers in sand

Flowers such as dahlias, zinnias, marigolds and roses can be beautifully dried in sand. Silver sand is suitable for this process and can be bought at any garden centre. It is a time-consuming method, but once you have got the hang of it you will want to carry on as the results can be startling.

You will need boxes, or plastic containers, with tight fitting lids. Place a layer of sand into a container. Onto this sand you can now carefully place the flowers, facing upwards, their stalks having been cut very short. Ensure that they are absolutely dry and that no bloom touches another. It is best to use separate containers for different types of flower. In this way each batch will dry at its own rate. Now you can carefully and slowly sprinkle sand into and around each bloom, until they are completely

Observe certain rules when out picking flowers in the countryside: only pick the plentiful, common types. Some rarer species are protected. Many wild flowers can be grown in a garden and will seed themselves if you don't do too much weeding. Many wild flower seeds can now be bought from seed suppliers.

covered. The boxes can now be closed and put away to dry. Some people like to speed up the process by placing the boxes near radiators, even in the oven; it is safer to try the simple way first. After 2 to 3 weeks most flowers should have dried. Brush some sand aside carefully, and feel a bloom; if it feels papery, then it is dry and the rest of the sand can be cautiously poured off. The next step is the wiring of each bloom to provide an arranging 'stem'. Flowers that have solid *calyxes* can simply be pierced by wires, and then secured. With flatter blooms, poke the wire up through the head so that it comes out at the face; bend the wire to form a hook, then pull it back gently to secure the head. Remember that the blooms are now very fragile. You can now make up a bunch of flowers for a vase that does not need water but which will last for a long time.

There are other desiccating materials besides silver sand that can be used for drying flowers. Silica gel is one; these crystals can be obtained from chemists. They work very quickly and must be dried out between uses. Silica gel can also be added to sand to speed up the process. Other substances used are alum and borax. The best mixtures and methods are generally found only after some experimenting, as conditions in every home will be slightly different.

Flowers that are suitable for drying
Flowers don't all have the same properties. Apart from shape and colour, each flower responds in a different way to being cut. Many blooms lose their sheen immediately and are only fit for the compost heap!

'True dried flowers', those that just naturally have hard, crisp, papery petals, are well known; these are the 'everlastings', or *Helichrysum*, which hardly need drying at all before being used as dried flowers. It almost seems as if their colour and sheen was always intended for use in drier states. Fortunately for flat-dwellers, and those without gardens, these everlastings are usually available at florists. Now and again you will see other dried flowers for sale. What you can also do is buy flowers from a florist or market, that are suitable for drying, and then dry them yourself. If you have your own garden then the possibilities are, of course, much greater. Nearly all flowers, with the help of one or other of the methods mentioned, can be dried. However, not every bloom looks

good when dried. Some become too brittle, whilst others, unfortunately, fall apart when touched. But many more than you would at first imagine, are suitable.

Flowers for drying
If not otherwise specified, these flowers can be dried by hanging upside down. Other methods of drying are also indicated.

Achillea (Yarrow)
The beautifully scented *A. filipendulina* blooms in mid-summer, with yellow, umbrella-shaped clusters of flowers. Other varities have pale yellow or rose blooms. The flowers must not be picked too young and should be firm to the touch. *A. millefolium* is a wild species, which also dries well; its grey-white or pinkish flowers are smaller than the garden varieties.

Achillea can also be dried after the flowers have faded, and the brown flower heads make an interesting addition to an arrangement. Don't make the bunches too big for hanging.

Aconitum (Monk's Hood)
A true garden plant, with sturdy stems and beautiful blue, hood-shaped flowers. Pick when fully open.

Dried flowers without stalks are given wire stems. Store them by pushing their 'stems' into an oasis block.

Providing a bloom with its wire stem.

From top to bottom:

Allium moly.

Astrantia major.

Dipsacus fullonum, the Teasel.

Alchemilla (Lady's Mantle)
Pretty leaves that glisten long after a shower has passed. Unfortunately, you can't dry these for bouquets, but you can dry the fine yellow and green flowers. Pick the flowering stems once all the flowers have opened.

Allium (Onion family)
This is a large family of bulbous plants, and includes both the onion you might use in soup, and the chives used in salad. They all have attractive, globe-shaped flowers. Care must be taken when drying them: they are inclined to fall apart.

Amaranthus (Love-lies-bleeding)
An annual that grows easily. Some varieties have red 'tails', others greenish-white. They dry well, but must be handled carefully as they are brittle.

Anaphalis (Pearl Everlasting)
An attractive plant with grey foliage with flat, white flower heads. Best picked before it is fully open. If picked after flowering they give off lots of fluff which blows everywhere.

Artemisia (Mugwort)
There are both wild and cultivated species of *Artemisia*. The garden type, with its pretty grey foliage, has long, sweetly-scented white flowers. Pick just after flowering, but when not too ripe or it will fall apart.

Astrantia (Masterwort)
These are hardy, herbaceous perennials, with fine, off-white flowers, tinged with pink. They can be dried hanging up, but look much better if dried in sand.

Calluna vulgaris (Heather)
After a summer's day in the country, you could return with a variety of heathers. When placed in a vase, they will last for months; a fair amount of bloom and foliage may drop but this can be lessened by adding glycerine to the water.

Cirsium (Spear thistle)
This troublesome weed grows along verges and hedgerows; it must be tackled with gloves as it is prickly. Pick when the first purple petals show, and it will open while drying. If picked when fully open, it will go to seed. The seed-heads are attractive, but only after the fluffy seeds have been removed.

Daucus carota (Wild Carrot)
A wild plant that grows along roadsides in summer, particularly in chalk areas. It has white umbels of flowers. As the flowers die, the heads curl over into a still-green lacy ball. When picked at this stage they dry well.

Delphinium (Larkspur)
The annual varieties have a good colour range, of pink or blue shades. For drying, the flowers should be picked just before they are fully open. If you wait too long, then flowers will fall off. Hang them in small bunches, or put stems in a glycerine mixture.
The perennial Delphiniums can also be dried. You may find it better to remove and dry the side shoots, as the main flower stalk is often just too thick. The dried seed heads can also be used in arrangements.

Dipsacus fullonum (Wild Teasel)
Once you have this biennial plant in your garden you need have no worry about losing it! It reseeds itself everywhere. The stems can be picked at any stage, but the later you leave it, the darker the colour will be. Teasels were used in years gone by for the carding of wool, and raising the nap on woollen cloth.

Echinops (Globe Thistle)
These thistle heads must be picked when the blue of the flower first appears, but just before it opens, otherwise it will fall apart when dried. Globe thistles are seen sometimes in florist shops.

Eryngium (Sea Holly)
This plant is not only grown for its attractive blue flowers, but also for the stems, as the whole plant has a steely-blue colouring. Wait until the plant is at its prettiest before picking. It is worth finding a sunny spot in the garden for this plant.

Gypsophila (Baby's Breath)
This is one of the most popular of dried flowers, and equally well used fresh in many bouquets. The finely branched flower stalks are extremely decorative. Gypsophila grows easily in a sunny position in a garden. The flowers must be fully open when picked. Placing them in a vase with only a little water is the best method of drying these blooms. Both annual and perennial species are suitable for drying.

Helichrysum (Strawflower)
An annual plant, known as 'the' Strawflower, or Everlasting, it comes in many colours. Picked as a bud, they will open in the vase as they dry. Do not remove too many leaves from around the flower-heads or they will look too bare. Mount on wire for floral use.

Helipterum (Everlasting)
There is some confusion over the naming of this annual everlasting. It is sometimes called *Rhodanthe*, or *Acrolinum*. They are small, straw-textured, daisy-like flowers. Pick as soon as they are open.

Hydrangea
This is a large family of plants. The best known of which are the garden shrubs with their large, round heads of pink, blue or white florets. There is also a climbing species, *Hydrangea petiolaris*, which has flat heads of creamy-white flowers. Flowers must be picked at the right stage or they will wilt. The blooms must be fully mature: wait until the petals start to feel leathery and change colour. They can be dried in a vase, with a little water which is allowed to evaporate, or hung singly upside down. They can be preserved with glycerine, but this tends to turn them brown.

Lavendula (Lavender)
This well known shrub not only adds colour to a dried arrangement, but also provides a lovely smell. Pick just before the flowers are fully open or they will fall apart.

Limonium (Statice)
Both annual and perennial species can be dried for flower arranging. *L. sinuatum* is one of the most popular types, as it has a wide colour range from yellow, through orange and red, to blue and purple. Perennial species have softer colours. All dry very well and last for ages.

Lonas indora
The golden-yellow umbrellas of this annual are similar to Yarrow. Pick when fully open. They dry well and are most useful in an arrangement.

Mentha (Mint)
The lilac shades of all the Mint species dry well and add a lovely scent to a bouquet.

Molucella (Bells of Ireland)
Grown as an annual, not for its flowers which are insignificant, but for the unusual green, bell-like bracts that surround the flowers. They can be dried by hanging, but don't dry them too quickly or else they fall apart. Their colour tends to fade somewhat. They can also be preserved in glycerine without changing colours. They are often sold by florists, as both fresh and dry blooms.

Mentha or mint.

Hydrangea

Monarda (Bergamot)
A hardy perennial, with aromatic leaves. Beautiful, bright scarlet flowers are produced in whorls. Pick once all the florets are open, all around the flower head.

Nepeta (Catmint)
The pale, lilac-blue flowers should be picked when fully open. Cats have an extraordinary affinity for this plant, which you should keep in mind if you have a cat, or your arrangement could be flattened by a rolling cat.

Polygonum affine (Knotweed)
This is a well known perennial ground-cover, with dark, rose-coloured flowers. Pick once flowers are fully opened. Very useful in small bouquets.

Rosa (Roses, in variety)
Whether a wild species, or a cultivated garden hybrid, all roses are well worth the trouble of drying. Pick while still buds or slightly open, and dry by hanging in a warm place as they need to dry rapidly. For the best results roses should be sand-dried. Never use fully opened blooms as they fall apart almost immediately.

Santolina (Cotton Lavender)
Dwarf shrubs, with attractive fine, silvery-grey foliage, and button-like yellow flowers. Retains its grey colour when dried.

Sedum:
This is a large family made up of many different types of succulent plants. *Sedum spectabile* and its varieties are very pretty in the rock garden, and you don't have to do anything to dry the blooms as they do this themselves if you leave the flower stems on the plant. Blooms from most rock garden species are attractive when dried, but are small in size.

Solidago (Golden Rod)
A lovely perennial cut flower, with golden-yellow fluffy panicles. There are also wild varieties. Pick in full bloom.

Tanacetum (Tansy)
A wild flower of dry, waste ground. The button-like yellow flowers form loose, flat heads. Pick when the buttons are bright yellow, and rounded. They can also be gathered after the flowers have faded; drier brown shades are also effective in arrangements.

Xeranthemum (Paper Flower)
This annual everlasting can be grown easily from seed. Its blooms have white and purple shades. Pick when fully open. The white blooms are useful in Christmas decorations.

Sedum sieboldii

Tanacetum vulgare, the Tansy

184

The grasses

The last few pages have dealt with flowers that can be dried successfully — blooms in many different shades, of white, pink, red yellow and blue. Some blooms retain most of their colouring after drying, others, though, fade to some extent. These shades give a dry bouquet a special charm of its own. There is another large group of plants, whose blooms are especially suited to drying. These flowers have no need for any bright colouring, as they do not need to attract insects, the wind, instead, is responsible for their pollenation — so bright colours wouldn't make any difference. This group is the huge grass family. Grass blooms are so numerous that many people tend not to realise that they are flower heads. There are a great many different grasses. Many species have minute greenish flowers, clustered together to form a plume, or ear, at the tip of a stalk. These flowering stalks are often very decorative, and not just in the wild, nor the garden, but also in dried arrangements. These plumes and ears provide a certain 'lightness', and their slenderness a contrast to the rounder and heavier blooms normally found in an arrangement. It would be impossible to describe *all* the different grasses, particularly as grasses are amongst the most difficult of plant groups to categorise and identify. If you become really interested in grasses and their identification, then you will need to acquire a good specialist book for this purpose.

With all types of grass, you should try to pick them before the flowers mature, and open. A 'ripe' grass flower will not remain intact after drying, but tend to fall into dozens of little pieces.

Grass-like plants: reeds, rushes and sedges

As well as the grasses, rushes, reeds and sedges also have flower heads that are very suitable for drying. While grasses have hollow stems, this group has stems filled with a soft pith. The stalks of reeds and rushes are round, while sedge stems are of triangular section. The blooms of these grassy types are well worth drying for their interesting forms.

Fruits and seeds as 'dried flowers'

Each living plant is involved in the great continuous natural life-cycle. As the plant matures, it produces flowers; these can develop into fruits and seeds. These fruits and seeds are worthy of our attention, as potential dried material. Many fruits dry out on their own, into very attractive features. Sometimes the seeds are retained within the dried outer casings. In other cases seeds will have been released when the fruit ripened and opened; it is only the husk or shell that remains for us to gather.

Dried fruits

A great variety of fruits, seeds, and parts of these can be dried and used with great effect in arrangements. Think of Horse Chestnuts *(Aesculus)*, Beech nuts *(Fagus)* and especially their cups, and fruits of the Alder *(Alnus)*. The round fruits of the Plane *(Platanus)*, can also be used, but pick them before they ripen; if you wait until they fall, they are likely to fall apart in the house, and spread fine fluff everywhere.

Cones

Coniferous plants bear their seeds in fruits known as cones. Cones of the Pine trees *(Pinus)*, are the most widely used and the best known, particularly at Christmas time. Spruce cones, *(Picea)*, are larger and longer, but are effective in larger arrangements. Larch *(Larix)* cones are smaller and more delicate. They are excellent for Christmas wreaths. In fact, virtually all types of cone can be used. The more exotically shaped cones are sometimes imported, and sold by florists.

Above:
fresh grasses.

Below:
dried fruits.

Grasses and grassy types are often difficult to identify accurately. The grasses belong to the family Gramineae. *The Bulrush,* Scirpus, *belongs to the family* Cyperaceae. *The Rush,* Juncus, *belongs to the* Juncaceae, *and the Sedges,* Carex, *to the family* Cyperaceae.

Fleshy fruits

Fruits of the Hawthorn *(Crataegus)*, Crab apple *(Malus)*, and the rose-hips of the various rose types, can all be preserved. The Hawthorn and Crab apple stems are best placed in a glycerine solution, but many of the rose-hips can be simply hung up to dry.

Branches

Branches with unusual shapes are worth collecting and drying. Thanks to their woody structure, they can be used immediately after picking. Walking through the woods after a storm would be a good time to search for interesting examples to take home.

Branches of the Corkscrew Willow or Corkscrew Hazel, with their twisted forms, are always attractive. If someone in your neighbourhood is pruning a grape vine, try to obtain some of the more interesting pruned branches. Vine stems can be most attractive when used with Ivy in an arrangement, especially if you can find sections that still have tendrils attached.

Leaves

With leaves, it is not necessary to mention species, as leaves of all types can be dried under a press. The most attractive are usually leaves with autumn tints. But be careful that the weather doesn't beat you to it, drying the leaves excessively before you can gather them. Leaves that are too dry will crumble if you put them in a press.

All fern fronds should be pressed as soon as possible after picking otherwise they will tend to curl up. Many ferns are used as houseplants, so you can easily cut a few of these to dry, the plant will soon grow new ones.

Those who wish to preserve fronds of the hardier deciduous types can try different ones in glycerine solution. Just remember that the fronds must be fully mature, and that this method is not suitable for delicate leaves. Beech leaves with an interesting red colour, which have been glycerine preserved, are sometimes available in florist shops.

Fruits and seeds from herbaceous plants

All the seeds and fruits mentioned so far have been from woody trees and shrubs. It

Dried fruit composition.

is important to remember that many herbaceous and perennial plants also produce fruits that are of great value in dried arrangements.

Fruits to be picked before they ripen

Anthriscus (Cow parsley)
Well known white umbels seen along roadsides. Pick heads before seeds ripen, and burst. Hang stems in small bunches.

Clematis vitalba (Travellers Joy, Old Man's Beard)
A climbing plant, whose fluffy seed heads are seen everywhere in hedgerows, and gives the plant its name (Old Man's Beard). Pick the seed heads as soon as flowering is over, and spray with hair lacquer, to prevent them falling apart. You can use the seeds from the cultivated types, as well.

Oenothera
A biennial, that seeds itself very freely, so you'll never be without, after your first crop! The yellow flowers have a lovely perfume at night, which attracts moths.

Typha (Reedmace)
Well known 'cigar' shaped reed, growing alongside rivers and canals. Those sold by florists are treated, to prevent them falling apart. They must be picked before they are fully mature, or the disintegrating fluff will cause quite a mess!

Fruit stems that must be picked green

Arctium (Burdock)
This fruit was much loved by little boys, for putting in girls hair, as the spines make it difficult to get out. Its main means of dispersal is in fact, by animals. Pick the stems before they are fully ripe, or else the fruits fall easily.

Astilbe
A perennial garden plant, that comes in different colours and sizes. The plumes with young fruits attached, are well-worth drying.

Digitalis (Foxglove)
A tall biennial, poisonous plant; the long stems with young fruits can be dried and used to good effect in large displays.

Humulus (Hop)
This climbing plant, though often found in hedges, would not be out of place in a garden. Fruits are found on the female plants. Fruit-bearing stems must be cut while still green, and are very decorative although they tend to yellow with age.

Arctium minus, or Burdock.

Fruits of the Ivy (Hedera helix).

Fruits to pick when fully ripe

Alisma plantago (Water Plantain)
A walk alongside a stream in September, might well bring you a chance of finding the dried seed heads of the Water Plantain. They look just like miniature trees, and can be dried by hanging them up singly.

Aquilegia (Columbine)
A lovely perennial for the garden, which comes in many colours and shades. The fully opened seed pods on their stems can be collected and hung until fully dry.

Epilobium (Rosebay willowherb)
This large wild plant with pink blooms is a pioneer on waste ground, and usually in large numbers. Only pick once the fruits have split open, and the fluffy, white seeds have blown away.

Hedera (Ivy)
Occurs in abundance in hedges and on trees, the common ivy is known to all. Its bunches of fruits can be seen in amongst the shiny green leaves. If picked when mature, they will dry well.

Heracleum (Hogweed)
The giant hogweed is quite a spectacular sight, with its tall umbels of flowers. It has several smaller relatives; all dry very well when picked with either green or ripe fruits.

Lunaria (Honesty)
The rather insignificant purple flowers that appear in spring give no clue to the beautiful penny-like, silver seed cases that will be produced in autumn. Once the two outer discs are removed, the seeds fall out, and the glossy centre disc remains.

Nigella (Love in the Mist)
The beautiful blue flowers are surrounded by a fine network of green bracts. The seed-pods are of interest as well; they are shaped like rose-buds, still with the lacey bracts around them.

Papaver (Poppy)
The pods of both wild and garden varieties can be used. They have a typical, interesting shape, with a flap top row of dispersal holes just below and a body which tapers down to the stem. Larger, imported poppy fruits can be found at florists.

Physalis (Cape Gooseberry)
The decorative attraction of this plant is not its fruit but the papery, green lantern-like case that surrounds it. Allow to ripen fully on the plant.

Zea Mays (Maize)
Ornamental varieties of corn are now available. These cobs have yellow, red, orange, and blue-purple seeds, which can be dried for winter arrangements.

Plants that do not grow in this country are often seen in dried flower arrangements. These have been imported by wholesalers. In this way blooms and fruits from South Africa, Australia and other countries arrive at local florists either fresh, or already dried. If you want to create arrangements that are 'different', you are sure to find many interesting specimens amongst these imported plants. Make sure that the very 'exotic' blooms aren't made up of several different pieces glued together! They may look good but aren't really natural.

Heracleum giganteum, the Giant Hogweed.

189

Materials and equipment

Even a gravy boat can be used with the aid of oasis.

The basic needs

To create a dried flower arrangement you will naturally need more than simply an assortment of dried flowers. The arrangement will have to be held, or supported, in some manner, and you will need certain materials and eqiupment well known to any florist, but which the average do-it-yourselfer may not have immediately to hand.

Tools and materials

Start with the simplest item: *a knife.* Of course, you could use any knife to cut the flower stalks, but not every knife is either convenient to handle, or safe on tougher stems. A small, sharp, vegetable knife serves well for most of the lighter work. A proper florist's knife is even better. These are sharp, easy to handle, and the blade folds into the handle for carrying, and also to protect the blade. For cutting thicker blocks of oasis and other plastic foams, a longer, sharp knife makes cutting both easier and smoother. You will need pairs of different sized *pliers and scissors.* You'll also need a pair of wire-cutters for cutting florists wire: these are usually pliers with a short nose. For thicker flower stalks, and branches, a good pair of pruning shears, or secateurs, will always be useful.

Dried flowers and plant material naturally lends itself to being stuck into blocks of *oasis-type foam,* for support, and as the base for arrangements. This foam is available in different densities and shapes. The blocks of water-absorbing oasis foam, which must first be soaked in water, are intended for use with fresh flowers. But it can also be used dry for dried flowers with thinner stems. There are other plastic foam products available specially intended for use with dried materials. Both types of foam are very versatile as they can be obtained in different shapes, or in sheets which you can cut up yourself into blocks, balls, cylinders, etc., or to the exact shape of your container.

Clay, or *plasticine,* is even more versatile than oasis, in that it can be kneaded and shaped into any form you can think of. This can be an invaluable asset in narrow-necked vases, or around the bases of objects such as candlesticks.

Blooms that have been dried in sand, silica gel, or some similar method, are very often without stalks. These can be made up with the aid of green painted *florists wire,* which is available in different thicknesses, for different purposes. Thin coils of binding wire have many purposes, such as securing of oasis in the neck of a vase. There are also special flower prongs, with self-adhesive bases, that are used for sticking oasis onto surfaces, or into vases.

Florists tape, usually green for fresh stems, can also be found in a brown colour, which will be much less conspicuous with dried material — it is especially useful for binding thin wire stems to disguise them and thicken them.

You would not normally associate Aerosol spray-cans of paint with dried flowers, but remember that hair lacquer is very useful for spraying onto seed heads that might otherwise fall apart. Gold or silver spray paint may be used to add a finishing touch to a Christmas decoration. Other colours can also be used for special effects, but their use must be limited if possible.

Before oasis foam was developed for floristry, *Sphagnum moss* was used as a supporting base for dried flower arrangements. You can still use it as a background, or to conceal a base of oasis. Icelandic Moss, was often used as a base for many of the smaller Christmas decorations.

Containers for dried flowers

Into what are you going to place your dried flowers? The answer, with very few exceptions, is: into anything that you wish! You don't need any special type of vase or pot, and they don't even have to be

water-tight. Simply look around the house, and you're sure to find something useful: a leaky tea-pot that you don't want to throw out, a fruit bowl on a stand, or even, an egg-shell that's still whole, the possibilities are limitless. Baskets can also provide wonderful settings for dried displays: Biedermeier bouquets, with dried wild flowers look particularly attractive. As a contrast, try a tall, slim vase. Delicate blooms in subtle shades should always match the vase, always try to create a harmony between the colour and form of the arrangement with that of the vase. There are certain basic rules that should be applied, but as you become more practised, you will get the 'feel' of which proportions and colours are appropriate, and which are not.

Dried flowers are more difficult to arrange in glass vases as oasis would be visible. If the vase has a narrow neck, you could make up a bouquet in the hand, bind it with raffia and place the whole bunch in the vase.

Creating decorations and arrangements

A dried flower 'painting'.

Being creative with dried flowers

By now you will probably have an attic full of dried flowers, branches, fruits, seeds, cones, etc! All the materials and accessories that are needed for the putting-together of an arrangement are at hand too, so now you can begin.

This is the most difficult but also the most exciting stage; you will have to ask yourself quite what you intend to do. Do you, for instance, want to brighten up the entrance hall with an arrangement? This would have to be made with a flat back as it would be viewed from the front only. Perhaps you need a decoration as a table centrepiece for that dinner party in a fortnight's time? One of the great advantages of dried flower arrangements is that you can make them up well in advance and at a time that is convenient for you. With dinner parties there is always so much last-minute preparation, so having the table decoration 'pre-arranged' is a great help.

You may wish to present a gift to a friend who has just had a baby. What could be nicer than a small bouquet made from flowers you have dried yourself? Round Biedermeier bouquets, or the more carefree, smaller bouquets will quickly become easier to make 'in the hand' as you get more and more practice.

Once you have filled all the flat surfaces in your home, and don't have room for another dried flower arrangement, why not start making gifts for all your friends? Perhaps there's still a small space on one of your walls where, with modern aids and materials, you'd soon be able to make up a wall-piece, or a dry-ball. From pressed, dried flowers you can make up attractive pictures. Try choosing a theme, such as 'the changing seasons': in this case it may be an idea to do four pictures that can be hung in a group, which represent the flowers of each season. But, whatever you do, and however you set about it, is purely

a matter of personal taste. Hopefully, you might also get some ideas of your own after reading some of the suggestions made in this book. Inspiration, and improved methods, will often come from the regular handling of dried material and observing its qualities. But whatever you do, be sure that the quality of your work is consistently high and remember that basic faults, such as leaving foam or wires visible in a completed display, can completely spoil the effect you are seeking to achieve.

A mixed fresh and dry display.

192

Dried bouquets with backgrounds

A dried flower arrangement that stands in the centre of a table will be viewed from all sides, so must be equally well made all around. If the arrangement is to stand on a mantle-piece, or on a hall table against a wall, then it needs only to be a 'one-sided arrangement'. Such displays do have a number of advantages: they are much easier to make than round ones, they also require far fewer flowers than a circular piece.

Choose an appropriate vase or container for your arrangement; the shape of the vase must suit the types of bloom and foliage you intend to place in it. As a general rule, do not choose a vase that is over-bright, or one that has too many colours on it — neutral shades are safest. Dried flowers are muted in colour, and slightly faded, any container that is too bright or dominant will detract from your arrangement. An average height for an arrangement is one and a half times the height of the vase (or its diameter, in the case of shallow bowls).

The weakest part of the dried flower is usually its stalk. This will either have been removed before drying, or will have become very brittle in the drying process. You can, of course, make wire stems for the flowers, but if all the stems are made of wire the appearance will certainly not be terribly attractive for the wiring cannot be entirely concealed. In taller arrangements this fault can be reduced somewhat by allowing the oasis foam to extend well above the rim of the container; this means that the tallest blooms don't require quite such long stems, and it's easier to provide 'body' lower down. The oasis must be firmly secured to the vase or the whole arrangement is likely to tip over. The portion of oasis that projects above the vase can be camouflaged with Icelandic Moss, and held in place with pieces of bent wire.

You can make a flat-backed, triangular-shaped arrangement in which all the stems radiate out from an imaginary centre-point, located just above the rim of the vase. Use round, larger and darker blooms in this area as the focal point, and graduate outwards with lighter shades and smaller blooms. Ensure that some blooms or foliage spill over the rim of the vase to provide a fuller display, and also to hide the oasis and any wiring.

A 'cradle' bouquet

Each time you are involved in the making of a new creation, you will learn a little more, and become yet more proficient. For the smaller type of bouquet you can experiment with all sorts of smaller flowers with shorter stems. Many will need to be wired to make their stems of usable length. If you watch a florist doing this wiring, it is made to look extremely easy. However, when you try to do it on your own for the first time you're quite likely to end up with very crushed little blooms. It does become much simpler after a bit of practice.

If the flower still has some stem attached hold this against a piece of florist's wire — thinner wire for more delicate blooms — twist the wire once around the stem, and then bend it down to lie parallel to the stem. Take the other end, and wind it a

Biedermeier bouquet of dried flowers.

couple of times around both stem and wire. The florets of plants such as Hydrangea can be wired into little bunches by this method. With bigger flower-heads, you can take the florets apart, and wire them one at a time. An *Achillea*, for example, would be far too large for these smaller types of bouquet. Smaller 'portions' of the flower-head on wire stems would be perfect.

The wiring of leaves is done in a slightly different way. Starting from the underside of the leaf, push one end of the florist's wire up through the leaf and then down again, on the other side of the mid-rib; on the underside make both halves of wire of equal length, and run them down towards the leaf-stalk; twist one wire around both stalk and the other wire, so creating an extended wire stem. Flowers that have a thick calyx can be wired directly through it; blooms with a prominent centre can have a wire pushed up from below, straight through the centre of the bloom; bend the end of the wire into a small hook, and then retract the wire, so that the hook embeds itself firmly into the centre of the bloom.

After these preliminaries you will have flowers that you can now work with, making them into the designs of your own choice. By twisting the wire stems together, as you add flowers to a small, tight bunch, you will end up with a sturdy piece of work. Bind the twisted wires and stems with florist's tape, and decorate with a coloured ribbon.

Dried flowers in baskets and bowls

No type of container is better suited for dried flower arrangements than baskets; the basket itself is made from natural materials and has natural colours compatible with the shades of dried flowers. If it is a small basket make sure the oasis foam is firmly wired or clipped into place. With a larger basket the space surrounding the oasis should be filled with gravel as ballast, and also to help in securing the oasis. In very large baskets, as with large pots and vases, it can be expensive to fill the whole container with oasis, and also let it protrude above the rim. You can fill the bottom of such baskets with a layer of clay, and fasten the oasis to it with wires. This, too, would give the basket added weight and prevent the whole display from toppling over!

There are special flower prongs available with adhesive tapes to hold oasis foam in

A dry white and blue arrangement matching its surroundings.

194

position. However, on the rough surface of a basket these probably will not hold very well, though when used in bowls and dishes they do work admirably. Since baskets and bowls are usually round, they naturally lend themselves to round arrangements that can be viewed from all sides. Such displays are more difficult to make than the one-sided types already mentioned. You have to keep turning your work so that all sides receive equal attention. Start a round arrangement in a shallow bowl by covering the base of oasis with Icelandic Moss, or a similar camouflage. Then establish the height you want with a few taller blooms. Such pieces don't necessarily have to abide by the rule of one and a half times the diameter of the bowl. They can be made up as a flattish 'mound' of blooms.

Dried flowers in a bowl would combine well with dried fruits, such as chestnuts, acorns, etc., or other exotic fruits.

Dried flowers for the table

As previously mentioned, it's a relief to know that your centrepiece for a dinner party has been completed long before you're involved with the turmoil of preparing the meal and tidying the house! For a base, or 'container', you could well utilise a piece from the dinner service you will be using on that occasion. A gravy boat or meat dish, or even some wine glasses filled with little festive bouquets, would be most attractive. If you use glasses, you won't be able to use prongs to anchor the oasis, as this would be visible. However, you could still use oasis, by filling the space between the glass and the oasis with flower petals, coloured paper, or aluminium foil to hide the 'works'. A piece from your dinner service may not be available, for whatever reason. In this case, you could simply use an oblong piece of oasis as the base. Cover the bottom and most of the sides with aluminium foil to prevent crumbs of oasis from getting all over the table cloth. Pin the foil in place with staples.

An alternative would be to use a wooden base of an appropriate size, with felt glued to the underside, and oasis glued to the top. The wood adds some weight to the base, and provides stability for arrangements provided that they are not too tall.

Candles add a nice touch to a dinner table. They can be very effectively decorated with

You can store bunches of dried flowers in baskets. Arranged according to height and colour, they look very attractive, and you will be loathe to disturb them when you need some of the contents.

Plasticine can be used as a base for dry arrangements and can be formed into any shape. For example, use a roll around the base of a candle for a Christmas decoration. For softer stems, first make holes with a knitting needle and the wire stems are then easily pushed in. When using lighted candles remember that dried material is inflammable.

dried blooms and fruits around their bases. Use a circular piece of oasis, cut to the right shape, to fit around the base of the candle-stick. A moulded mound of plasticine would be equally good as a base. Such displays are usually low, and the use of fruits with the blooms, plus ribbons can be very attractive. Your choice of materials and the size of the display, will depend on the style of the candle-stick and the table setting. A table decoration must never be too high or too broad. It should conform to the shape of the table, and its colours should complement the colours being used on the table.

A garland for the door

A lot of work is involved in the making of a garland, the result, though, is very rewarding and attractive.

The easiest base material to use is, once again, oasis foam. Garland 'rings' are amongst the ready-made shapes that are available in different sizes. If you are attempting to make a garland for the first

A dried table arrangement.

A dried flower garland.

Christmas garland of fresh and dry material.

time, begin with one of a smallish size. You could cut your own base from a flat piece of oasis (the same type as used for fresh flowers); use two different-sized plates to draw an inner and an outer circle, and then use a sharp knife to cut them out. Round off the upper edges by gentle rubbing with sandpaper — the back rests against the door and so requires no shaping. Cover the upper surfaces of the oasis with Icelandic Moss to hide the foam; it is much easier to work with after it has been soaked for a while in luke-warm water; then attach it with staples.

You will need quite a number of small flowers and leaves to fill in a floral garland. There are several different ways of tackling the project. You can insert the blooms, one type or colour at a time, so that they are evenly spaced around the garland. Continue in this manner with each type of flower or leaf, until all the spaces are filled; all the blooms and leaves are closely packed.

The other way is to start at a point, and fill in solidly as you work your way around, ensuring that the different species and colours are evenly distributed. Pay special attention to the inner and outer sides of the garland, as a lack of covering in these areas can detract from the overall effect.

You could also make a garland without using foam at all. This method involves bending lengths of heavy gauge wire into a flat circle; to increase rigidity, and create a 'mesh' effect, thinner wires are interwoven with these rings. The whole garland is then bound with florist's tape to conceal all the wires. Each piece of flower, fruit or greenery which you want to work into your garland, has to be wired individually to the frame or in little bunches. Be careful to get them evenly spaced and all facing in the same direction. You will have to overlap each piece slightly to hide the wires of the previously fixed stems.

Dried flowers screened from dust.

A Biedermeier bouquet

A Biedermeier bouquet is a round bouquet of flowers, put together in the hand, and bound so as to be all ready to present as a gift, or to be placed in a vase as it stands, without further arranging.

If small flowers are to be used they will all have to be individually wired. You will also need a sturdy flowerstalk or branchlet as a centrepiece, around whose stem you can start attaching the wire stems of the other blooms and foliage.

These bouquets are, in effect, a 'ball' of flowers on a 'stalk'. The stem wires must be cut off evenly below the 'hand grip', but should not be too short if it is to be put in a vase. This whole stem of wires is then bound with florist's tape, both to neaten the appearance and to hide the wires. Florists formerly used special papier mâché cornets to place over the stems. A lacey paper doyley, with a hole cut in the centre for the stem, can be used with good effect to set a bouquet off.

A more modern version of bouquet can be made very easily, without the need to wire all the stems. Again, you form the bouquet in your hand, but hold the stems higher up, just below the blooms. The blooms must be placed firmly against each other until you have created a 'ball'. At this stage, you can tie the whole bundle of stems by binding it firmly with florist's wire. Cut off the lower ends evenly and cover the whole 'handle' with florist's tape. This 'stem' will be thicker than the stem of a traditional wired bouquet. Biedermeier bouquets can be enhanced by the use of velvet ribbons in matching shades.

Dried arrangements in other forms

With oasis foam in the shape of a ball, one can create some different and interesting hanging flower arrangements. The simplest method of doing this is to pin the flowers on, one by one, either with pins or pieces of wire pushed right through the ball.

There are, of course, any amount of different effects to be obtained through the use of different sized balls, and different types and colours of flowers. Try at all times to keep the spherical shape regular in outline.

Dried picture with poppy flowers and seeds.

Dried 'fantasy' composition.

198

Care and maintenance

Keeping the arrangements attractive

The greatest enemy of dried flower arrangements is dust. Larger fruits and cones can be dusted very easily, but flowers are far too delicate and brittle to be treated in this way. A certain amount of dust can be blown off or dusted with a very soft paint brush.

During warmer weather the whole arrangement could be lightly sprayed with water (using a garden type sprayer), and then placed in a warm spot to dry. The blooms should recover most of their freshness. A display can also be rejuvenated by adding newly dried blooms and removing any that appear to be past their best.

Dried flower pictures on the wall

Construct a wooden frame to contain a flat sheet of oasis foam, or similar material. You can now pin dried flowers onto this layer to create a decorative wall hanging.

Choose the size you want to use and use polystyrene foam, which is sold in sheets of different thicknesses and sizes as insulation in most decorating and hardware shops. The idea is to completely cover the whole surface with dried material held in place with pins or bent wire where necessary.

'Pictures' can be created by choosing a theme or subject; as inspiration, you could choose natural scenes, such as the setting sun, woods in autumn, or a sea or river scape. Subdivide the surface with different colours and types of plant material as if you were weaving a tapestry.

Press-dried flowers, grasses and twigs can also be made into pretty pictures. Arrange the blooms on a suitable background, and paste them down carefully with a transparent glue. Mount these pictures in either modern or older-styled picture frames. Pressed flowers have many other applications, for example, on menus, greetings cards, or on your very personal stationery.

Sending home made greetings cards while on holiday would be a nice gesture. Holidays are not usually long enough to collect and dry flowers to put onto cards, but there is a short-cut. Choose small, thin-petalled flowers or smaller grass ears and glue these onto pre-cut cards. Paste a transparent plastic sheet (cling film) over this, and write your message on the opposite side. This will certainly be different from the usual postcard. Remember to take along some prepared cards, etc. on your next holiday.

Tools and materials

Use and maintenance

Even with cacti in a glasshouse, temperature is important.

and sowing accessories. No matter what essential tools you may need for indoor gardening you can always find an alternative that doesn't have to be bought. A spoon can replace a trowel; string will do the same job as raffia; egg boxes can serve as seed trays, and so on. In the long run, it pays to use the right tool for the right job, and the most satisfactory results are assured. It is also a false economy, in most cases, not to buy the best quality of tool that you can afford. Storage of all your tools and equipment should also be given careful consideration. The ideal is to have a special cupboard where everything can be kept together. There is nothing more frustrating than not being able to find items as and when they are needed. Thus organised storage will pay considerable dividends.

Care of equipment

All equipment should be of good quality and, even though any single item may cost more, its durability will make up for that extra cost and will, usually, do the job better. But you will have to look after your equipment if it is to provide you with good service over many seasons. Always rinse off your tools after use, and dry them thoroughly before you put them away. Whenever any piece of equipment made of steel is to be stored for a period of time, give it a light coating of grease to prevent rust. Any moving parts will need to be oiled regularly. Cutting and clipping tools will need their cutting edges sharpened now and then. A knife sharpener can be used for this purpose. The edge can be kept longer if it is rubbed regularly with a small oilstone.

Peat pots

When growing your own plants from seeds or cuttings, you will find the smaller peat pots very useful. Although ready-made pots are generally available, it is possible to use a small press to make your own smaller

Buy the best

Growers of houseplants will need less equipment than their counterparts with outdoor gardens. A sharp knife, a pair of pruning shears, plant sprayer, two watering cans, and a sponge would be sufficient to undertake all of the more important tasks. For those who become involved with indoor 'gardening', a few other items are also needed, in addition to the basics. Useful extras would include a seed-sower, humidifier, peat-pot mould, ventilators, and various meters.

And now, onto the subject of materials and aids for indoor gardening, and you will discover the great diversity of binding materials, pots and containers, propagators

A small block-making press.

Pruning tools must be kept sharp.

planting 'blocks'. These presses are available at garden centres, and can save you a fair amount of money if plants are to be grown in quantity. Peat pots come in many sizes, and the starter packs for seedlings are ideal for the home grower who only wants a few plants.

Pruning knives

For pruning, and taking cuttings from houseplants, a good, sharp knife is essential. You could do the job with a small, sharp vegetable knife, but a proper pruning knife is much easier to handle. A good pruning knife has a blade approximately 10cm (4ins) long; the curved blade types are preferable to the straight blade types, and provide a better, cleaner cut when pruning.

Pruning shears (secateurs)

Secateurs can be used for the same tasks as a pruning knife. Choose a pair with a good quality blade with scissor action, that is comfortable to handle and provides a close, clean cut. Ensure the centre nut that holds the two halves together can be tightened easily; loose blades will tend to tear rather than cut and will damage your plants.

Sponges

When the leaves of houseplants become very dusty or greasy the plant will start to suffocate. They must be dusted off regularly, but this has to be done carefully. Plants with larger leaves can be wiped with a soft sponge. Make your own leaf-cleaners for smaller leaves by glueing smaller pieces of sponge onto thin canes, dampen them, and then gently wipe smaller leaves. It helps to support each leaf with your hand whilst wiping. Special leaf-cleaning devices can be bought at garden centres; some work reasonably well.

Sprayers

Some type of sprayer is essential for the spraying and misting of your plants. Small,

plastic sprayers with a hand-pump action are all that's really needed for the care of a few houseplants. Most will have adjustable nozzles, so that the droplet size can be regulated. For those who have more plants, and who find the constant hand-pumping too tiring, there are various types of pressure sprayer: the hand-held versions work on the same principles as the larger garden sprayers. The liquid is put under pressure by pumping air into the can. One is able to spray continuously, until the pressure becomes too low, when you simply do a little more pumping.

Thermometers

When growing plants in an unheated room,

A maximum and minimum thermometer records temperature extremes as well.

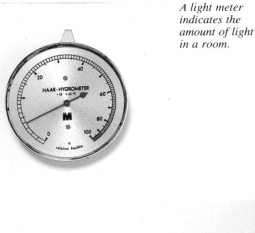

Right above: *Both hand-action and pressure sprayers are effective for indoor gardening.*

A hygrometer measures the relative humidity of the air.

Above: *A moisture meter shows exactly how much water is present.*

you will have to keep a careful watch on the temperature as large fluctuations are bad for plants. Some type of thermometer is therefore essential. The most useful type of thermometer is the 'maximum and minimum' type, which provides that essential information as to when it is becoming too cold for plants.

Ventilators

Many indoor gardeners would argue that the installation of a ventilator is an unnecessary extravagance. Good air circulation is of great importance to plants, so if you are seriously concerned about the health of your plants, you could consider buying a small electric ventilator to help the air to move about; if you occasionally warm the room with an electric heater this, too, will help to spread the warmth.

Moisture meters

It is not always easy to tell when a plant needs watering. A moisture meter can solve this problem. Various types are available from florists and garden centres; they have prongs which are stuck into the soil of the pot, and register the exact moisture content of the soil. There are also meters that

measure the humidity of the air — called hygrometers. When one is growing a number of plants indoors, such a meter can provide an accurate indication of whether the air is too dry for healthy plant-growth.

Forks

Sometimes the soil in a pot can become compacted from all the watering; the top layer of soil will need to be loosened now and then. This can be done with a miniature rake or an ordinary table fork.

Binding materials and other aids

A good many houseplants don't grow in a neat and orderly fashion and need to be 'trained'. Frames and trellises of wire, wood, cane or plastic are available to train plants up, and the simpler 'ladders' can be made up easily from thinner canes.

All too often plants are tied with wire or cotton, which can cut into the stems severely. Raffia has long been the most useful of tying materials, but there are also many artificial fibres that are equally good.

Taller plants may need a bit of extra support, which can be provided with canes, which are available in a whole range of sizes.

Top:
Ties, canes and supports for more orderly growth.

Above:
A radiator panel humidifier.

Humidifiers

The atmosphere of a house is often too dry to suit the needs of tropical houseplants. This is certainly the case in houses with central heating. Dryness can be alleviated by placing shallow bowls of water in the room. Better results are obtained from the reservoir type humidifier hung from the radiator panels; this increases the rate at which water is evaporated into the air.

The best results are obtained with electric humidifiers which can be set to maintain a particular level of humidity in a room. A relative humidity of 50% to 70% suits most houseplants. Some humidifiers are more like 'air conditioners', and can also remove smoke or dust from the air.

Watering cans

The most important part of a watering can is its rose; here the water is broken down into separate gentle streams. The finer the holes, the finer and softer the jets of water, which helps to lessen the compaction of the soil.

A watering can that has been used for some other purpose, such as applying fertiliser, insecticide or weedkiller, should never be used for normal watering. For this reason, one must have at least two watering cans. The can used for insecticides should be clearly marked, so that no mistake whatever can be made.

Cans with a longer 'spout' are most convenient for indoor watering.

Seed sowers

It's not always easy to obtain an even spread when sowing the very fine seed of many houseplants. A seed sower can help. It is usually a plastic device with an adjustable aperture through which the seed is allowed to drop; this avoids the usual 'clumps' of seedlings from normal sowings.

Light meters

Plants need a certain minimum amount of light if they are to remain healthy and grow well; not all plants need the same amounts of light.

Where light from windows is inadequate, special lights to stimulate growth can be installed. To determine the light intensity in any spot one needs to use a light meter. This is the instrument normally used by photographers. If the meter indicates that there is insufficient light then the correct amount can be supplemented artificially.

Planting trowels

A planting trowel can be useful when re-potting indoor plants. For this, use the smallest size for smaller plants; of course, this job can also be done with a spoon.

Some trowels are made entirely of metal, and others have a wooden handle. The former are the stronger.

Plant protection

208

The prevention of disease

The healthy plant

Plants, like people, don't look well if they are not too healthy! Sometimes it isn't too obvious what the matter is, but with regular observation you may discover what is wrong at an early stage and do something about it. Sometimes the causes are obvious. If a plant is being attacked by aphids, for example, it will soon begin to look unhealthy. The aphids are easily visible on the shoot tips so the problem should be seen easily.

If your plant starts to drop leaves, the problem becomes a little bit more difficult to diagnose as there could be several causes. First, check to see whether it has enough water. If it is not dry, then perhaps it has had too much water. More plants die from over-watering than almost any other cause. If watering has been regular and adequate, then the next possible causes are draught or cold. If these are excluded, then you can consider deficiences of a specific nutrient, or perhaps a virus infection.

Unhealthy plants: finding out the problems

It is important to establish at an early stage whether the plant's distress is being caused by incorrect management, the wrong conditions, or attack by pests or disease. You can only begin treatment once you have found the cause. The best cure is, of course, prevention. Unfortunately, this is not always possible, so it is important that you identify the problem in time, diagnose its likely cause and start treatment, or rectify conditions before the plant succumbs.

Avoiding problems

Prevention is better than cure and you should keep this in mind from the time you start choosing a plant at a garden centre. Only buy your plants from reputable suppliers. The plant must look healthy (but not over-lush), and be of a good natural colouring. Don't buy plants that have yellowed or deformed leaves (except, of course, if they are variegated types). Examine the plant carefully, particularly under the leaves, as this is where many pests make their home. Avoid buying plants that have been standing outside a shop, in the wind and cold, or in a setting that is substantially cooler than your home. At this early stage problems won't be visible, but plants don't always adapt to sudden great changes in temperature.

In cold weather, when you buy a plant at a heated garden centre, remember to wrap it well for the journey home. When you get home don't place the plant directly into a very warm room. Let it acclimatise first in a cooler spot. Sometimes you bring home a healthy plant which deteriorates after a while. In such cases it is possible that the plant you have chosen is the wrong type for the climate in that room.

When choosing a flowering plant, don't buy one with its blooms fully open or you will only have the pleasure of their colour for a short while. On the other hand, choosing a plant with very immature buds could result in their failing to open, or to drop off which could be caused by the change of climate or position. Such problems are almost impossible to overcome.

Provide the right conditions

Houseplants will only thrive if you care for them properly and give them a suitable growing environment. Healthy plants are less prone to disease infection. Each plant type has specific needs and also some definite dislikes. For example, Azaleas and other acid-loving plants, will not stay healthy if planted in a chalky soil. Ensure that the air is not too dry, especially for tropical plants. Some pests, such as red spider mite, thrive under drier conditions and can seriously harm your plants.

Diagnosis

When houseplants start suffering from a lack of some vital nutrient, they show their needs in characteristic ways:
Nitrogen: *leaves become paler and remain small;*
Phosphorous: *root development stagnates and blooming is poor;*
Potassium: *yellow or brown markings appear on the leaves;*
Lime: *generally weaker growth and plants are more prone to diseases;*
Magnesium: *yellow-brown discolouring on leaves between the veins; older leaves wither.*

Deficiencies

Let us start with deficiencies and then try to link them to faulty care and handling.

Wilting leaves: due to *lack of water.* You can tell by looking at the soil, and if it also feels dry. If the pot is of clay then its lighter colour will also indicate water shortages. In this case, watering from the top in the normal manner, will not be enough to revive the plant. A better method is to plunge the pot, up to its rim, in a basin of luke-warm water and allow it to soak up all it can. Allow the pot to drain before putting it back in its place.

Too much water can also cause the plant to wilt. You may be tempted to water your plants each day, regardless of whether they need it. It is better to feel the soil each time and if it is still damp, skip watering until it has dried out a bit more. Too much water causes a more serious problem than not enough. It is likely to cause the roots to rot and if it isn't discovered soon enough the plant can die. Quick action with this problem is essential. But what can you do? Firstly, stop watering. Then, if the soil doesn't dry out quickly, you will need to re-pot after removing as much of the sodden soil as possible from the roots (without disturbing them too much) and plant in a more porous mixture.

Plants with hairy leaves are often more susceptible to over-watering. African Violets *(Saintpaulia)*, and *Gloxinia* are best watered from below, as they dislike water on their leaves. Wilting foliage can also be caused by an *excess of fertiliser.* Never exceed the dosages specified on the instructions and don't feed when the plants are not actively growing. When plants are dormant, they aren't absorbing anything so feeding could cause damage.

Excessive light or *excessive heat* are other causes of wilting. You can usually solve these problems by simply moving the plant to another position.

A plant that is not looking well and is not standing on a window sill, could be suffering from a *lack of light.* Moving it to a position with more light, but not direct sunlight, could bring about its recovery.

Now take the example of a beautiful, large plant that you are very proud of. Suddenly, it stops growing and starts looking 'seedy'. Remember that plants only grow in spring and summer and are virtually, or completely dormant in winter. However, with the protected and artificial indoor climate, the seasonal changes are hardly felt and the plant has an unnatural life-style. If you try to stimulate the plant's growth by providing fertiliser at the wrong time of the year you could cause damage.

Some plants, such as succulents and Clivias, require a definite rest period at a certain time of the year and if they don't have this they are likely to 'go off'.

If it is summer and your plant isn't growing then you must tip it over and have a look under the pot. It is very likely that the roots have grown out through the drainage hole. No wonder that the plant can't grow any more! Its roots have nowhere to grow to and so can't absorb enough water and nutrient. Re-potting into a larger pot should get the plant growing again.

Of course the problem could have been caused by one of the other problems already mentioned: too much or too little water, too much or too little light, and too much or too little feeding.

No two plants need exactly the same handling. What is excessive for one could be a deficiency for another. Look on each plant as an individual, with its own peculiar needs and try to imitate its natural conditions as closely as possible. A well-tended plant thrives well.

Yellow leaves

Any plant can produce the occasional yellow leaf. This is as natural as is the production of new leaves. A mistake that many people make is to pick the yellowing leaves before they are completely dead. Admittedly, the plant will look better without any yellowed foliage, but it is preferable for them to remain on the plant, until all natural processes have been completed, and the leaves are ready to fall off. This is a completely natural process as most plants lose some leaves while they are forming new ones. The exceptions are deciduous plants which lose all their leaves in autumn, and those evergreens which keep their leaves for many years. If a plant loses an abnormal number of leaves, at the wrong time of the year, then something is not quite right. If the plant's leaves turn yellow and then fall off this could be the result of *standing in a draught* or having been subjected to conditions that were *too cold*. During the winter you can, without realising it, be placing your plants in a 'refrigerator', by simply closing the curtains. It would be better to move the plants off the sill or at least have the curtains between the plants and the glass so that they are not excluded from the warmth of the room.

Dry air, especially in a centrally heated room, can cause leaves to yellow. You can increase the air's humidity by spraying, placing bowls of water about, or by using an automatic humidifier, although these are often less efficient than you might think. The best way to maintain a reasonable humidity level is by having lots of plants. Each plant releases the water it has absorbed back into the air (by transpiration) and so contributes towards a more humid atmosphere. When the yellowed leaves remain attached to the plant, then the fault lies elsewhere. Let's take the Azalea as an example: it prefers an acid soil so that when it is planted in a *soil containing lime,*

its leaves may change colour in protest. This problem could also be caused by the water. If you live in an area where the *tap-water is 'hard',* i.e. it has a high lime content, you may also get an adverse reaction from acid-loving plants. You will need to collect rain water for your watering.

Yellowing of leaves can also result from an incorrect potting soil. If the ailing plant has been in its pot for some time, it might be an idea to try re-potting it into fresh potting-soil, that has a good balance of nutrients. The plant should then pick up quickly. Feeding plants with a general fertiliser isn't always enough. The potting soil could be deficient in one or other of the trace elements, such as iron, manganese or magnesium and these won't be found in a general fertiliser. A balanced potting mixture or matured cow manure are likely to contain all necessary nutrients. Plants are usually fed via the soil. Another effective way of feeding houseplants is by using a *foliar feed.* This is a solution containing all the essential minerals a plant needs. It is sprayed onto the leaves, from where it is absorbed by the plant. The response can be dramatic if the plant is suffering from a mineral deficiency.

Leaves with brown tips

In winter this fault is usually caused by *cold or frost* and in summer by too much *heat or direct sunlight*. Plants prefer a more uniform temperature and don't take well to extreme or sudden changes.

Without some protection a Hydrangea, for example, could be 'burnt to death' on a hot, summers day. By the time you have noticed the brown, dried-up shoot tips, it could be too late. If the plant doesn't die, it most certainly won't look good and will need drastic cutting back. As there is no ready cure for such problems you should ensure that any of the more tender plants are screened or shaded from direct sunlight. Take adequate precautions in winter against the cold. Browning of leaves could be caused by some defect in the potting soil, in which case, re-potting would be the solution and should prevent further spoiling of leaves. Spraying with a foliar feed that is too concentrated or spraying too closely with an aerosol-insecticide could also cause this symptom.

If a plant develops lighter patches on its leaves or tiny bumps on the surfaces or flowers that are deformed when the buds open, it could have become infected with a virus. There is no cure for plant virus diseases. Infected plants should be destroyed before the problem can be spread to other plants. Virus infection is transmitted via tools or hands, and not through the air. Any tools, knives or pruners that are in general use should be disinfected if a virus is discovered and the plant itself must certainly not go on to your compost heap. Dispose of plant, pot, soil and stake by throwing them out. One particular virus strain causes stripes on blooms. Tulip breeders use this to create the striped blooms of certain varieties; only in this rare instance is a virus of some benefit. Virus diseases do not occur all that frequently but sooner or later, most indoor gardeners will come across an infected plant. Plant care is not always easy; there is so much to watch out for, but when your plants thrive, you are rewarded with their good appearance and your self-satisfaction. Perhaps you are one of the lucky green-fingered gardeners, who can do no wrong. In this case your plants should remain free from problems.

The plant's enemies

Fungi are a very elementary form of plant-life. They prefer growing in moist conditions. You'll see fungi in abundance amongst the decaying leaves and rotting twigs of an autumn woodland. After you have sown a batch of seed indoors and they have germinated well, they could suddenly start collapsing even though they have been given plenty of water. The cause is most probably *damping off,* a serious fungus infection that originates in the soil. To avoid it you should use sterilised soil mixtures for your seed trays, in which all fungus spores have been killed. Don't over-water, or keep the glass covering over the seedlings for longer than the first few days after germination. There is no cure for seedlings affected by damping off and it spreads rapidly. You will need to use an insecticide immediately, to save any plants that have not yet been infected.

Rust

The name 'rust' covers a group of fungi that cause brown or black spots on the leaves of host plants, and have characteristic spore-sacs on the undersides of the infected leaves. Diseased leaves turn yellow or brown and fall off. To prevent the spread of these diseases you should remove infected leaves and burn them, before the whole plant and possibly its neighbours too, are affected. Rusts are not all that common on indoor plants, they seem to prefer leaves with hairy surfaces. Some geraniums and Fuchsias are prone to attack. Excessive humidity and poor ventilation will encourage the invasion of these fungi. After you have removed the infected leaves, you should spray the rest of the plant with an appropriate fungicide, to kill off any remaining spores.

Grey mould

This is a troublesome and very common fungus disease. Dead leaves and twigs are especially prone to attack, which can soon spread and infect healthy foliage. Furry grey patches appear on the leaves, and soon cause them to rot. Keep pots and soil clear of all fallen dead leaves and other loose material; remove all infected parts and burn them. African Violets (Saintpaulia), are extremely susceptible to attack by this fungus. Each time you remove an old leaf and a short piece of stem remains you will be providing an ideal chance for grey mould to enter the plant. Removing all traces of infection is often sufficient control, provided you watch closely for any recurrences, otherwise use a fungicide. A still atmosphere encourages this fungus so good ventilation is important.

If the African Hemp (Sparmannia) gets irregular brown spots on its leaves, then the sun is the most likely culprit. This plant prefers not to be in directly sunlight.

Yellow blotches on the foliage can result from too much sunlight. African violets are very susceptible. With excess sunlight, Cissus leaves can develop dry spots called 'windows'.

The white-coloured *mildews* are related to the moulds. *Downy mildew* (Spaerotheca) appears as a dusting of fluff on the leaves. This can be wiped off with the finger but the leaves may become misshapen.

Powdery mildew appears as a powdery white dust on infected leaves and stems. At the first signs, remove any infected leaves. If this doesn't stop the disease, then it has probably penetrated the plant fairly deeply and you will need to apply a sulphur-based fungicide. If the infection is severe, and the plant not valuable, it would be better to discard it.

To prevent mildews, try to avoid excessively moist conditions, especially when the foliage is also damp. Lower light conditions will also suit fungi.

Controlling fungi

This is the classic situation where prevention is most decidedly better and easier than cure. In a great many cases by the time you have discovered the disease it is already too late to save the plant. Most fungicides are preventative, rather than curative. In nurseries, fungus-prone plants are sprayed regularly to protect them from fungal attack. Once the plants have become infected, spraying can only prevent the disease from spreading further, by killing off its spores.

In the majority of cases, attack by fungi can be traced either to mismanagement or incorrect growing conditions.

Good air circulation, not too much humidity, and not allowing water to remain on leaves for any length of time provide the basis for a preventative programme. In addition you should keep the whole plant growing area clean of fallen leaves and blooms.

The latest method of keeping houseplants free of fungi, is by using 'fungicide spikes'. These are inserted into the soil of the pot in the same way as you use the popular 'feeding spikes'. The fungicide is absorbed by the plant and in this way makes the whole plant distasteful to any free-floating fungus spores.

Insect pests

Insect pests pose the greatest natural threat to houseplants. Keeping your plants healthy and well maintained is no guarantee against attack by pests or diseases but the plants will be in a better condition to withstand the onslaught.

Once you have discovered insects on your plants, it is essential that you act quickly to limit the damage and prevent their spreading to other plants. Insects can multiply at the most alarming rate so that to put off spraying is to court disaster. Most people who notice an insect invasion will grab for the nearest spray can without stopping to examine exactly what it is that is attacking the plant. The next time you find insects on a plant, take the time to study them a bit more closely with a magnifying glass. This examination is well worth the time, as not all insects are sensitive to the same sprays. You may spray and find a few days later that the pests are still flourishing.

There are two main groups of insect pests: the *chewing insects* and the *sucking insects*. The first group includes all the caterpillars, weevils and snails which are best caught by hand as you discover them. The second group includes all the pests that cause so much damage to plants, by their persistent drawing-off of the plants sap. This includes aphids (the largest group), red spider mite, scale (also many types), white fly, mealy bug, and a few more. These insects are specifically adapted to this method of obtaining nourishment. Aphids, for example, feed mainly off the soft, growing-tips by boring holes with their sharp proboscis and sucking out the sap. They are usually found in large numbers, on each tip of a plant. Other types will draw their nutrients from the leaf surface.

This is a parasitic existence where the insects survive at the plant's expense. But why should they attack houseplants? We have already mentioned that strong, healthy plants are less prone to attack, but houseplants cannot be totally immune, as they are in an unnatural environment and so will rarely be in perfect health. Naturally some plants are more susceptible than others, but if pests are found on one plant, it is best to spray them all as a precaution. Before describing several pests and effective control measures, here are a few general facts:

Insect control
Insect pests should be controlled as soon as they are discovered before they damage the plant and start to multiply.

There are various home remedies that have been in use for many years and are just as effective today. Spraying the plants with

Scaly marking on the leaves of some plants (e.g. Ficus) can indicate an attack by a fungus, commonly called leaf-spot. Infected leaves must be removed to prevent the disease spreading. Further treatment requires the use of fungicides.

A plant is not particularly keen on being sprayed with either household or chemical substances. Before spraying, make a protective cover for the pot by taking a square piece of plastic, cutting a slit to its centre and placing it over the pot. Fold the ends over the rim and keep in place with an elastic band.

cold water is one such remedy and catching the pests is another. However scale insects are not going to be bothered by a bit of cold water, and white fly is not easily caught.

By examining the pests more closely and finding out more about their life-cycles, you will be able to tell at what stage they will be doing the most damage to the plant, and when they are most vulnerable.

Mixtures, such as soap and spirit solutions, or dabbing with alcohol, are also home remedies. If these don't work, you'll have to resort to modern chemical controls.

When using insecticides you must take all possible precautions, as all chemical insecticides are poisonous and potentially very dangerous, especially to animals and children. If you have to use them, make sure that you read the instructions carefully and follow the directions exactly. Only use the chemical for the designated pest; don't be tempted to save an extra spraying by making up a 'cocktail' of different insecticides and fungicides in the hopes of killing 'everything'. These ingredients won't always be compatible and can damage the plants. Whenever you need to spray your plants it is advisable, weather permitting, to do this out of doors. If plants are too large to move, screen them from adjoining furniture with newspapers, before spraying and remove foodstuffs, pets or children from the room.

An insect that is troublesome to a great variety of plants is the *aphid* (Aphididae). This is a large family with many different species — the commonest varieties are green, yellow or brown. They can multiply rapidly, without fertilisation, and in most instances invade the young, growing tips of plants, where the stems are softer and easier for them to penetrate with their sucking mouth-parts. An invasion by aphids can be recognised by the deformed younger foliage. Look more closely and you'll see the stem seething with the pests, some adult and some tiny. Aphids secrete a sticky substance called honeydew which encourages a black-coloured fungus *(sooty mould)* to develop and feed off

the honeydew. This infection results in a blocking of light from the infected leaves and the blackened foliage is most unsightly.

What can be done about these pests? First try one of the older remedies: a concoction can be made by adding to 1 litre of lukewarm water, 1 teaspoonful green soap and 1 tablespoonful methylated spirits. Mix the ingredients well and spray on to the plant. Spray daily for the first few days and thereafter once a week until all trace of the aphids has disappeared.

Don't allow the spray to fall on to the potting soil or on to polished furniture. Cover the pot with paper or plastic while spraying. Be sure to spray the undersides of the leaves as well as all the young tips.

Another home remedy to try is made from *stinging nettles* (Urtica dioica). This is not only effective against aphids but will also discourage many other insects. If you gather the nettles yourself pick them before they have started blooming and don't forget to wear gloves! You can sometimes buy dried nettles. Soak the fresh (or dried) leaves in rain-water for about 24 hours. Don't soak them for much longer or the mixture won't work as an insecticide and will only be fit for the compost heap. The potion must be diluted with 4 to 5 times its volume of fresh water and then sprayed on to the plant.

As with the soap and spirit mixture, this spraying must be repeated several times. There are of course many very effective chemical insecticides that you can buy.

Leaves that have become sticky with honeydew and sooty mould can be washed off with a little green soap and lukewarm water, and then rinsed well with clean water. This should only be done to plants with tougher leaves. Finer and softer foliage that has become badly infected should rather be removed.

Scale insects (Coccidae) are an equally large family as the aphids. They can become serious pests amongst plants in greenhouses or in the home. Infestations are often also accompanied by unsightly sooty mould, as these

A plant with aphids? Try to catch some ladybirds and place them on the plant. Aphids are their favourite food. Once they have finished eating all the pests, you can place the plant at an open window to allow them to escape again.

Aphids do not like smoke. You can make use of this fact with smaller sized plants. Place the plant in a large plastic bag, blow in a few large breaths full of cigar or pipe-smoke, and securely close the bag. After an hour you can remove the plant. Repeat this process after a week, and you will find their numbers have been reduced.

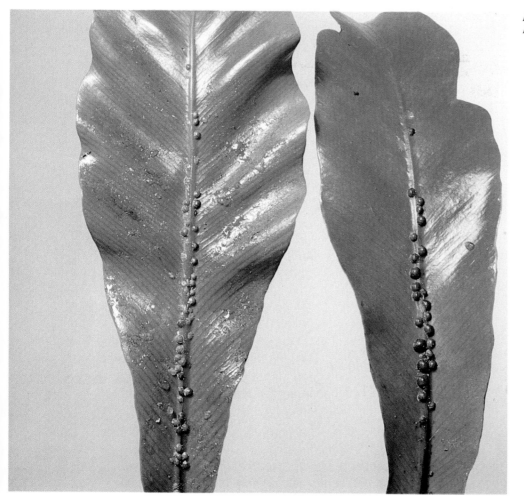

Brown scale on Bird's nest fern.

An extract from Wormwood (Artemisia absinthium) *can be used against a variety of insect pests. The fresh (or dry) leaflets are placed in water in a pot and brought to the boil. Let it draw for an hour and then strain off the leaves and dilute the brew with 1 part brew to 4 parts water. This can now be sprayed onto the plant, making sure that all parts are wetted.*

insects also give off honeydew. The adult insects form colonies of brown yellow or white waxy scales on either stems or leaves. These larger scales are the females and don't move about. They lay their eggs under their protective shell and when the young hatch they crawl out and spread to other parts of the plant. Each scale can produce large numbers of young so the invasion can be rapid and the effects soon become apparent. In a warmer situation, they can breed throughout the year, so you need to be vigilant. Scale insects are often difficult to get rid of with normal insecticides, as their scales offer good protection. Add the insecticide to a heavy oil-based spray. This has the effect of totally blanketing the insects until the poison can take effect.

A close relative of the scale insects is the *mealy bug* (Pseudococcidae). These look like small, woolly lice covered in a waxy, whitish substance, which acts as protection. They gather in colonies, tightly clustered together, usually in leaf-axils and near the tips of younger stems. The adults don't move about, but are very persistent and repeated spraying is needed to control them.

If the infestation is fairly limited, or has just begun, you can mix up a small quantity of well-diluted methylated spirits in water and paint it directly on to the mealy bug with a soft, small paint brush.

As in the case of aphids, all scale insects have a tremendous multiplication rate and can soon disrupt a plant's growth processes. How do you recognise when a plant is infested with scale? They very often establish themselves on the undersides of leaves and appear as small, brownish spots that can be easily scraped off. They'll usually be clustered closest to the midrib (whereas mealy bug prefer the leaf axils). The young and mobile scale are very small and barely visible until they settle, and develop their hard shells.

Red spider mite: if you notice very fine webs on the surfaces of your houseplants' leaves, don't blame the

215

Eggs of the red spider mite.

Centre:
Mite eggs and juveniles.

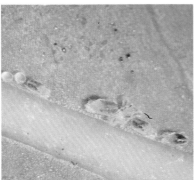

Impatiens with severe mite infestation.

dusty atmosphere as it is more likely to be the typical symptom of red spider mites. These mites are not insects but belong to the spider family. They are so small that you will usually only see them with the aid of a magnifying glass. Mites are easy to overlook as they invariably choose to live on the undersides of leaves and are happiest in a dry atmosphere. They do their damage by sucking the juices from the leaf which results in tell-tale pale blotches on the upper surfaces. The fine web is spun as a protective screen, between the mites and the air, and a severe infestation has the appearance of moving dust. Like most insect pests, mites have an enormous reproductive capacity.

The first step in controlling mites is to alter the atmosphere in their growing area and give the plant more water. By spraying the foliage regularly with water, cutting off any deformed and very heavily infested parts, and perhaps re-potting into better soil, you can discourage the mites to such an extent that they could leave in search of a more neglected host plant.

A pyrethrum-based insecticide can be used as a repellant. The mites eggs are resistant, so repeat the spraying every few days. A soap and spirits solution is also worth trying.

If one of your plants appears less healthy and develops small, silver-coloured blotches on its leaves it could signal an attack by yet another leaf-sucker called *thrips* (Thysanoptera). These are up to 3mm (approx ¼in) in length and their colour can vary from yellow to black. They are not fussy about which part of the plant they attack and can be found on stems, leaves or flower heads. Conditions of warmth and dryness are also preferred by this

pest. In fact low humidity is its first preference. Control is similar to the treatment for other leaf-suckers.

Sprays made of home made mixtures are usually disliked by the insects and the insecticides you can buy are very effective.

Another, more physical method, is to shake the plant vigorously over a sheet of white paper and collect the insects that fall off.

The next pest makes itself visible when a plant it is inhabiting is bumped. Then a cloud of small white insects flies out and settles again after a few seconds. This is *white fly* (Trialeur odes vaporariorum). The wings of this small fly are a dusty white and they prefer occupying the undersides of leaves. The eggs and the young are a yellow-green colour, and also live on the lower surface; they look similar to young scale insects but have a white, powdery covering.

And the damage they can cause? As with so many insects they extract plant sap and can do so on such a scale that the plant dies. They also like the conditions preferred by so many indoor pests: warmth and lower humidity. They also secrete the sticky substance honeydew on to the surfaces of the leaves below them, and so provide nutrition for the fungus sooty mould. This upsets the plant's growth processes, by reducing the amount of light that can reach the leaves.

Obviously these pests have to be eradicated or chased off, for the plant to survive.

If you can change the atmospheric conditions around them sufficiently you could persuade the pests to move to other parts more to their liking. You can provide more humidity in the air by

Centre:
*Thrips-damaged
Saintpaulia
bloom.*

Right:
*Thrips
magnified many
times.*

Left:
*Brown marking
on
Dieffenbachia
caused by
thrips.*

*Desert-dwelling cacti
don't like humid
conditions and prefer
alkaline soils. If you
don't take these factors
into account, the cacti
are likely to become
infected with rust or
mildew, which can often
prove fatal.*

regular syringing of the plant's foliage,
placing bowls of water near radiators
and never allowing the plant to dry out.

Bright light is liked by white fly but not
to the same extent by the plants it lives
on.

They can be further discouraged with a
soap-spirit solution, a nettle brew, or a
pyrethrum-based insecticide. Spray
every 3 days for at least 2 weeks to
ensure that both adults and newly
hatched young are caught by the
chemicals. Despite their size white fly
can cause considerable damage to
indoor plants where conditions
encourage their fantastic breeding rate.

Having dealt with the most troublesome
of the pests, unfortunately there are
other creatures that may attack your
plants. There are even some that cannot
be effectively controlled, and others
that you don't even need to kill.

You may find the drainage in a pot is
upset, or seedlings in a tray being
pulled down into the soil. These are
possibly the result of an earthworm,
which is normally an active humus-
eater, but in the confines of a pot it can
upset the roots and its casts can block
the drainage. It will eat seedlings only
when very hungry. The easiest way of
getting the worm out of the pot is to
stand it in lukewarm water. The worm
comes to the surface to breathe, and can
then be caught and taken to the outdoor
garden. The presence of earthworms is
often revealed by their heaps, or casts,
on the soil's surface. These twisted by-
products are composed of humus mixed
with loam or sand.

Sometimes when plants are brought
inside after a spell out of doors, slugs
or snails can be inadvertently brought in
as well. You will only discover them
after finding holes chewed in the leaves

or along their edges. Their other tell-
tale sign is the slimy, silver trail they
leave behind. Snails and slugs are
nocturnal so it would be best to surprise
them at night with a torch, or first thing
in the morning when you could pick
them off by hand. Snails like to hide
amongst fallen leaves or under
containers, where daylight is excluded.
Cleanliness will help but poison snail-
pellets, containing metaldehyde, are
most effective. An alternative method is
to entice them to a glass or container of
beer, which they drink and while
intoxicated become easy to catch!

*White fly on
Calceolaria
leaves.*

Classifying houseplants

Plants can be classified in several different ways: according to botanical characteristics, their country of origin, choice of climate, mode of growth, or manner of propagation.

These divisions are of little practical use to the amateur gardener. What is needed is a system that divides plants according to their appearance, and the manner in which they can be used.

Apart from the alphabetical index at the back of this book, each of the following chapters has its own alphabetical list of plants. It must be realised that any type of classification can never be complete or too precise. For example, a plant such as *Spathiphyllum* can be listed under the heading 'foliage plant', and also under 'flowering plants'. It might also happen that some plants listed under 'succulents', for example, might be found under 'foliage plants' instead, if their 'foliage' aspect is deemed to be more important than their 'succulent' aspect.

The advantages of this system are largely compensated for by the exceptions listed in the introductory sections at the start of each chapter. In this way, you will know where to look for plants that can't be found in a particular section.

It is important to know the exact plant you are dealing with, as some plants that resemble each other closely, or which are even closely related, may need entirely different care or conditions.

Once you know the plant's correct name, you can buy exactly what you want, and you should also be able to find out its exact requirements.

The use of common names is to be discouraged, as the same common name can often apply to completely different plants, either in different parts of the country or in other countries. Some common names refer to a whole family of plants and do not denote the species at all. Many plants don't have common names at all. For these reasons the botanical names of the various species will be used in the following chapters, and only some of the better known common names will be indicated.

The following lists of plants are by no means complete but constitute a general selection. You will soon realise why every plant cannot be described, when you discover that amongst the Orchid family alone, there are between 40,000 and 60,000 species and varieties. And this is only one family!

Foliage plants

Green plants

*Variegated
Tolmiea, with
'baby' on leaf.*

Under this heading you will find plants that are sometimes described under the collective term of 'foliage' plants. Either term is appropriate for this most varied group of plants, whose common feature is that they are grown, or bought, primarily for their attractive green (or coloured) leaves.

This does not mean that foliage plants don't flower, but rather that the flowers are perhaps insignificant, not particularly attractive, or the blooms only remain out for a very short while.

These decorative plants are usually fairly large in size; smaller foliage plants have a more limited use. These leafy plants are popular because they remain uniform throughout the year and, by and large, they are easy to care for. They are generally less prone to diseases and other problems than, for example, variegated plants, or plants grown for their flowering display.

When looking at the choices available, foliage plants become very desirable, as there is such a variety of leaf-forms from which to choose. You only have to think of the leaves of the *Monstera, Ficus elastica,* or one of the Palms.

Plant collectors with a more refined taste in colours will discover an infinite variety of green shades and textures to be used in a hundred different ways and places.

Collections can be made according to botanical groupings (Palms, Ferns, etc.), or leaf shapes.

You must not forget that the plants in any group must have fairly similar needs as far as climate and general care are concerned if maintenance is to remain simple.

Foliage plants are often used as a background for other plants, and especially as the permanent 'base' for seasonal plantings.

If you wish to extend the group of green plants even further, you will find many more examples under other headings. Nearly all Ferns are 'foliage' plants, as are many of the climbing and hanging species and houseshrubs.

But, as we've mentioned before, each section is based on the primary characteristics that are common to all plants of that group.

Araucaria heterophylla

Araucaria
Norfolk Island Pine
This evergreen, coniferous tree will grow to 60m (or approximately 200ft) in its natural habitat. It grows well as an indoor plant, reaching 1m (3ft) or more in height. Prefers cooler, well-ventilated indoor conditions, and doesn't like direct sunlight. It will, in fact, tolerate fairly dark conditions. Use as an accent plant (specimen) on its own. Water regularly in spring and summer and less often in winter, when it does not like too much 'heating' which can cause lower branches to die and leave the stem bare. Re-pot annually, and feed sparingly.

Chamaedorea elegans

Chamaedorea elegans
Parlour palm
This is a true indoor palm, in that it grows well indoors, even when light levels are fairly low, and in more northerly climates it will not survive outdoors except perhaps in midsummer, but only out of direct sunlight.
The Parlour palm likes a warm and humid atmosphere. Spraying the foliage with water during the summer is beneficial, as is summer feeding. Water regularly in the summer, but less in winter. Palms have an extensive root system and grow fastest in larger containers. Re-pot every year in spring, while young, and less often once the plant is older. Red spider mite is its commonest and worst pest, so watch for it especially carefully, particularly on the undersides of fronds.

Asparagus 'Sprengeri'

Asparagus
These useful and hardy plants are much used by florists for greenery in flower arrangements. *A. densiflorus* is a foliage plant with slightly glossy, needle-like leaves of an attractive light-green. *A. plumosus*, better known as Asparagus Fern, whose dark green leaves are very fine and arranged in flat fronds, growing at right-angles to the stem, can be treated as a climber under the right conditions. All the Asparagus members like good light and warm temperatures, but tolerate some cold.
Water moderately taking care that the root ball does not dry out. They do not need a rest period and respond well to feeding. Propagate by division.

During a very hot summer, or during warm spells in winter, plants will need extra watering. You can place them outside during a shower of rain, to give them pure water and wash off all the dust. Just remember that all watering can cause certain soils to compact; this can cause problems to plants in glazed or plastic pots. The simple solution is to regularly loosen the topmost layer of soil with a stick.

Many houseplants 'go off' in winter. This is more likely to be caused by the fluctuations in temperature, rather than from the lowest temperature reached. A sitting-room temperature may reach 20°C (70°F) during the day and evening, and drop to 10°C (50°F) in the early morning. Changes will be greatest closer to the windows. Plants such as Anthurium, Aphelandra, Aglaonema and Dieffenbachia react quickly to these adverse changes.

Watering with cold tap water can be equally harmful.

Aspidistra elatior

Aspidistra
Cast iron plant
This plant lives up to its common name and is extremely tough. It will withstand just about any conditions and was very much beloved by the Victorians for use in dark hallways. It has handsome, broad, strap-like leaves of a glossy dark green. There are variegated varieties too. Prefers shady, cool conditions and moderate watering. Does not like 'wet feet' or direct sunlight. This is the plant for that spot in your home that is too dark for anything else. An older plant with a lot of leaves can be most attractive. They, in fact, prefer to be potbound, so only re-pot every few seasons. Propagates easily by division of rhizomes.

*Cyperus
alternifolius*

Cyperus
Umbrella grass
In their natural habitat these plants grow on river banks and even in the water. The plant has long slender stems with a feathery 'umbrella' of leaves at the top. Very attractive as a specimen plant standing on its own. Prefers good light and cooler conditions. It does not like a dry atmosphere or higher temperatures, so placing the pot on a shallow tray of water can provide the watery conditions it likes, and this also maintains a higher humidity. Regular feeding provides lush growth. Multiply the plant by dividing the rhizomes, or take cuttings of the 'umbrella', and place in sand or water. The commonest species is *C. alternifolius*.
A smaller species, *C. diffusus* also does well, but likes less moisture and more warmth.

Fatshedera lizei

Fatshedera
Ivy tree
This is a hybrid between *Fatsia* and *Hedera* (Ivy), with typical *Fatsia* shaped leaves, but a bit smaller. It is a hardy plant that will grow up to 2m (6ft) or more on long, thin stems, and needs support. The variegated types are very attractive, and the appearance is improved if the plant is pruned back to encourage it to bush out. Watering and conditions are as for *Fatsia*. Re-pot regularly for best growth, and water well while growth is active; less water during winter. Prune in spring, and use cut tips for propagating. Plants may be brought outdoors during summer.

*Dizygotheca
veitchii*

Dizygotheca
False aralia
A slim, elegant tropical shrub, with long dark green, serrated leaflets arranged in open, fan-shaped 'hands'. Can survive for many years with good handling. *D. elegantissima* has fine redish green leaves, while *D. veitchii* has broader dark green leaves.
They prefer a well-lit situation, but out of direct sunlight. Warm conditions and high humidity are also beneficial. Water moderately but do not allow to dry out. Spray the foliage to maintain a higher humidity.
Requires a winter rest period, but not too cool (i.e. above 15°C (60°F)). These are naturally slow growers, and should not be over-fed, or their stems 'stretch'.

Ficus carica

Ficus carica
Fig
This is the common fruiting fig. Some varieties can even be induced to fruit indoors, in particular, plants of the strain 'Brown Turkey'. It does best on a poor but well-drained soil, but this does not mean poor watering! It needs plenty of water when fruiting but stop in winter when the tree is dormant. Fertilising before fruiting must be light. Likes warm conditions but is generally very tolerant. Propagate from cuttings in spring.

Fatsia japonica

Fatsia japonica
The Fatsia is a native of Japan, and is a hardy attractive plant with large 'hand-shaped' leaves, with pointed lodes. In a pot it will grow to about 1m (3ft). It likes good light conditions and can be placed outdoors in summer but not in direct sunlight.
It does well as a permanent outdoor shrub but its general condition will then not be good enough for it to be used as a 'houseplant'.
Water regularly in spring and summer but less frequently in winter. Indoors it prefers a cool atmosphere, and is likely to suffer if the central heating is too hot and the air too dry. Excessive heat or draught will cause leaves to drop, with a resultant bare stem.

Ficus elastica

Ficus elastica
Rubber tree
Of all the members of this enormous family the rubber tree is probably the best known. It has long been a favourite houseplant with its large and glossy, dark green leaves. It can grow very large if well looked after. Control height by cutting out tips, this also leads to a more bushy plant. Good light and ventilation, moderate temperatures, and regular water will suit best, but it will tolerate fairly dark conditions.
Water less during the winter, when temperatures should not drop below 12°C (54°F). Keep the leaves clean and shiny by regular wiping with a damp cloth. Fertilise sparingly and regularly, as growth is normally fairly rapid. Re-pot annually in spring.

Ficus benjamina

Ficus benjamina

Unlike *F. elastica*, *F. benjamina* has small, pointed leaves and an attractive weeping habit. It is useful as a tall background to a group of plants, or used as a specimen on its own. Likes good light but not direct sun in a well-ventilated position. Water regularly in spring and summer, ease off the watering in winter. In a large container, with regular summer feeding, growth is fairly rapid. Prune for shape or to control height. Most of the tropical *Ficus* need similar handling. *Ficus lyrata*, with its large, flat leaves is more difficult as it needs constant higher temperatures and humidity. All *Ficus* are sensitive to draughts and sudden temperature changes.

Jacaranda mimosifolia

Jacaranda mimosifolia

Fortunately, the well known Jacaranda won't become as large indoors as in its native Brazil. There it reaches 20m (60ft) and produces masses of lilac blue flowers. You can only use it for its foliage indoors, where it may reach 2m (6ft) if carefully managed, and given the right 'tropical' conditions. For healthy growth provide a spot with good light, out of direct sunlight, with high humidity, and water sparingly. Soft water must be used (lacking lime). Higher temperatures are preferred, though during winter temperatures should not drop below 16–18°C (60–64°F). During active growth, fertilise fortnightly but avoid lime. Jacarandas will suffer from any 'excesses', too wet or too dry, too hot or too cold. They will not survive for more than a few years indoors. Propagation: in spring from seed, and in summer from young tip cuttings.

Grevillea robusta

Grevillea robusta
Silky oak

This hardy native of Australia can grow to 2 or 3m (6 or 9ft) tall in a pot and at a very great rate. It has fine, feathery leaves and in its natural habitat it produces masses of golden flowers. Unfortunately, it won't flower indoors. Water moderately and give it a position in good light but not direct sun. It likes a cooler atmosphere and can be placed outdoors during summer. Re-pot regularly, as the Silky Oak can soon become rootbound. Propagate from seed or stem cuttings.

Howea forsteriana

It's best not to re-pot houseplants later than August. As you know, a pot should be neither too large nor too small. In a pot that is too small the roots are cramped, and in a pot that is too large, as the saying goes, 'it can't keep its pot warm'. If you re-pot after August, there is a chance that the roots won't have fully grown into the new soil before winter. This may not sound too bad, but the risk of disease is increased, and so it is best avoided by re-potting only in spring and early summer.

Humidity can be increased around a single plant by the 'island' method. For a group of plants, construct a shallow tray of a large enough size to accommodate your plant group, and fill this with a layer of gravel, which must be kept damp. The plants are placed on this tray but without their pots becoming damp; in other words, this tray is a source of humidity to be evaporated into the air around the plants. If you have enough space, you can make a larger trough out of timber and heavy plastic sheeting. The timber forms the sides, and the plastic is the waterproofing.

Howea forsteriana
Kentia palm

There are only two species of Howea (also known as Kentia). They appear very similar when grown in pots. *H. belmoreana* has more upright fronds, up to 2m (6ft) in length, and *H. forsteriana* can produce fronds up to 3m (9ft) with a more drooping habit. They are valuable houseplants, as their needs are simple and care straightforward. These palms will tolerate good to fair light conditions throughout the year, and they prefer their soil on the dry side. Over wintering is no problem indoors, unless temperatures approach freezing or the heating is excessively warm.

Neanthe bella
Parlour Palm
This is a slow growing miniature palm from Mexico, which has long been used as an indoor plant as it tolerates fairly low light levels and a degree of neglect! Older plants develop a bare stem; they drop their lower fronds regularly. Flowering shoots are commonly produced on plants that are a few years old, but will not form fruit under the conditions found in the house. This palm prefers a light situation and regular watering, but let the soil dry out between waterings. Feed sparingly during summer. Young plants are very effective in cases, terrariums and bottle gardens, and as 'accent' in small mixed-plant displays.

Neanthe bella

Phoenix
Canary and Date Palm
These two palms from the Canary Islands and North Africa and South East Asia, grow huge in their natural habitats. They also make fine pot plants with their dark green and rather harsh fronds with spiny bases. Both in the Canary Island palm and *P. dactylifera*, the date palm, need plenty of light, air and water, and can be placed outside in the sun during the summer. They will tolerate cooler positions. Must have good drainage but need plenty of feeding from spring until mid-summer. Water somewhat less in winter, but don't let the roots dry out completely. Over-hard water is best avoided. Propagation is by seed.

Phoenix canariensis

Mimosa pudica
Sensitive plant
This is not the Mimosa that produces the fluffy yellow flower sprays one sees in the florists. This species is kept not so much for its attractive foliage as for its curiosity value. This spreading, slightly spiny plant has feathery, pinnate leaves. When the plant is touched, during daylight, the leaflets fold together down the midribs. After a few minutes, if left alone, they will return to normal. All the leaves fold up at night. Needs good light but *not* direct sunlight and daytime temperatures of more than 20°C (68°F) with fair humidity. Water freely in spring and summer. With correct care they flower freely, producing pink, ball-shaped blooms. Plants grow readily from seed sown in early spring. Pruning will limit flowering, but it will stimulate more bushy growth.

Mimosa pudica

Pittosporum
These are hardy, evergreen shrubs from East Asia, with shiny green leathery leaves in various colours. *P. tobira*, the best known, has dark green, shiny leaves and creamy clusters of sweet-smelling tubular flowers. *P. tenuifolium* has paler green leaves, blackish stems and red flowers. There are several other species, some variegated, to be found at nurseries. All their blooms have the added bonus of producing strong perfume that will fill a room. All types need good light conditions, cool temperatures, but keep them well watered. They can be moved outdoors in summer. Over wintering is a problem, as they require a resting temperature of about 5°C (40°F) and less water. Propagate with seed in spring, or heel cuttings in summer.

Pittosporum tobira

Pandanus
Screw Pine
An evergreen tree or shrub from Indonesia. *P. utilis* is the largest and most vigorous species with dark green leaves with red spines along the edges. It cannot withstand winter temperatures of less than 16°C (60°F). *P. sanderi* is smaller, with narrower leaves, striped yellow and green. These can grow up to 75cm (2½ft) in length. *P. veitchii* is similar, but has darker green leaves, with greeny yellow stripes. Neither will tolerate temperatures of less than 18–20°C (64–68°F). All *Pandanus* species need good light, but not direct sun, and relatively high temperatures throughout the year are best. Water generously with a bit less in winter and keep humidity fairly high. *P. utilis* is grown from seed and the others from side shoots formed at the base of a mature stem.

Pandanus sanderi

Schefflera
This distinctive evergreen tree from Australia and New Zealand has glossy, dark green compound leaves, arranged in groups of 3, 5 or 7 leaflets, depending on the age of the plant. These plants are extremely sensitive to temperature during their over-wintering period, which must remain between 12°C (52°F) and 18°C (64°F). If lower, the plant may not survive. Adequate light is needed throughout the year, with shading in summer when it can be taken outside. Beware of early frosts or leaves will be lost. Humidity must be maintained and spraying of foliage can help. Red spider mite is a likely pest under drier conditions.

Schefflera actinophylla

*Selaginella
martensii*

Selanginella
Creeping moss
This flowerless, moss-like plant is related to the ferns, and is widely used as a ground-cover amongst the bases of groups of plants. All these mosses are shade-lovers, but need a fair amount of light and moisture (soft water) at all times. There are about 700 species, mostly inhabitants of tropical rain forests. *S. martensii* is a trailing species that has flattened stems with small oval leaves; there is also a very popular variegated form. *S. apoda* is a creeping form, resembling moss that forms rounded hummocks. Propagation simply involves cutting off any smaller rooted portion.

Yucca aloifolia

Yucca
The trunk-forming species is most suitable as a houseplant; *Y. aloifolia* also has a variegated form, with long, spiky leaves. Some of the stiffer leaved varieties have almost lethal spikes on the leaf-tips, so don't stand the plant where a child might bump into it. Yuccas like a sunny position and can be taken outdoors in summer. Water sparingly in summer; its pot must have good drainage. Do not water in winter, during the rest period, and keep the plant in a cool position. Mealy bug is an occasional pest, especially under warmer conditions.

*Sparmannia
africana*

Sparmannia
African hemp
An evergreen shrub or small tree, growing to 2½m (8ft) in height. *Sparmannia* has large, pale-green hairy leaves. It is suited to well-ventilated, cooler situations in the home (halls or bedrooms). After re-potting, in spring, it can remain outdoors for the summer, but in the shade. Its rest period is late winter, when watering must be reduced, but not stopped completely. Once growth starts, water and feed regularly. Draughts are likely to encourage thrips and white fly, so beware! During summer sprays of white flowers are produced. Propagate by hardwood cuttings during summer.

Larger specimens of green foliage plants can be bought from florists and nurseries. They are, however, fairly easy to grow from cuttings, and the propagation from a tiny slip to a large plant gives great satisfaction. It is not as widely realised that many of these plants can be grown from seed. If you look through a spring seed catalogue, you'll come across quite a few foliage plants, besides the annuals and vegetables. You could try one of the Asparagus types, or a dwarf coffee plant? Or even an umbrella grass if you can create the correct conditions.

*Tolmiea
mensiesii*

Tolmiea
Piggy-back plant
The common name of this plant originates from the plantlets that are formed on the surfaces of adult leaves, and ready to take root when the leaf falls. It is a member of the *Saxifraga* family. Grows to about 20cm (9in) in height, and spreads well as a ground-cover, indoors or in the garden. There is also a variegated variety. It is a useful subject in a hanging basket, and soon forms a round green 'ball' of fresh green foliage. Fresh air (but no draughts), plenty of water and light are the main needs. Direct sun will scorch its foliage. Reduce watering during winter.

Variegated plants

The term 'variegated' describes plants that have leaves which contain two or more colours. This multi-colouring could be one of many combinations of green and yellow shades, red or white marks or edgings, stripes, spots, mottling and many more; the whole leaf can be multi-coloured. The range of colours to be found in the plant kingdom is very wide.

Variegated plants, like any others, don't all have the same needs, but one common factor is their usual need for more light than their all-green relations. They are also slightly more difficult to keep healthy. However, because of their great attractiveness, they are all worth a bit of extra effort.

Variegated plants need the extra light, as their growth processes (photosynthesis) are slightly retarded, due to the lesser green (chlorophyll) content of the leaves. Chlorophyll plays an important part in the process of photosynthesis.

It is tempting, because of their lighter colour, to use variegated plants in darker corners, to brighten them up a bit, but this will almost certainly lead to disappointment when the plant starts to decline.

There are always exceptions. In the section on 'Hanging plants' you will find details of the light yellow and green *Chlorophytum comosum variegatum*, which is very tough, and will tolerate quite dark conditions. The best examples remain those that prefer better light conditions.

On the other hand, the more sensitive variegated plants that might prefer good light, have to be protected from direct sunlight, especially during the hottest times of the day between April and September.

Self-control has to be exercised when grouping these multi-coloured plants, as too many different colours and species will either detract from one another, or clash, and the effect won't be at all satisfactory. Remember that combining colours is governed by personal taste, so use your judgment.

Some variegated plants will be found under other headings as well. There are examples listed in the sections on Hanging and Climbing Plants, Bromeliads and Houseshrubs.

A sea of Coleus colours.

Aglaonema hybrid

Aphelandra squarrosa

Begonia Rex hybrids

Aglaonema

This is one of a group of variegated plants that will tolerate low light conditions. It is sometimes mistaken for a *Dieffenbachia*, but has narrower, more pointed leaves and does not develop a stem or grow into as tall a plant. *A treubii* 'Silver King' is the commonest variety, with silver variegations. By contrast, *A. commutatum* is grey with green markings. The best situation is a well-lit, warm and humid spot. Temperatures around 20°C (68°F) are optimum. Water freely in summer, using lime-free water, but less frequently in winter. Misting the foliage during hot weather is beneficial. *Aglaonemas* do well in plant cases and terrariums. Propagate from cuttings or seed; bottom heat will aid rooting.

Aphelandra
Zebra plant
The yellow or white variegations on the *Aphelandra* highlight the veins of the glossy dark green leaves. Flowers range in colour from yellow to orange at the tips of the branches of the different varieties. After blooming they tend to drop their leaves. You can prevent this by letting them rest for a few weeks. At this stage the plant can be cut back and allowed to re-shoot. *Aphelandras* are very susceptible to temperature fluctuations and will not tolerate lower temperatures at all. They prefer good light and high humidity. Watering, with tepid, soft water, must be regular while the plant is growing; drying-out is fatal. Leaves are very sensitive to chemical sprays. Propagate from tip cuttings.

Begonia
The whole family of Begonias have been popular houseplants for a long while. Their many different leaf and flower colours and shapes provide a selection for most situations. Many are perennial, and can be kept alive and flourishing for many years without too much effort. All Begonias prefer a high atmospheric humidity and must be watered regularly. Spraying with water is not recommended, as the flowers tend to become soggy, and the leaves are prone to rotting. Light should be good but not direct sun. Regular re-potting and feeding will ensure healthy growth. The best known of the foliage Begonias is *Begonia Rex*, with an infinite colour range, from deepest purple to pale pink, green or metallic silver. Propagation is by division or leaf cuttings during summer.

Caladium bicolor hybrids

Codiaeum variegatum hybrid

Coleus blumei hybrids

Caladium

This is one of the most colourful of the foliage plants, with a wide range of colours and pattern on the large, heart-shaped leaves. Mostly reds, pinks, greens and white. The leaves have a delicate papery texture, some are almost translucent. They will grow well if you can provide the right conditions. They need a shady position and warm temperatures. High humidity is important. Use the 'island' method, by placing their pots over damp gravel, and mist the foliage with tepid water. Water and feed regularly until July when feeding stops. From August give them progressively less water. *Caladium* has a tuberous root and needs to be dried out and over wintered in its pot in a warm place, with temperatures between 15°C (58°F) and 20°C (68°F). Re-pot tubers in spring.

Codiaeum
Croton
The leaves of this colourful shrub can vary from long and narrow to broad or oval, depending on the variety. They may be veined, marbled or spotted yellow, white, red or green. Being a tropical plant they like good light, even sunlight, but should be protected from scorching through glass. They tolerate warmer temperatures in summer and cooler in winter, between 16°C (60°F) and 18°C (64°F). They need high humidity and like to be sprayed regularly with water. Water well in spring and summer, less in winter, but do not let them dry out or the leaves may fall. Susceptible to red spider mite and mealy bug attack if conditions become too dry. Propagate with young tip cuttings in sand.

Coleus
A very popular pot plant with a wide range of multi-coloured, velvety leaves. Also popular are the frilly leafed varieties; they come in all shades of red, brown, purple, green, white and yellow. The plants can grow vigorously to 75cm (2½ft) in height. Branch tips and flower buds should be pinched out regularly to encourage bushy growth. Good light is essential to keep colours bright; lack of light causes leaves to turn green. Warm temperatures, plentiful watering with soft water, potting in lime free compost and feeding every two weeks are their main requirements. *Coleus* are usually treated as single-season plants, but can be over wintered quite easily. Otherwise, take tip cuttings in water or sand of any of the worthwhile varieties.

229

Cordyline
Cabbage Palm

Cordyline terminalis

The family includes small trees and shrubs from South East Asia and Australia. *C. terminalis* has rosettes of dark green or bronzy-red sword shaped leaves. Many of the red leaved varieties are seen as houseplants. *C. stricta* has long, thin sword like leaves of dark green above and purple below. These plants are often confused with *Dracaenas* and have much the same needs and problems. They may need some climate adjusting after being bought — from a humid glasshouse to your drier home. They need plenty of warmth and protection from direct sunlight. In winter temperatures should not drop below 15°C (58°F). Water sparingly. Do not allow them to dry out. They do not like to stand in water. Re-pot annually in late spring and feed regularly.

Episcia

Episcia reptans

Attractive low trailing evergreen plants from South America, *E. cupreata* has downy, wrinkled leaves of pale green with red and silver stripes down the mid-ribs. *E. reptans* has darker, coppery-green leaves and pale silvery mid and lateral veins. They need good light out of direct sunlight, warm temperatures and need to be kept moist in spring and summer, but with less water in winter. Likes fairly high humidity. Both species are very effective in hanging pots or baskets. Leaves are sensitive so, when fertilising, be careful not to touch them. They will flower during the summer from April to August. Trailing stems tend to root as they go, so propagation is simply a matter of cutting off rooted pieces.

Dieffenbachia
Dumb Cane

Dieffenbachia maculata

Attractive foliage plants with large oval, slightly pointed leaves, heavily mottled with yellow or white. They have fleshy stems with regular, close nodes, and can grow to a height of 2m (6ft) or more. Care should be exercised when handling this plant as *its sap is poisonous*. A position in good light but not direct sun, away from draughts, is most suitable. It needs warm temperatures and fairly high humidity. Water well in summer, easing off in winter. Wash leaves with lukewarm water occasionally. When temperatures drop much below 15°C (58°F) in winter, the leaves are likely to drop. A dormant stage during cold weather is quite normal. The best-known species are *D. maculata, D. Seguine* and *D. bausei* with its many varieties.

Fittonia

Fittonia argyroneura

Another low trailing plant with fascinatingly marked leaves of mid-green with veins highlighted in contrasting colour. *F. verschaffeltii* has red veins, *F. argyronevra* has silver veins. Both are very effective as ground-covers at the base of taller plants, as they trail over the edge. There are other glasshouse varieties as well. All do well in cases or terrariums. They will tolerate fairly low light conditions, but prefer a warm position out of direct sunlight, and one in which humidity is high. Water regularly but ensure that soil is well drained. Feed with low doses of houseplant fertiliser. Propagate in the same way as *Episcia*.

Dracaena

Dracaena fragrans

The palm-like *Dracaenas* have long pointed leaves arranged in whorls around their stems. It is commonly confused with the *Cordyline*, but their needs are similar. The many varieties have a range of leaf colours, stripes in green and white, yellow, or silver or simply plain green. They are all good houseplants, especially if they have enough humidity. A warm position in good light, but not direct sun suits them. Water moderately in summer and less in winter, but do not allow the plant to dry out completely. Re-pot annually in late spring. Propagate from sections of stem or tips during summer.

Iresine herbstii

Iresine herbstii

This is a perennial, but is usually treated as an annual, with tip cuttings taken at the end of summer to provide new plants for the following year. There is a fair amount of variation in shape and colour of the leaves from blood red to purple. Blooms are nondescript, and the plant needs to be cut back regularly to encourage branching and production of more foliage. They are often used outdoors for summer bedding. They need to be in sunlight to maintain their colour. Like a warm temperature and good humidity. Water well in summer.

Maranta
Prayer plant

The *Marantas* are low growing tropical plants from Brazil, and kept for their highly decorative leaves. *M. bicolor* has a dark green surface with brown blotches at regular intervals on either side of the midrib. The underside of the leaf is purple. *M. leuconeura* has red or pink mid and lateral veins and regular patterns of green on the leaf, colouring varies according to the variety. They prefer good light without direct sun but they will tolerate fairly dark situations. Water well with lime free water in summer, less in autumn and winter. Needs regular re-potting and feeding for lush growth. Very useful in mixed arrangements and in cases and terrariums. Propagate by division, re-potting.

Maranta leuconeura

Sansevieria
Mother-in-law's tongue

A leathery leafed desert plant from Africa with upright spear shaped leaves with marginal stripes of yellow. They can grow up to 60cm (2ft) in height. They are very tolerant and easy to grow. They like good light and warm temperatures. Water regularly in summer but allow to dry out in winter. Humidity is hardly a factor for them. In contrast to most houseplants they prefer a chalky soil and lime in the water. They are often regarded as 'old fashioned', and were used in dark Victorian interiors. Modern hybrids are much more compact, and have fairly bright variegations and markings. Re-pot when they outgrow their containers, cut off shoots with a rhizome to propagate new plants.

Sansevieria trifasciata hybrids

Pilea
Aluminium plant

This genus of evergreen perennial plants are grown for their decorative foliage. *P. cadierei* is an erect, branching plant with oval leaves, patterned with silver, and grows 20—25cm (8—10ins) high. *P. spruceana* is a smaller plant with bronze, quilted leaves on purple stems. The genus has other varieties too. Reasonable light conditions, with good ventilation, but fairly high humidity are needed. Moderate temperatures are acceptable, but never below 10°C (50°F) in winter. Plants tend to go 'off' a bit during winter, so may need cutting back in spring, to start off new growth. Use prunings as tip cuttings.

Pilea cadierei

Saxifraga
Mother of thousands

S. stolonifera is a strawberry-like species that sends out long runners that bear numerous new plants. 'Tricolor' is a variegated form that has attractive pink and white markings on its leaves. Place in good light shaded from the sun. Likes warm conditions but it won't tolerate excessive heat. Winter temperatures should be above 10°C (50°F). Water regularly in summer but less regularly in winter. They are very useful for hanging pots and baskets. Their trailing stems with plantlets can become quite dense. Good as a 'filler' in mixed groups.

Saxifraga stolonifera

Rhoeo

An attractive foliage plant with spear shaped fleshy leaves, related to *Tradescantia* (the trailing garden plant). The leaves are 20—35cm (8—14ins) long and grow in whorls around the stem. There are several colour varieties of *Rhoeo spathacea*, some have purplish leaves and others green and yellow stripes. Place in semi-shade in summer and in good light in winter, but not direct sunlight. Likes fair humidity in summer and regular watering but drier conditions in winter. Can grow vigorously and will send out numerous side-shoots. Remove the surplus to keep it under control.

Rhoeo spathacea

Tradescantia
Spiderwort

A popular creeping and trailing plant with succulent leaves and stems. The leaves are oval, pointed, and green with white stripes in the case of *T. albiflora*, or white, pink or purple in the 'Tricolor' variety. Can be used equally well in hanging pots on a sill or together with other plants in a trough. Likes good light and moderate temperatures. Water well in summer easing off in winter. They are shallow rooted and will do best in a light, humus-rich soil. Curbing vigorous growth is usually more of a problem than getting plants to grow. Temperatures below 10°C (50°F) in winter will affect Tradescantia adversely.

Tradescantia fluminensis variegata

Ferns

Finely-divided leaves of the Maidenhair fern (Adiantum).

In their natural habitats ferns are shade-loving plants. This certainly does not mean that they must be expected to survive in a dark corner of the home. Usually, in their home environment, ferns have enough light, but it is often not bright enough for plants that would otherwise compete with them.

Although some ferns will be happy in full sunlight, most of them need situations that are fairly light but not in direct sun. On a window sill, the sun and accompanying heat can be regarded as a real enemy by most ferns. If the fern fronds become very pale, then the light intensity is probably too bright for them and this is a clear indication that you should find them another position. It is worth noting that ferns don't like artificial light.

Another important problem area is atmospheric humidity. Virtually all ferns prefer a high degree of humidity. This is easy enough to organise for either a single or a group of ferns. It can be done in the same way as for a small collection of orchids. Provide a shallow, waterproof tray filled with gravel that is kept moist. If this is used as a platform for the plants and is put near a radiator then the evaporating moisture will provide a humid atmosphere for those plants on the tray. This situation also helps the plants tolerate the higher temperature. The degree of humidity needed will depend on the specific fern types.

Without increasing the humidity no fern is going to grow well (or even survive) in a centrally heated room. Hot, dry conditions are not tolerated. Lower temperatures will not affect ferns provided they do not fall much below 8–10°C (48–50°F).

Another method of providing and controlling humidity for certain small ferns is to use an enclosed glass container, or terrarium, after the fashion of the once widely used Wardian cases. Here the moisture is perfectly contained and many fern species thrive under these closed conditions. Temperature fluctuations are usually fairly minor. For the fern collector, a closed case is ideal for growing and propagating many of the species which are particularly difficult.

You can easily make one of these cases yourself or use an old fish tank. Provide an angled roof so that condensing water droplets do not drip onto the plants but run down the sides of the case. Such a case, when the lid is closed, keeps the same moisture in circulation making watering almost unnecessary, and the retained moisture ensures that the humidity also remains high. In general, the most important aspect of the care of ferns involves keeping humidity at an adequate level and the plant's roots moist (but not wet). If conditions become too dry the fronds will shrivel. If too wet then the roots can rot. Ferns also dislike lime and salts, so rain-water, or hydro-culture with soft water suits them best. You will be well rewarded if you give your ferns the necessary attention.

Adiantum

Maidenhair fern

There are many species and varieties of this attractive, delicately foliaged fern. The differences are comparatively minor and cultivation requirements are fairly similar. The best known species include *A. capillus-veneris, A. raddianum, A. tenerum* and *A. pedatum.* This last species was one of the first North American plants introduced to Britain. It grows 30–45cm (12–18ins) tall with brown wiry stems, and pale green fronds bearing delicate fan-shaped leaflets. It is surely one of the prettiest of ferns. These ferns prefer a shady, draught free spot, moderate temperatures, and high humidity. They are good subjects for cases and terrariums. Water regularly with tepid, soft water. Give less in winter. Do not re-pot too frequently, as growth is best when the roots form a solid 'ball'. Propagate from spores.

*Adiantum
capillus-veneris*

*Cyrtomium
falcatum*

Cyrtomium

Holly fern

This fern is a houseplant that will tolerate very low-light situations, in fact, in places where nothing else would serve at all. Its fronds grow to about 30cm (12ins) in length, with dark green pointed leaflets on arching fronds. *C. Rochfordianum,* the Holly Fern, has wavy leaflets and a prickly appearance similar to holly. It is easy to look after requiring regular watering during the summer growing period, but with cooler temperatures. In winter, temperatures can drop to 10°C (50°F) when much less water is needed. Spray with lukewarm soft water now and then; whilst higher humidity is enjoyed, it is not essential. Propagate either by division or from spores.

*Asplenium
nidus*

Asplenium nidus

Bird's nest fern

Asplenium nidus has a different appearance to the other ferns in this genus. It has undivided, tongue-shaped fronds that are a glossy light green colour, growing in an arching rosette. They can reach up to 60cm (2ft) in height. In its natural habitat it grows as an epiphyte — other *aspleniums* have divided fronds. Grow them in a shaded position with warm termperatures, though not below 18°C (64°F) in winter. High humidity and regular watering, with soft water warmed to room temperature. Feed regularly for healthy and large fronds. Don't re-pot every year.

*Blechnum
gibbum*

Blechnum

Under the right conditions, *Blechnum* is an outstanding houseplant. The mid-green fronds are deeply indented, and fairly hardy in appearance. *B. brasiliense* will eventually form a small scaly trunk, with the rosette of fronds on top. *B. gibbum* grows to about 1m (3ft) with light-green fronds of glossy leaves, and makes a handsome specimen. A shady position with good ventilation suits them best. They prefer warmer temperatures in summer when growth is active, but less warm in winter. Maintain reasonable humidity. Propagation is by spores.

Houseplants need a fair amount of water as we all know. This consumption is explained through uptake by the plant and eventual transpiration, by evaporation from the soil and, in many cases, also through porous walls of pots. This last factor can be so bad that the soil ball can dry out completely. This can't happen so easily in non-porous pots. Always make sure that the pot has drainage holes. Porous pots can, of course, be treated with some type of coating. Remember to adjust the watering frequency as the soil will remain damp for longer.

233

*Davallia
canariensis*

Davallia
Hare's foot, Ball fern
A species that is becoming more popular, these ferns come from temperate climate zones. Their elegant, finely divided fronds grow 30–45cm high (12–18ins). *D. canariensis*, the hare's foot fern, gets its common name from its hairy roots that tend to grow over the edge of the container. *D. mariesii*, the ball fern has rhizomes that grow into ball shapes and has taller fronds. Likes a lighly shaded position, warmer in summer and cooler in winter. Water well in summer, less in winter. The hare's foot fern makes an ideal subject for hanging baskets, where their roots can completely wrap themselves around the basket. Baskets frequently leak, so hang them over a bath or in a conservatory so the frequent watering can't cause too much damage.

*Nephrolepis
exaltata*

Nephrolepis
Sword fern, Boston fern
Sword ferns, and especially the frilly types, are always in demand and make outstanding houseplants. They can carry on for many years and form large plants. There are a great many varieties with all manner of leaf formations and plant sizes. Some are best grown in pots, others better in hanging baskets. During the growing season regular feeding is advised, the results of which are soon apparent. A trough will soon be filled if just a few ferns are planted, as they can be vigorous growers. Propagation is thus very simple. Good light is preferred but fairly dark situations are tolerated. Drought, draughts and sudden temperature changes will adversely affect growth. After the more dormant winter period the fronds can be cut off, the plant re-potted, and summer growth restarted.

*Didymochlaena
truncatula*

Didymochlaena
A hardy fern, with fairly easy requirements, and a tolerance of fairly dark conditions. Its glossy, somewhat leathery leaflets start off light green, becoming darker as they mature. Fronds reach lengths of up to 45cm (18ins). A shady situation with warm temperatures in summer and regular watering. But it prefers cooler conditions and less water in winter. Spraying with water in summer is beneficial. Propagation is by means of spores sown in the usual manner onto a damp peat surface.

When insects are found on plants, you should examine both the plant's situation and the way it is being cared for. If a plant that prefers shade and high humidity is placed in a draughty, dry and sunny spot, it is far more likely to be attacked by mites. Controlling insects on ferns has to be done carefully. Scale and mealy bug, the most common invaders, are best removed by hand; mealy bug is easily killed when dabbed with a paint brush containing diluted spirits. But be careful as ferns have sensitive foliage. Some chemicals can do more harm than the pests will. Always remove badly infested fronds.

*Doryopteris
pedata*

Doryopteris
(sometimes listed as *Pteris*)
These are smaller tropical ferns with distinct hand-shaped fronds. *D. pedata* has two kinds of fronds, the broader one-piece sterile leaves on short stalks, and the taller and larger fertile leaves are deeply divided. Older foliage is of a darker green than that of the young fronds, and the stems become nearly black.
A bright situation, screened from direct sunlight, and high humidity are its primary needs, together with regular watering. Be sparing with feeding, and don't re-pot too soon. Day temperatures of about 25°C (76°F) and at night down to 15°C (60°F) are suitable. Propagate by spores or pinning leaflets with buds onto damp peat.

Pellaea rotundifolia

Pellaea rotundifolia
Button fern
In contrast to most ferns, this type requires good light and high summer temperatures. Neat, mid to dark green, round leaflets are to be found on alternate sides of the fronds with their slender rust coloured stems. They are low growing, being only 15–20cm (6–8ins) tall.
They make good ground-cover at the base of taller pot plants. Winter temperatures can drop to about 12°C (52°F). Regular watering is necessary but lower humidity is preferred. The foliage should not be sprayed. Hard water is tolerated. They are propagated from spores, but not terribly easily.

Platycerium bifurcatum

Platycerium
Stag's horn fern
The well known Stag's horn, with its hanging, deeply incised fronds is a very adaptable houseplant, and is less demanding than most fern species. These epiphytic ferns from the East Indies, will thrive in a cool greenhouse. The plant has two types of leaf — round, barren fronds that lie flat against the log or container in which they are growing, and the fertile, antler-shaped fronds that grow out from it, which start off narrow and then broaden and branch. It can be grown in a pot, or basket, or on a log. Watering is sometimes a bit tricky and may be replaced by the spraying of the roots only. The roots should be kept moist throughout the summer, and only slightly drier in winter. Try to keep the fronds dry but do not dust them with anything rough. Propagation by spores is difficult without the correct facilities.

Phlebodium aureum

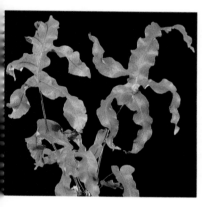

Phlebodium
(also known as *Polypodium*)
This large group of ferns has many differently shaped and sized plants. Their leathery fronds develop from creeping rhizomes, with shallow root systems. They are good plants for hanging baskets or shallow pots and some, such as *P. aureum* and its varieties are quite happy indoors. Provide a fair amount of space, as the fronds can grow to 1m (3ft) or more in length, and so can be quite spectacular as solitary specimens. They need fairly bright, indirect light, and as with most ferns, a fairly high level of humidity. Winter or night temperatures are best kept above 15°C (60°F) with day temperatures between 20 and 25°C (68 and 76°F). Keep soil moist but not soggy. Feed established plants monthly during the growing season with a diluted mixture. Propagate with spores or root cuttings.

Pteris cretica

Pteris
Brake
This is a genus of over 250 evergreen species, a few of which are very attractive small houseplants, and are widely grown commercially. These have deeply divided fronds, with leaflets in many shapes and colours. Most are fairly low growing and 'bushy'. They will not tolerate any sun. What they need is a relatively high humidity, especially when new fronds are forming. Water must be given regularly, preferbly soft water. Winter temperatures as low as 10°C (50°F) can be tolerated though slightly warmer for variegated types. The smaller growers are useful subjects for cases or bottle gardens. Re-potting is needed annually (twice per year for some). The easiest method of propagation is from spores.

Phyllitis scolopendrium

Phyllitis
Hart's tongue fern
Another fern which does not like direct sun, but otherwise is tolerant of lighter or darker conditions inside or outside, and at all times of the year. A hardy, upright-growing fern, with undivided, strap-like fronds. *P. scolopendrium* has several varieties, including *undulata* which has frilly edged fronds. Preferring a shady position, it will tolerate fairly poor light conditions. Water generously in summer, keep moist in winter. They originate in limey soils so do not mind chalky (hard) water.

Most ferns are forest species, but can be grown indoors, as long as the right conditions can be provided. Humus-rich soil, humidity and shade are most important.

Hanging and climbing plants

Hanging plants are generally easier to handle than climbing plants. The only major factor that distinguishes them from normal houseplants is their choice of location — they must be placed higher up, so that their trailing stems and blooms have 'downward' space in which to grow before they reach the floor. In this respect, it is most often found that baskets and pots provide an answer. A row of plants in pots located higher up in front of a window can form a 'green curtain', which can be very effective if not so dense as to block out too much light. Otherwise, pedestals, wall brackets or window sills provide good spots for them.

Hanging baskets or troughs and pots of hanging plants out of doors must be firmly secured, so that they cannot be dislodged as the plants become larger and heavier.

Climbing plants, whether indoors or out, need some type of support or framework up which they can climb. Whatever type of trellis or frame you use, do ensure that it can be readily extended, as many of the indoor climbers are fairly vigorous and can come to form fairly large plants.

Some climbers attach themselves to walls with their aerial roots *(Hedera, Philodendron scandens)*. They will grow happily on trellises as well, but keep a lookout for 'stray' stems. Most climbing stems will need to be tied to their support.

Plants that could be included in this chapter will also be found in other sections. *Saxifraga stolonifera* is listed with 'variegated plants', *Thunbergia alata* is to be found with 'flowering plants'.

Well-developed plantlets on Chlorophytum, soon become new plants when potted up.

Aeschynanthus speciosus

Aeschynanthus

If the correct conditions are provided this trailer can form a most attractive display. This epiphyte with ovate, pointed leaves arranged in opposite, alternate pairs is an ideal subject for hanging baskets. *A. speciosus* has pale green leaves and orange tubular flowers. *A. pulcher* has mid-green leaves and scarlet flowers with yellow necks. These species need warm temperatures and high humidity in summer, with regular watering and spraying during the main growing period. From spring until August feed with a lime-free fertiliser, use soft water if possible. High humidity is preferable in a lightly shaded spot. Winter temperatures should not drop below 13°C (56°F).

Ceropegia woodii

Ceropegia
String of hearts
The common name describes the well known trailing, succulent plant with small fleshy leaves arranged on string-like stems. *C. woodii*, commonly grown in hanging baskets, has grey-green mottled, heart-shaped leaves and small purple flowers. Good light and warm temperatures are needed, though cooler in winter. For a 'fuller' plant, one needs to put several plants in the pot, so that their stems can become entwined. They root easily from leaves. Growth is fairly slow. Normal potting soil can be used and less water is needed than for most plants. During the winter allow the soil to nearly dry out. Only feed sparingly while there is active growth.

Ampelopsis brevipedunculata

Ampelopsis

A plant that can be used as either a climber or trailing plant. It is sometimes sold as *Vitis* as it is a member of the vine family. *A. brevipedunculata* is a variegated form with mid-green leaves marbled with white and pink. Its blooms and its white, red or blue berries are not attractive, but the foliage and growth habit are rewarding. To maintain leaf colouring, the plant needs sun or strong light, and can be grown equally well in or out of doors during the summer, but it must be over wintered inside under cool conditions. Feed lightly as growth can be vigorous. Prune in spring for bushiness. Propagate from cuttings.

Chlorophytum comosum 'Variegatum'

Chlorophytum
Spider plant
A grass-like trailing plant from South Africa, it is one of the least demanding of indoor plants. Its narrow leaves arch gracefully and it sends out long slender runners which bear young plants on their tips, giving the plant its common name. *C. comosum* is plain green, and 'Variegatum' has a yellow-white stripe down the central rib. Light and temperature are not critical with this plant, so it can be tried in dark spots as well. Water regularly during the growing period, less in winter. With better care, *Chlorophytum* grows vigorously, and its roots form thick storage tubers. Does well as a hanger if given the space to produce an abundance of stems with plantlets.

Campanula isophylla 'Alba'

Campanula
Bell flower
Campanula is a genus of hardy and half hardy annuals, biennials and perennials. They bloom profusely in summer bearing their typical white or blue flowers. *C. fragilis* and *C. isophylla* are the trailing species most commonly grown indoors, with their star-shaped flowers they make ideal subjects for hanging baskets. They need good light, but keep them out of direct sunlight. They do not tolerate frost and need warm spring temperatures to start them off. They are rapid growers and so need plenty of water (often several times a day in hot weather). At the end of summer the plants can be cut back, almost to the ground, and can be over wintered in a cool spot, with less water. Propagate from tip cuttings, in spring, rooted in water.

Cissus antarctica

Cissus
The two best known hardy climbers of this genus are both excellent houseplants, and can be used as trailers as well. *C. antarctica* has shiny, simple leaves with toothed margins, while *C. rhombifolia* has its leaves divided into three leaflets. They do not like direct sunlight, but can tolerate fairly shady situations. They are also likely to suffer if their soil remains too moist. Being evergreen foliage plants, they have no real 'off' season, so can be kept in the same spot throughout the year. Support is needed, as tendrils need something to cling to. Tie unruly stems into the support. They prefer lime-rich soil, so use limed compost rather than peat. Re-pot in spring when cuttings can be taken.

*Clerodendron
thomsonii*

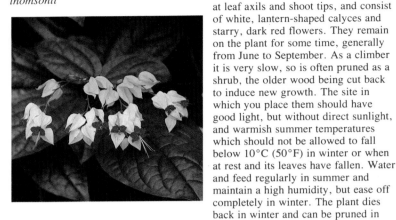

Clerodendrum

Another plant group, where many of its members are well known as houseplants. The climber, *C. thomsonii,* is the most important. It has glossy, dark green, oval-shaped leaves. The flowers are to be found in clusters at leaf axils and shoot tips, and consist of white, lantern-shaped calyces and starry, dark red flowers. They remain on the plant for some time, generally from June to September. As a climber it is very slow, so is often pruned as a shrub, the older wood being cut back to induce new growth. The site in which you place them should have good light, but without direct sunlight, and warmish summer temperatures which should not be allowed to fall below 10°C (50°F) in winter or when at rest and its leaves have fallen. Water and feed regularly in summer and maintain a high humidity, but ease off completely in winter. The plant dies back in winter and can be pruned in spring to stimulate new growth.

*Dipladenia
sanderi*

Dipladenia

Handsome climbing plants with mid-green oval, pointed leaves and trumpet-shaped pink or white flowers. The best species for indoor use are *D. splendens* with large, deep pink flowers, *D. sanderi,* with blooms of pink with yellow throats, and *D. boliviensis,* whose white blooms have yellow throats. Blooms last for some time and each cluster provides a continuous show during summer. The difficulty with these lovely climbers is that they need high humidity and spraying every day during hot weather. Place in reasonable light, but not direct sunlight, and water well in spring and summer making sure they are in a well drained potting mixture. Gradually decrease the amount of water in autumn and winter but do not allow them to dry out. Winter temperatures for dormancy should not be below 12°C (54°F) nor above 15°C (60°F).

*Columnea
hybrid*

Columnea

An epiphytic genus of sub-shrubs, and perennial climber, they make excellent hanging basket specimens. *C. microphylla* and *C. gloriosa* are the two most commonly grown, for their bright orange and yellow hooded flowers that appear at the leaf axils all the way down the long trailing stems. The leaves are small, dark green and velvety. Newer hybrids are brighter and easier to care for. They need good light but not direct sunlight, warm temperatures all year round, and high humidity. Water regularly with tepid lime-free water. The soil mixture should be light and well drained, but feed them only when growth starts and then with an orchid-growing fertiliser. For summer blooming types, winter temperatures may drop to 10°C (50°F) while winter flowerers need about 15°C (60°F). Propagate in spring with tip cuttings (heat may be needed).

Ficus pumila

Ficus pumila
Creeping fig
This member of the *Ficus* family has none of the usual *Ficus* characteristics. It can creep, climb or trail, depending on its habitat. It can be used as a ground-cover or, better still, in a hanging pot, where the stems are allowed to hang and trail informally. The neat, slightly wrinkled, little oval leaves are its juvenile stage. Larger leathery leaves develop on mature plants that are some size. When grown in a pot the smaller leaves are usually retained. If the plant becomes too large it can be cut back quite easily. This will provide you with tip cuttings which can be rooted in sand or water.

Hanging and climbing plants are best pruned in early spring. At the same time, you can use the prunings as cuttings, and they should root easily in water. Don't leave them in the water for too long; once the roots are about 2cm (¾in) long, pot them into light soil.

If hanging plants are too high, watering can become difficult. Also, these higher plants will need more frequent watering, as the air is warmer nearer the ceiling.

Gynura
Velvet plant

The startling purple-coloured foliage is the most striking feature of this smaller climbing or trailing plant, which grows to about 1m (3ft) in height. Its longish pointed leaves, with roughly toothed edges are covered in purple hairs. These give the plant a velvety appearance. Its summer needs are a sunny or light position, and warm temperatures, with regular watering and feeding. In winter don't feed, and water less. Keep temperatures at about 15°C (60°F) so that the plant can rest. To keep plants compact, pinch out buds, and keep cutting them back. It is often better to take cuttings in the autumn for the next season's plants. Older plants can become very straggly after a season's growth. The flowers produced in autumn have an unpleasant smell.

Gynura aurantiaca

Hedera
Ivy

Ivy is probably the best known indoor climber and includes several species and a whole assortment of varieties in all shades of green and variegation. They are all evergreen, non-flowering, and can be used as ground-cover, as climbers, or as trailers. Some varieties produce aerial roots freely and need watching if you don't want them clinging to your walls. They are generally tolerant of most conditions to be found in the home and many are good in darker situations. Water, in moderation, is needed throughout the year, as there is no proper resting period. Small-leafed varieties are suitable for cases and bottle gardens, and others can be very effectively allowed to trail from hanging baskets. Keep a lookout for red spider mites and scale insects.

Hedera

Hoya bella

Hoya
Wax flower

These attractive climbers with glossy, somewhat leathery, dark green leaves, have clusters of pendulous, waxy, star-shaped flowers. *H. carnosa* has several variegated forms. The flowers are pale pink to white with red centres. The wiry stems with leaves set wide apart look best when several stems are entwined to provide some denseness. *H. bella* is lower growing and is better suited to hanging baskets. It has silvery spots on its leaves, which are also more pointed. Hoyas need good light and warm temperatures without direct sunlight. Do not allow temperatures to fall below 10°C (50°F) in winter. To induce flowering a spring temperature of at least 16°C (62°F) is needed. Water moderately in summer, but keep just moist in winter.

Jasminum officinale

Monstera deliciosa

Passiflora caerulea

Jasminum
Jasmine

There are over 300 species of Jasmine, some are tender, some are winter-hardy. The Winter Jasmine (*J. nudiflorum*) is found in many gardens; other species are suitable for growing and flowering indoors. The typical 'Jasmine' flower is tubular, opening out to a star shape, often found in clusters, and sweet-smelling. They are usually white, white tinged pink or yellow. They need good light, warm summer and cool winter temperatures. Water generously in summer, less in winter. *Jasminum officinale* is a deciduous climber, which grows well indoors, and has highly perfumed blooms in summer and early autumn. It should be treated in the same way as the average houseplant with light, airy conditions in summer, with regular feeding and watering and a cool, drier spot for its dormant period, where temperatures of 5–10°C (40–50°F) are adequate.

Monstera
Swiss Cheese Plant

Large, leathery leaves with deep indentations or holes have given this group of plants its common name. These divisions are partly or wholly absent in juvenile leaves. The most commonly grown species of this group are *M. deliciosa* which develops deep indentations in its leaves; *M. obliqua,* a smaller growing species and *M. pertusa* which has denser foliage and smaller leaves. There are several other varieties too. These plants are heavy, and need support and tying for them to grow upright. They can eventually become quite large but can then be cut back. This provides cuttings and the plant will soon shoot out again. Plants are well adapted to indoor cultivation and can tolerate a wide range of conditions. A shady position with moderate temperatures and regular watering all year round are its primary needs. Spray occasionally in summer and wipe leaves with a damp sponge. Feed in summer, either via watering or spraying.

Passiflora
Passion Flower

Most Passiflora species grow best out of doors in summer, but are set back by winter frosts. They are flowering vines from the tropics and have complex, very exotic looking flowers and lobed leaves. They need good light with direct sun and good ventilation. Moderate temperatures and generous watering in summer, less in winter. Can be cut back in spring. Apart from *P. caerulea*, several other species and varieties are known, and many will grow well in a protected corner of the garden in summer but need protection in winter. Indoors, only very good light conditions will do, and a cooler winter temperature of about 10°C (50°F). Before re-potting, cut back older stems to 6–8 eyes. Summer pruning can encourage blooming.

Philodendron

Philodendron scandens

A genus of South American climbing and trailing plants, and some non-climbing species, that are probably the best known group of pot plants. *P. bipinnatifidum* and *P. selloum* are non-climbers which have dark green, deeply incised leaves, emerging from a central stem. *P. scandens* is a climber with small mid-green, heart-shaped leaves. *P. andreanum, P. panduriforme,* and *P. erubescens* are larger climbers, with larger, heart- or arrow-shaped, dark green leaves. There are a great many other species. They will tolerate a wide range of temperatures but not below about 10°C (50°F) in winter. They prefer good light and fair humidity, but not direct sunlight. Water regularly all year round. Pruning is very often necessary to control size, as some species are strong growers.

Rhoicissus

Rhoicissus rhomboidea

Hardy evergreen climbers, grown for their decorative foliage. *R. capensis* has woody stems and vine-like leaves that are dark green and glossy. *R. rhomboidea* has dark green leaves of three-lobed leaflets with deeply dentated edges. The former has been popular since Victorian times. Both make excellent houseplants, and can be trained up trellises into screens or columns of glossy, evergreen foliage, usually as a multi-stemmed plant. They prefer cool to moderate temperatures, and good ventilation. They need good light and regular watering all year round. Re-pot annually and feed during the growing season. Propagate from stem cuttings.

Piper nigrum
Pepper

Piper nigrum

This is the plant from which our black and white peppercorns originate. It comes from tropical East Africa and from India, and needs warm, humid conditions. It has attractive, dark green, oval pointed leaves and needs a lot of support for its weak stems. *P. ornatum* can be used as a trailer or climber: its foliage is more attractive but it has no berries. Both can be grown in good light with shading from direct sunlight. Feed and water regularly in summer and spray to increase humidity. Apply less water in winter but maintain temperatures at a minimum 12°C (52°F). Plants will die if their roots dry out completely. Propagate from cuttings, using heat.

Stephanotis
Madagascar jasmine

Stephanotis floribunda

Another pleasant smelling and easy climber whose blooms have long been used in bridal bouquets. The blooms are borne in clusters on slender, twining stems that need support. If conditions are right, growth is very vigorous and they can become quite large. This results in their being less 'portable', which can be a problem as they prefer cooler winter temperatures, of 10–14°C (50–56°F), which may be too low for your living-room. Re-pot regularly while young to keep pace with growth (at least once a year). Flowering will increase as growth slows. They prefer good light, warmer conditions in summer, and regular watering and feeding.

Rhaphidophora (syn. Scindapsus)
Devil's ivy

Rhaphidophora aurea

This trailing or climbing plant is popular as a pot plant. It can grow to 2m (6ft) or more *R. aurea* has oval, pointed leaves as a juvenile, and more heart shaped when mature. These are yellow-cum-cream and green, while the variety 'Marble Queen' is cream with green spots. They need good light without direct sunlight, and warm temperatures which should not fall below 15°C (60°F) in winter. Water generously all year round. Moderate humidity is preferred. They respond well to feeding in summer, but need support for climbing. Moss sticks for rooting as they grow are most suitable. Propagate them from tips or stem of a leaf.

A hanging container should both be of an adequate size and contain a water retentive soil. The traditional wire baskets with most linings are best used out of doors, unless they are first lined with a plastic sheet to reduce the chance of water dripping. Moss can be used to camouflage the plastic.

Tradescantia

Tradescantia

Spiderwort or Wandering Jew
These well known creeping plants are part of a much larger group, with many species and varieties suitable for the house or greenhouse. Those suitable for the house need fair light conditions, fresh air and average temperatures. They do best as ground-cover, or in hanging baskets. The best known species, *T. albiflora* has several colour varieties, in whitish shades; they need regular trimming to keep them in check. *T. blossfeldiana* is a robust, more upright type with hairy, dark green leaves, purple underneath, or with green and white variegations. Plants can either be treated as annuals, with new plants grown from cuttings, or they can be 'carried over' for several years. Feeding must be moderate, and soil kept moist, but never too wet.

Zebrina pendula

Zebrina

This group is closely related to *Tradescantia*; the plants look similar but their requirements differ. While *Tradescantia* will tolerate darker conditions, these plants need bright, screened light and adequate warmth. They have several colour variations, but all variegated. Their runners can easily reach lengths of ½m (18ins). Care of these plants differs too. They dislike water with any lime content and the same applies to soil. Any feeding should be diluted and infrequent. They will not tolerate cold conditions (below 15°C (60°F)), so care has to be taken in winter. Cuttings from stems or tips are easily rooted in sand or water.

Ferns can be grown from spores. It is easier than one might think. The spore sacs are found on the undersides of mature fronds. Tap the frond gently over a sheet of white paper, and you can gather the dust like spores. Sprinkle these onto the surface of a sterilised, peaty potting soil in a sterile tray. The soil must be damp but not wet. Cover the tray with a sheet of glass.

It is important to know something about the growth and habitat requirements of a hanging or climbing plant, before deciding on a more permanent spot for it. If, for example, you place a Philodendron scandens on a low sideboard, it'll soon be spreading along the floor, which was probably not the intention. A higher position would suit better, and you can train the stems up and down on some type of trellis.

Flowering plants

Short-term colour

One of the many pretty Primula hybrids.

In this section, plants that only have a short life-span (and so are treated as annuals), are described. The characteristic of an annual is that it grows from seed into a plant that produces flowers, fruits and seeds, and then dies off, before the winter. A great many of the popular garden flowers, ornamental grasses, herbs and everlastings belong to this group.

Because of its rapid burst of growth and flowering, the plant has huge demands made of its system, and is soon exhausted. It is commonly seen that insects and disease will attack plants shortly after their peak blooming, as their resistance becomes lower. For this reason some perennial plants, that don't die off completely after flowering, are best dumped rather than trying to induce them to produce more blooms. However, if you are inclined to, it is possible to over winter some flowering houseplants and then to get them to flower again the following season. The boundary between 'annual' and 'perennial' is vague, and often depends on your own treatment of them once the plant has bloomed. Thus, in the section on perennial plants, there are some that could just as well appear in this section.

Begonia

From this large family we will only be dealing with the specific flowering types: the fibrous-rooted begonias *B. 'Gloire de Lorraine'*, *B. elatior* hybrids, and hybrids of *B. semperflorens*. These are the three most important blooming groups, and the latter two types can also be grown outside. Temperatures that are too high are harmful, as all prefer somewhat cooler situations — approx. 20°C (70°F). *B. 'Gloire de Lorraine'* flowers in winter, bearing pink single flowers. *B. semperflorens* make small mounds of various colours (often used as summer bedding plants). *B. elatior* hybrids bear larger blooms of more distinct colours. These plants all need good light and a cool position. Water regularly with soft water. Spray to keep humidity high. Two common diseases, mildew and stem rot, are not easily cured so it is best to destroy the plants.

Begonia 'Gloire de Lorraine'

Chrysanthemum indicum

Chrysanthemum

One of the best known flowering houseplants, much beloved by the Japanese, *C. indicum* and *C. morifolium* are very commonly grown as indoor pot plants. They are available in a wide range of colours and sizes, some reaching a height of up to 45cm (18ins). As they are not permanent houseplants their needs, while their blooms last, are basic: they like a well-lit spot, fairly cool but not draughty, and regular watering. After flowering they can be cut back severely, and then planted in the garden. Otherwise, they are best over wintered in a glasshouse or conservatory with a temperature of about 8–10°C (46–50°F) and fairly dry conditions. Propagate from young shoots in spring.

Calceolaria

Calceolaria

Slipper flower

The common name originates from the weirdly shaped, brightly coloured blooms. Growing to about 30cm (12ins) high, with slightly hairy leaves, these annuals have flowers with a balloon-like lower lip in shades of yellow, orange or red, with darker blotches. It flowers in early summer; the flowers last for some time. Place in a cool position with good light but not in direct sunlight. A north-facing window sill would suit. Water regularly and see that air circulation is good, but keep these and any other plants out of draughts. Grow from seed, but cuttings are possible.

Exacum affine

Exacum affine

Persian violet

A sweet-smelling, busy annual bearing pretty lilac-blue flowers with yellow centres. Blooms in mid-summer, for about 6 weeks and can then be discarded. It should be placed in good light, but out of direct sunlight. Cooler temperatures and regular watering with soft water are best. This is a succulent plant and will not recover if the roots dry out. Grow from seed sown in December in a warm case.

Capsicum annum varieties

Capsicum

Ornamental peppers

These annuals are grown for their brightly coloured fruits rather than for their insignificant flowers. They are available in a range of sizes and fruit colours, from dwarf to 45cm (18ins) in height. Fruit colours can vary from green, red and yellow to purple. The fruits remain on the plant for a long time and are very popular at Christmas time. Care is simple: they need good light without direct sunlight, in a spot that is cool but not too dry, and need to be watered regularly. If conditions are unsuitable, the fruits will soon shrivel. Save some of the fruits to provide seed for the next season. Although the fruits look appetising, these types are not edible.

Impatiens walleriana

Impatiens

Busy Lizzie

These plants earned their name from their rapid growth and free-flowering habit. They form bushy plants with thick, fleshy stems and bright green leaves. The flowers, from white, pink, red, orange to purple are slightly succulent and translucent. There are several hybrids available, some with semi-double flowers or with multi-coloured blooms. They are equally good out of doors during the summer. Make sure the potting soil drains well and water freely, but do not spray the foliage. Place them in a good light shaded from direct sunlight, in an airy but not too cold a spot. They tend to suffer from dry air during winter (from central heating) but cuttings are easily taken, and will root easily in sand or water. Sowing is also easy and the newer varieties are always tempting.

Ixora hybrid

Ixora

An attractive evergreen shrub from India with leathery, shiny green leaves, it can grow up to 1m (3ft) high, and bears clusters of blooms in summer, ranging from red to orange and pink (according to the variety). During summer, this plant needs high humidity, fairly high temperatures and good, shaded light. Temperatures about 18°C (64°F) in winter are suitable. Water generously in spring and summer, less in winter if you are trying to over winter it. Problems arise with over wintering; it requires bottom heat to maintain roots at 18–20°C (64–68°F) (throughout the year), although air temperature can be a bit lower. Lime, in either soil or water, is not tolerated.

Thunbergia alata

Thunbergia

Black-eyed Susan
A quick-growing climber, usually treated as an annual, it is very effective in hanging baskets or trained up a small trellis. They are also easy to over winter. Different varieties have blooms of varying shades of yellow. Provided with a sunny situation, adequate water and feeding, Thunbergia will flourish. A chalky soil is preferred. In a hanging basket, plant more than one seedling to make for a denser mass. Sow seeds in the spring. Within 10 to 14 weeks you should have plants in flower. It is easiest to sow the seed directly into the pot or basket.

Primula vulgaris

Primula

Primrose
Commonly used as spring flowering bedding plants, some *Primula* varieties will also grow indoors under coolish conditions. Typical compact growing rosettes of mid-green leaves bear clusters of flowers on short stems in a wide range of colours. *P. malacoides* is a scented, smaller flowered species, *P. obconica,* with hairy leaves that can cause an allergic reaction in some people, has larger flowers at the top of erect stems. *P. vulgaris,* an older type, has various coloured blooms on shorter stems. All three types can be grown indoors and require similar conditions. They need good light but definitely not direct sunlight, and are especially sensitive to drying out, draughts and too much humidity. For over wintering, temperatures can drop to 10°C (50°F). Propagate from seed.

Senecio cruentus

Senecio cruentus

Cineraria
These are true throwaway plants, but they certainly give value for money. With good care you can enjoy a full month of colour from each plant, and they are available in such a wide range of colours and sizes that it is often difficult to make your choice. Bought plants are specially grown under glass for indoor conditions, but they are otherwise fairly hardy. In the home they prefer not to be too warm. Temperatures between 10 and 15°C (50 and 60°F) are adequate, semi-shade and tepid water are also appreciated. Seed sown in April can produce plants that will flower between December and June, but handling is often full of pitfalls.

Impatiens balsamina, an exceptional 'Busy Lizzie'.

Perennial and permanent flowering plants

Cyclamen blooms are equally attractive on the plant or in a vase.

The range of flowering plants suitable for indoor use is very large, and very fortunately so. A few colourful plants on the window sills, or in selected positions within the home make a welcome addition to the decor. There are spring flowerers, that include certain *Primula* and *Medinilla's*. Others can flower all the year round, for example, think of *Stephanotis* and *Streptocarpus*. Unless the flowering plant has attractive foliage, you must reckon on it not looking at its best after it has finished flowering. This is easily solved by moving such plants to less conspicuous positions. Together with foliage plants, flowering plants form the basis of most indoor plant displays. If you wish to enjoy them fully you will have to pay attention to their individual needs and environmental demands. To get them to produce their very best, flowering plants need good light and temperatures that are not too high. Adequate water and the absence of draughts are of equal importance. Light, water and draught-free conditions can be regulated fairly easily, but the temperature in most homes is very often higher than the plants actually need. This can be overcome to an extent by placing the plants as low down as possible, and at night putting them in a draught-free position on the floor, thereby making use of the lowest temperature in that room. Flowering plants must be watered with more care than foliage plants. The more sensitive plants will show you immediately when they are short of water, often by dropping flower buds or leaves. An overflowing window sill containing a flowering mass of only one or two different types of plant can look very impressive. For instance, a trough-full of *Gazania* or *Pachystachys,* can be quite spectacular. If the plants are all in pots of matching colours, the effect is improved even more. Compare this with a display of four different plants on a sill, each in a pot of a different colour and size. Uniformity is usually more harmonious. When choosing flowering plants you should not forget to take into account the foliage plants you already have, and especially the variegated types, with stronger colouring. The blooms must harmonize with each other, with the plants close by, and with the surroundings. Combining colours becomes more difficult with variegated plants, as too many different colours in a group can give a confused and unattractive effect. Plants that will combine well with the plants listed in this section will be found in the chapters on Hanging and climbing plants and on Orchids.

247

*Abutilon
megapotanicum*

Abutilon
These are evergreen shrubs from the tropics, a few species of which are grown as pot plants. *A. megapotanicum* is a spreading shrub with bright green leaves on hanging branches, and pendulant flowers with yellow petals and red calyces, in summer and autumn. There is also a variegated type. *A. striatum* is a more delicate, upright shrub, with pale orange or salmon flowers, with darker veining. The variety *'Thompsonii'* has yellow mottling on the leaves. Plants need pruning in spring as they tend to become very twiggy. They need good light without direct sunlight. Warm temperatures in summer and cooler in winter. Water regularly in summer while they are growing, and less in winter. The plant should be put outside if possible in summer. Summer feeding is beneficial. Allow winter resting, at about 15°C (60°F).

*Anthurium
schezerianum*

Anthurium
Flamingo flower
Grown both for their attractive glossy, large green leaves and spathe-like flowers these plants originate from the tropics of Central and South America. The flowers consist of a brightly coloured, waxy spathe, ranging from white through pinks, orange to red, and a spadix or central spike, which may be curled. They need good light without direct sunlight and reasonably high temperatures, though never below 16°C (62°F) in winter. Because they should be planted in a loose, well drained potting mixture, they should be regularly watered with soft water. The humidity also needs to be kept high. This and feeding are the two vital tasks (use a hydroponic-type fertiliser). Propagate from seed or by division.

*Acalypha
hispida*

Acalypha
Chenille plant
A genus from the warmer parts of the world, usually grown for their brightly coloured leaves. The flowers are usually insignificant, except for *A. hispida* which has bright red tail-like blooms in summer. *A. wilkesiana* is a shrub with coppery foliage with red markings and patterns, (depending on the variety). The plants need good light and warm temperatures, not below 18°C (64°F) in winter. Water regularly during the growing period, and provide humidity throughout the year. Plants are very sensitive to cold water. Dead blooms should be removed, and the plant pruned regularly, for bushiness, and resultant new foliage.

*Begonia
metallica*

Begonia metallica
One of the perennial, fibrous-rooted group of begonias, this one is from Brazil. It grows into a handsome shrub with ovate, pointed leaves with a green, metallic sheen. The flowers are pinkish-white or red shades. Plants can grow to 1m (3ft) or more in height. *B. foliosa,* or fern-leaf begonia, has tiny leaves on twiggy stems, which arch downwards. It has small red, white or pink flowers. All these Begonia types need a draught free position with good light. Temperatures should not drop below 18°C (64°F). Water regularly but allow plant to dry out in between. Lime-free fertiliser during the growing season is best although lime in the water does this group no harm. Over winter in a cooler spot, and prune heavily in spring, before new growth starts.

*Astilbe
'Straussenfeder'*

Astilbe
More usually seen outdoors, especially around garden pools, the shorter growing varieties of this plant make good pot plants. They have deeply divided, dark green foliage that has coppery tints when young, and plumes of small flowers, usually pinks, reds or cream. *A. chinensis pumila, A. x crispa* and *A. glaberrima* are some of the lower growing varieties. Pot up in September or October and leave in cold frame or cold glasshouse until December. Gradually increase temperature to about 15°C (60°F) to encourage flowering. These plants need to be kept constantly moist, and stand in a light position. After blooming, plants can be planted in the garden.

*Begonia
semperflorens*

Begonia semperflorens
A fibrous-rooted *Begonia* that flowers all year round and can be kept for several seasons, but is usually treated as an annual. Hybrids have been developed with compact, branching habits and glossy green, purple or red leaves. Among the popular green-leaved varieties are 'Flamingo', with white blooms edged with pink, 'Organdy' a mixture of white, pink and red flowers and 'Pandy', with deep red flowers. Place in good light and even a bit of sun. Water regularly with soft water and keep humidity high. They prefer a loose, humus-rich soil in a shallow, wide container. If plants are attacked by either stem rot or mildew, the two main enemies, it's best to discard the plants, as the conditions are probably unsuited.

Beloperone guttata

Beloperone
Shrimp plant

A smallish, twiggy upright plant, from Mexico, grown for the strange flower heads, which are made up of overlapping pinkish-brown bracts and protect the white flowers. It has oval pointed leaves of mid-green, and flowers throughout the year. Although a shrub, it is commonly treated as an annual. Grow in a cool, well ventilated place, in good light but not in direct sunlight. Water freely from April right through the summer, but ease off in winter, and give only enough to prevent drying out. Winter temperatures must remain between 12 and 15°C (54 and 60°F). Young plants need to be disbudded to encourage bushy growth. Older dormant plants must be heavily pruned in February, and then re-potted. Can be put outdoors in summer. Use prunings as cuttings.

Clivia miniata

Clivia
Strap-like, dark green, glossy leaves and a flower spike with ten or more trumpet-shaped orange flowers, make this a popular pot plant, which has been in use since Victorian times. *C. miniata* from South Africa is the most showy. They are undemanding as to conditions and would benefit from being put outside in summer, in a semi-shaded position. Their biggest asset is their tolerance to darker conditions, (where most plants would not survive). Dry air and occasional lack of water also pose no problem. They prefer good light and a cooler position in summer. Water regularly but do not allow soil to remain wet. Do not allow the plants to become frosted during winter rest, when they barely need any water. Re-potting should be infrequent, as they bloom best when pot-bound, growing in a clump.

Bougainvillea glabra

Bougainvillea
A vigorous climber from Brazil, its beauty is not in the flowers, which are insignificant but in the brightly coloured, papery bracts which surround them. These bracts can persist on the plant for a long time, through spring and summer. A very common climber in warmer climates, it dislikes too much cold, and won't survive more than a mild winter outdoors. The best species for pot cultivation are *B. glabra* of which there are several hybrids and *B. buttiana* 'Mrs Butt' which has crimson flower bracts. These are normally sun-loving plants and can benefit from being placed outside in summer. They need good light, and an airy warm position. Water freely but ease off in winter, keep them just moist. Winter temperatures should not drop below 8–10°C (48–50°F). Beware of early and late frosts. Prune after flowering to keep the plant compact.

Brunfelsia pauciflora

Brunfelsia
An evergreen shrub from Central and South America, it really belongs in the conservatory but can be grown in the living room. It has oval pointed, mid-green leaves and flat-faced, round petaled flowers, either lilac/blue or white that are very sweet smelling. These can be produced during most months of the year. Needs good light and can be put outside during summer in a semi-shaded position. Also needs good light in winter, when temperatures can be allowed to drop a little. Water generously in summer and maintain reasonable humidity. Less water in winter, dislikes drought, draughts and dry atmosphere. Can become prone to attack by mealy bug and red spider. Prune carefully, as cut branches don't always shoot again easily as with most shrubs.

If flowering plants are combined with others in a trough, you shouldn't only use plants that you find attractive. First ensure that all the plants have similar needs. It is also more attractive to use a few plants of the same variety, amongst or against contrasting foliage-plants. This can accentuate the blooms and appear more harmonious.

As a rule, most plants will enjoy a bathe under a real or artificial shower of rain. This includes flowering plants. In general, blooms will be spoiled by water, so either avoid getting them wet, or make up some type of screening from cardboard or plastic before spraying with water.

Crossandra infundibuliform- is 'Mona Wallhead'

Crossandra

A tropical evergreen sub-shrub, growing 30cm–1m (1–3ft) high. It has dark green, glossy leaves and terminal clusters of salmon pink flowers, consisting of a slender tube ending in five, lobed petals, three of which form a lip. Flowers from April until the autumn. Place in a warm spot with good light, but shaded from direct sunlight. The temperature must be kept above 18°C (64°F) throughout the year, and humidity kept reasonably high. Water regularly with tepid, soft water, and feed during spring and summer. If spraying for humidity, avoid wetting the blooms. Propagate from cuttings in spring, using bottom heat.

Fuchsia

One of the most versatile of summer-flowering shrubs (native to Central and South America) it can be planted in hanging baskets, pots and garden beds. The hanging, bell-like flowers have calyx and corolla in contrasting shades of pink, red, purple, or white. The variations in colour combinations and flower formation are extremely great, and there are many collectors and specialist growers. Some types can be grown indoors but they tend to 'stretch' from lack of light, are best put outside in summer, or grown in a conservatory. They need a well ventilated position with good light but need to be shaded from direct sunlight. Warm temperatures in summer, with high humidity. For winter rest, temperatures can drop to about 15°C (60°F). Water regularly in summer, less in winter and feed weekly during the whole of the growing season. Prune in March, but regular nipping of buds may be needed during the season.

Fuchsia

Erica

Erica
Heather

A genus of over 500 species, Heathers are found in a variety of sizes, colours and flowering habits. The autumn and winter flowering varieties, *E. gracilis* and *E. hyemalis* are commonly grown as pot plants for the Christmas trade. These are lime tolerant. They have pink or pink and white bell-like flowers, and fine needle-like leaves. Other species can follow in a succession that can provide colour throughout the year. They like good light and can be put outside in the sun in summer. Cool temperatures in winter 6–8°C (42–46°F). Water regularly in summer, less in winter. Virtually all the heathers dislike lime, either in water or soil. Propagate by division or cuttings, with rooting powder.

Gardenia jasminoides

Gardenia

A tender evergreen shrub with handsome glossy, dark green leaves. Bears rose-like, semi-double, waxy white flowers. These have a strong perfume. *G. jasminoides* is the best species for pot cultivation. The variety 'Fortuniana' is an excellent double-white, with full flowers 7cm (3ins) in diameter. This is another shrub that needs good light and will benefit from being in a sunny position outside in mid-summer, but beware of early and late frosts. They need average temperatures indoors in summer, not too low humidity, and regular feeding in summer, though slightly less in winter. The water and soil should be lime-free. Propagate from tip cuttings, under glass. The well known *Camellia* requires similar treatment.

Euphorbia pulcherrima

Euphorbia pulcherrima
Poinsettia

A deciduous shrub from Mexico that is very popular as a Christmas decoration. It has eliptical, dark green leaves with shallow lobes. The terminal bracts are bright red, pink or white, with insignificant flowers arranged at their centres. All varieties need 'short day' treatment, to induce them to bloom. They are placed in controlled situations for a while, with less than 10 hours of light per day, which starts the flower development. In this way, the time of blooming can be controlled too. Prune back after blooming, remember that the *milky sap is poisonous*. They need good light, without direct sunlight. Warm temperatures in winter, not below 18°C (64°F). Water regularly with tepid water.

Gazania splendens

Gazania

A low perennial, herbaceous plant from Southern Africa. They have large daisy-like flowers, very often with zonal markings, in a wide range of colours, yellow, orange, pink, and red with bronze or brown markings. Foliage is either mid-green or grey. They are most commonly used as annuals, and are not usually regarded as being suitable for use indoors, but they can do quite well. Regular feeding and re-potting, and plenty of light are their primary needs. They grow quite vigorously, and a group of plants can produce a sea of colour. Grow from seed, or slips of better varieties.

Hibiscus

Hibiscus
rosa-sinensis

H. rosa-sinensis is a warm-climate evergreen shrub, suitable for pot culture, and for tubs when larger. It must be protected, indoors, during winter, as extremes of cold will kill the plant. It is related to the deciduous *H. syriacus*, which is equally attractive in bloom, but is only suitable for conditions outside.

Hibiscus, with its many colour varieties, needs careful handling to ensure good flowering. Winter rest, with temperatures between 10 and 15°C (50 and 60°F) are needed. In spring, a light and warm spot is needed, to prepare for blooming, with average watering and feeding provided. If the conditions are not favourable, then flower buds are likely to drop off. Pruning is only needed for shaping and controlling size.

Jacobinia

Jacobinia
carnea

Two species of *Jacobinia*, a smaller tropical shrub with pink or orange terminal flower clusters, are suitable for growing indoors. *J. pauciflora*, the more difficult of the two, has red or yellow hanging blooms. *J. carnea* needs semi-shade and high humidity, and a minimum winter temperature of around 20°C (68°F). Needs regular watering and spraying, plus feeding while actively growing and blooming; use luke-warm water.

J. pauciflora needs over wintering at a temperature of 10°C (50°F) until February, if it is to flower. During summer, 16–20°C (62–70°F) is adequate. Place outside after flowering. Pests are likely if humidity becomes too low. *J. carnea* needs heavy pruning in spring, and a spacious pot.

In most cases, the stakes supporting plants will be found to be too short. This outright statement may sound harsh, but look around: plants everywhere are outgrowing their canes or trellises. The need for longer stakes is ever-present. You have probably seen vain attempts at lengthening stakes by tying on all manner of 'extensions'. Could this perhaps provide a suggestion for a Christmas or birthday present? A selection of canes, ranging from about 50cm (19½ins) to about 3m (9ft 10ins) in length could be a useful present to a keen indoor gardener.

Plants that need to be pruned and re-potted in spring, need to be handled with extra care. Obviously, you can't do both operations together; this means a test of adaptability for the plant. The pruning wounds have to heal and the roots need to establish themselves in the new soil. It is a fact that if a plant loses some roots, you can compensate by removing some top-growth. In general, the best time to prune will be in March, and to re-pot in April.

Medinilla

Medinilla
magnifica

This tropical plant is not really a plant for the living room, but rather for a heated glasshouse or window case. It forms an attractive evergreen shrub, with elliptical, dark green leaves with prominent veins, and rosy pink, pendulant flowers. These are carried in clusters that can reach 30cm (12ins) in length. The plant should be placed in a room with good light and high humidity whilst in bloom. Water generously, using soft water. In a case, temperatures should be above 20°C (70°F) in summer, and 15–17°C (60–62°F) from November to February, whilst the flower buds are forming. Temperature changes must be made gradually.

Myrtus

Myrtus
communis

Myrtle

A half-hardy shrub with aromatic leaves. *M. communis* has dark-green, shiny, oval pointed leaves and white saucer-shaped flowers and a prominent spray of stamens. Can be grown in a pot either as a bush or a standard. Place in the garden during summer, until the arrival of the first frost. Indoors, they need good shaded light, and ventilation. Winter temperatures can be between 5 and 12°C (40 and 52°F). If too warm or too dark, then diseases are likely. Water with soft water, and use a lime-free soil. Propagate by cuttings, in summer.

251

*Nertera
granadensis*

Nertera

This flat-growing little plant is really bought for its berries rather than its flowers. It has moss-like, pale-green foliage, and a creeping habit. It flowers from April to May, but is covered in orange berries from August until the end of the year. For best growth, it needs a cool position in summer, with plenty of light, and in winter must be kept above 10°C (50°F). Water regularly, taking care not to over-water. Feeding must also be moderate, especially with nitrogen, or growth will be too lush to the cost of the blooms. Multiply by seed or division.

*Pentas
lanceolata*

Pentas

A soft, winter-flowering shrub with light-green, down covered leaves. Flowers are born in terminal clusters, in shades of red, pink or white. They are tubular, opening at the ends into a star shape. Plants are inclined to become straggly if not pruned, or if tips are not nipped out. They need good light, and would benefit from being outdoors during summer. Warm temperatures are needed in winter. Water regularly while growing and flowering, then ease off. Feed from spring until they flower. Prune young plants to form framework of stems, and cut back heavily each spring. Use prunings as cuttings.

*Pachystachys
lutea*

Pachystachys

Very similar in appearance to the Shrimp plant, *Beloperone,* this small and slender shrub has small white flowers that emerge from a protective head of overlapping yellow bracts. These appear at the tips of shoots (like candles) and remain on the plant for a fair while. Leaves are narrow and pointed, mid-green in colour. Plants need good light and warm temperatures during growth. Water freely in summer, and somewhat less in winter, when the temperature can drop to 15°C (60°F). Pruning should be done in early spring; cut back all stems to encourage new growth and a more compact plant. Use tips as cuttings.

Plectranthus

Plectranthus

A vigorous creeping and trailing plant usually grown for its attractive foliage, it makes a good subject for hanging baskets, but can become too big for a window sill. *P. coleoides* is a trailing plant with furry leaves, pale green with white margins. The leaves are oval with scolloped edges. The blooms are 'candles' on erect stems of white and purple. They appear in October and will continue until spring. *Plectranthus* likes a sunny position, with moderate temperatures, but in winter not below 15°C (60°F). Water well throughout the year. Feeding and humidity in moderation too, fairly dry conditions are tolerated. Light, humus-rich soils are best, in spacious pots.

*Pelargonium
radens*

Pelargonium

There are three main groups of *Pelargonium.* The first group, which includes *P. radens,* has attractive aromatic foliage. The second group is formed of *P. grandiflorum* hybrids, and the third flowering group comprises hybrids of *P. zonale,* the well known 'Geranium'. Members of the first two groups can be grown indoors, provided there is sufficient light to prevent 'stretching'. Protect from sun during hottest times of day; plants can be placed outside during summer. Warmer temperatures are preferred in summer, slightly cooler in winter, but do protect them from frost. They like an alkaline potting soil and water. Propagate from cuttings or seed.

*Plumbago
auriculata*

Plumbago

A rambler rather than climber, *P. capensis* from South Africa has terminal trusses of pale blue flowers. The flowers are narrow tubes, opening at the ends to five starry petals. The leaves are an attractive pale green colour. A plant will flower from April until November. Likes good light but not direct sunlight, and can be placed outside in summer in dappled shade. Beware of early frosts though! Water regularly during summer. Needs temperatures above 14°C (56°F) in winter, and less water, but still needs light. Will drop most of its foliage in autumn. Re-pot in spring after heavy pruning. New shoots can be cut later, as cuttings.

*Primula
praenitens*

Primula
Primrose
For their lasting ability, *P. sinensis* and *P. obconica* are both useful species. *P. obconica* has light green leaves that are hairy, and can *cause an allergic reaction in some people.* The flowers are 'umbels', carried on upright stems, in pink, red and shades of purple. *P. sinensis* has darker leaves that grow in rosettes. Flowers are similar to *P. obconica,* but petals are dentated. Place in a position with good light but not direct sunlight, indoors or out. Cool temperatures and regular watering is needed to prevent roots from drying out. *P. obconica* is more lime-tolerant than most. Winter temperatures should be about 12°C (52°F). Plants will bloom from January to April, and are grown from seed.

*Spathiphyllum
floribundum*

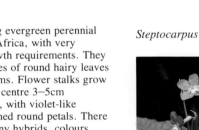

Spathiphyllum
White Flag
A tropical evergreen perennial, these lily-like plants are popular and hardy pot plants. Bright green, spear-shaped shiny leaves grow up from the ground. The flowers grow on long, slender stems and produce a white, leaf-like 'spathe' with a yellow 'spadix'. *'Mauna Loa'* is a good hybrid that flowers all year round. *Spathiphyllums* are able to tolerate conditions that are far too dark for most other plants. Their preference though is for good light, without direct sun. In autumn and winter place in the best light position available. Lack of humidity causes no problem, the temperature should not be below 16°C (60°F) in winter. Water regularly throughout the year. Feed sparingly in summer, when buds are forming. Re-pot in spring, in rich compost, roots should first have filled the pot completely.

*Saintpaulia
ionantha*

Saintpaulia
African violet
A low growing evergreen perennial from Central Africa, with very particular growth requirements. They produce rosettes of round hairy leaves on straight stems. Flower stalks grow from the plant centre 3—5cm (1½—2ins) tall, with violet-like flowers, flattened round petals. There are a great many hybrids, colours range from purple to blue, pink and white. Many double varieties are also available. Provide a shady spot in summer, and more light in winter, but never direct sunlight. Dislike any draught. Winter temperature must be at least 15°C (60°F). Warmth is always needed, but conditions should not be too dry. Watering with soft, tepid water should always be from below, and never onto leaves and flowers. Re-pot only when necessary. Propagate by leaf cuttings.

Steptocarpus

Streptocarpus
Cape Primrose
A low growing herbacious plant from South Africa that has been developed into many hybrid forms. They produce a rosette of short strap-like leaves with a corrugated surface. The trumpet shaped flowers are borne on slender stems, colours range from shades of pink and red to deep blue and purple. Plants are better suited to glasshouses and conservatories, so beware of draughts, direct sun and dry air. Place in good light and in a well ventilated position. Winter temperatures should be warm, a minimum 18°C (64°F) are needed. Keep humidity high, and water regularly during summer, though less in winter, using soft water that is not cold. Propagation is by seed or by leaf cuttings.

*Solanum
capsicastrum*

Solanum
Nightshade
Half-hardy evergreen shrublets from Brazil, *S. capsicastrum,* and the larger *S. pseudocapsicum* are popular pot plants. They have dark green, oval pointed leaves and white insignificant flowers, the decorative value of the plant lies in its attractive fruits that form after flowering. They start off like green marbles changing colour as they mature through yellow to red. Plants can become quite large under the right conditions. Place in a sunny position which is warm in summer, but cool in winter. Water regularly while plant is in berry. Ease off later. Prune in spring, and increase heat and start feeding.

*Zantedeschia
elliottiana*

Zantedeschia
Arum or Calla Lily
A genus of rhizomatous plants that flower in spring and summer. They have typical green, fleshy arrow-shaped leaves and well known arum-lily flowers. *Z. aethiopica* has white blooms, *Z. elliotiana* has bright yellow, and *Z. rehmannii* has pink flowers. After the plants have bloomed, they need a rest period, as the foliage fades, watering should be reduced completely. After a while, new growth recommences, and the plant can be placed outside and even in the garden. In October they can be lifted, and brought indoors, at a 10°C (50°F) temperature, until the end of November. The rhizome is left in the pot until it has again flowered. Propagate by division of sideshoots.

Indoor Shrubs

*A camellia
blooms freely
under the right
conditions.*

Plants with woody stems are called shrubs.
Under the heading, 'Indoor Shrubs', are
grouped shrubs that are grown in gardens
both here and in warmer parts of the world.
The distinction being that they can be
brought indoors for at least a part of the
year. In other words the shrub is grown in
a container, so that a part of its growth or
flowering can be shared and appreciated at
closer quarters — indoors. The container
can either be brought indoors or placed on
the terrace so that it can be seen from
indoors. When the flowers are over, the
shrub can be moved away, and something
more interesting brought into view. Such
practical arrangements can provide a
continuous change of scene.

Many of the shrubs mentioned in this
chapter will do quite well indoors all year
round, but they would benefit from a few
refreshing months outdoors in summer. A
few examples of this group include,
Aucuba, Camellia, Euonymus, some
Hydrangeas, Ligustrum, Rhododendron and
Rosa.

Shrubs originating in warmer climates are
best kept indoors for at least the winter
months. During the summer they could be
taken out of doors, but this is not essential.
You must however be careful of the higher
temperatures that can build up inside a
window, avoiding prevention of draughts is
also important. The plants from warm
climates might be able to withstand high
temperatures out of doors, but behind glass
they can be as intolerant as any other plant.
There are some persistent misconceptions
about plants. Winter-hard species do not
die during winter from freezing, but from
the drying out of the root ball when
moisture has frozen, causing the rest of the
plant to die of drought. That is why it is a
good idea to protect cold-resistant plants
like *Aucuba* and *Ligustrum* from drought
through freezing, by applying a mulch of
damp leaf-compost or straw. Use chicken
wire or something similar to hold the
mulch in place. If you then water the plant
occasionally, you will find that it will come
through the winter unscathed.

Aucuba

*Aucuba
japonica
'Variegata'*

A. japonica is a hardy evergreen shrub from Japan, growing to 2m (6ft) or more, and has shiny dark-green leaves. The variegated variety is a mottled yellow. They bear insignificant flowers on separate male and female bushes, while female plants can develop attractive red berries. As outdoor shrubs they tolerate all but the harshest of conditions; they are equally adaptable indoors. They need a shaded, cool position. Water moderately in summer, and less in winter when they prefer a temperature of about 15°C (60°F). Too warm a situation attracts scale and mealy bug. Re-pot in spring, if needed, and cut back to shape or reduce height.

Camellia

*Camellia
japonica*

C. japonica, from Japan, is a hardy shrub with glossy, dark-green leaves and beautiful single or double blooms. The flowers occur in shades of red, pink and white, and some hybrids have striped or spotted petals. They flower in late winter or early spring. Though they have a very 'exotic' appearance, they are easy to grow. They were also very popular as 'orangery' subjects, and are also common as garden shrubs. They must be grown in a lime-free soil, enriched with leaf-mould. They need a semi-shaded position, preferably outdoors in summer, with cooler conditions for the roots (and pot). Water moderately with soft water. Keep humidity up in winter, in a cooler room, where they can also bloom. Do not move or turn the plant once it has started forming flower buds or they will fall off.

Ardisia
Coral berry

Ardisia crenata

An attractive, very slow growing evergreen shrub, that can eventually reach 1.2m (4ft) in height. It has glossy, dark-green leaves and sweet-smelling creamy-white flowers in autumn. These are followed by scarlet (or white) berries that can last on the plant until the following season's blooms, especially if the temperature is not too high, or humidity too low. It needs reasonable light conditions, but does need to be shaded from the sun. Make sure plants are well ventilated in summer. Needs an over-wintering temperature of not lower than 8°C (46°F). Water freely in summer, and feed regularly. In winter, keep the soil just moist. Easy to grow from fresh seed.

Citrus

*Citrus
microcarpa*

These hardy evergreen trees and shrubs from Asia produce lemons, oranges, grapefruit, and all the other edible types. Some dwarf varieties are very suitable for placing in containers in the home. *C. mitis,* the Calomondin, grows to a height of around 50cm (18ins) and is amongst the best for pot culture and can bear bright little fruits while still young. It produces clusters of sweet-smelling, white, waxy flowers. The fruits can remain on the plant right through the year until the next seasons blooms. They need good light, and can be placed outdoors in summer. Citrus were the traditional 'orangery' subjects. Water freely in summer, but keep just moist in winter, when the temperature should be around 6°C (42°F). Higher temperatures, and excess moisture in winter can cause leaf-fall. Prune in spring, and re-pot as necessary.

Callistemon
Bottlebrush

*Callistemon
citrinus*

These evergreen shrubs from Australia are hardy, but don't like very cold winters. *C. citrinus* grows to 2m (6ft) or more, and has a habit of spreading. Its grey-green leaves are borne on arching branches. The flowers form a typical 'bottlebrush' of scarlet stamens on the tips of the branches. Other species have different coloured blooms. Flowering is usually from June to August. Callistemons need to be grown in fairly large pots or tubs, and must be fed regularly. Re-pot at least every second year. They were, formerly, popular as 'orangery' specimens, and so can be brought outside for the summer. Indoors, they need good light conditions in an airy spot. Keep cooler in winter: minimum 6°C (42°F). Water well in summer, and less so in winter. Prune in early spring.

Coffea

Coffea arabica

The Coffee tree is an evergreen shrub, with glossy dark-green leaves and sweetly-scented white flowers, followed by red berries. Lower growing varieties are suitable for growing in pots; they will not, unfortunately, flower for the first few years. Place in good light, but shade from direct sunlight, and keep indoors permanently. Light must also be good in winter, and the temperature must be kept above 15°C (60°F). Water freely in summer, and ease off in winter, using soft water, as these are lime-haters. Propagate from seed.

*Euonymus
japonicus*

Euonymus
E. japonicus is a densely foliaged evergreen shrub, that can grow up to 2m (6ft) in a container. It has leathery, oval leaves and upright branches. There are several attractive variegated varieties: *'Albomarginata'* has green leaves edged with white; *'Aureomarginata'* has dark-green, edged with yellow; and *'Aureo-variegata* has yellow splashes on green. All are equally good in pot or garden, but they dislike too much frost, especially when in containers. If they are over wintered indoors, a temperature of 5°C (40°F) will suffice, but adequate light is needed as these are all evergreens. Water freely in summer, but less in winter. Prune in autumn, if needed.

Laurus nobilis

Laurus nobilis
Bay laurel
This hardy shrub, with its glossy green, lanceolate leaves is the same laurel that was used in Roman wreaths, and provides the bay leaves used in cooking. There is also a variegated variety. The plant looks best in a container when grown as a 'standard', with a clear stem, and kept in shape by regular pruning. They tend to throw suckers from the roots, which need to be removed too. Place in a sunny position, and water regularly. Outdoor conditions are fine in summer, but extremes of cold in winter can cause damage; it is best to over winter the plant indoors. Make sure the potting mix is well drained, and water less in winter. Plants are susceptible to scale insects.

*Hebe
andersonii*

Hebe
Half-hardy small shrubs from New Zealand, with green, grey or variegated foliage. These shrubs are resistant to salt-laden winds, and so make a useful terrace plant for seaside situations. They are mostly sensitive to frost. *H. andersonii variegata* grows to about 1m (3ft) and has oblong, pointed leaves of mid-green with cream variegations. Lavender coloured flowers are borne in dense upright spikes in mid-summer. A well-drained chalky soil suits them best. They are sun lovers, and need plenty of water in summer. A winter temperature above 5°C (40°F) should be maintained for over wintering indoors. After re-potting and pruning in spring, place in sun or light shade, indoors or out. Seldom bothered by pests or diseases.

*Nerium
oleander
'Variegatum
Plenum'*

Nerium oleander
Oleander
In Southern England and Europe this shrub can be grown in sheltered positions out of doors. It can form a large shrub 2m (6ft) or more tall, with leathery, narrow lanceolate leaves, of mid-green. There is a variegated variety with cream margins to the leaves and pink flowers. The flowers are borne in trusses in a range of colours from white, pink and orange to red, in both single and double forms. This plant is undemanding but should be protected from frost. Water freely during the growing period, but less in winter when temperatures should not drop below 7°C (44°F). Do not spray foliage. Prune, and cut back older stems in spring. Please remember that this shrub is very poisonous.

*Hydrangea
macrophylla*

Hydrangea
Hydrangea macrophylla is the best known and most popular species for growing in pots, and can bloom for lengthy periods from early summer. The flower head is composed of a mass of flattened florets, forming the typical round 'ball'. Flowers are in all shades of pink, blue or white. The shading is influenced by the acidity or alkalinity of the soil, which can be changed with chemicals, to alter the colour of the flower. Alkalinity encourages pink tones, while blue is enhanced by acidity. As the blooms finish, they don't always need to be pushed out of sight, as they can dry on the plant, into acceptable 'dried' blooms. *Hydrangeas* need a shaded, well-ventilated position, and may be kept indoors or out. In winter, after leaves have dropped, maintain in a cool place at around 5°C (40°F). Water frequently in summer, but allow the soil to almost dry out in winter; in spring the temperature must be increased gradually.

*Pernettya
mucronata*

Pernettya
A hardy, low, evergreen shrub with small green, narrowly-pointed leaves, closely packed on the branches which gives the plant a heather-like appearance. This is heightened when the plant flowers, as the small, bell-shaped, white flowers closely resemble heathers. The plants are unisexed, so both male and female have to be grown for berries to be produced. Berries vary in colour from white through pink to rose and red, they have a metallic sheen, and last on the plant for a very long time. They are not really houseplants, but the attractive berries are well-worth displaying. An acid soil is essential as is good watering during summer. Plant outside once berries have fallen.

Plumbago

Plumbago auriculata

This indoor trailing plant is popular because of its pale green leaves and pale blue or white, phlox-like flowers. In a large container on a terrace it can reach 3m (10ft) or more if trained up a trellis. It is a sun-lover and needs good light, even in winter when its leaves have fallen. A well drained soil and regular watering are necessary. It is not frost hardy, so needs protection in winter. Propagate new plants from young, soft shoots in a heated bed.

Punica

Punica granatum

Pomegranate

P. granatum from Iran is a spiny deciduous shrub, known since ancient times. It has shiny, mid-green leaves; bronze when they first appear, but yellow in autumn. The flowers are brilliant orange-red, with a bell like, waxy calyx from which the petals emerge looking like crumpled tissue paper. Modern varieties are very full 'doubles'. The fruits are bright orange-red and remain on the plant for a long time. The plant will tolerate very alkaline soil and needs lots of sunshine to flower and fruit. It is drought resistant and needs well drained soil. Water regularly when in flower. Protect indoors during winter, and prune in early spring.

Rhododendron

Rhododendron

This is the group of plants that we all know as *Azalea*. There are several hybrids suitable for growing indoors. Dwarf varieties are best for pot cultivation. The range of colours, and forms of the flowers is enormous. From white through pink and from red to mauve, and single or double. Flowering periods range from mid-winter to summer. Plants are acid lovers and should be watered only with soft water. They need a well ventilated position and good light without direct sunlight. A cool atmosphere is preferred. Water moderately and see that the roots do not dry out. Maintain reasonable humidity. Plants can be placed out of doors during summer, after they have flowered.

Rosa

Rosa polyantha

These plants are too well known to need description. The many miniature rose hybrids are suitable for growing in pots. Most are derived from *Rosa chinensis 'Minima' and Rosa noisettiana*. These miniature roses are not full indoor plants and so should be over wintered outside protected by a mulch of straw. If left inside they 'stretch' and the leaves will drop. Leave them outside until the flowers have formed, then place inside in the best-lit position. Return them to the garden as soon as flowers are over.

Many indoor shrubs 'disappear' during winter, into cellars or garages. Regular watering can be recommended during March. Even when no re-potting is to be done, the topmost soil can be replaced with fresh soil to which some fertiliser has been added. Examine each plant carefully for disease or pests; spray if needed, and do any pruning before sending the plant out into the new season.

Water conservers

Cacti

A large hobby needing only a small space.

This group of plants stands apart from others, not only because of the obvious physical differences, but also because of the special conditions they demand.

The three major demands concern the type of nourishment they need, the way they over winter, and the manner of propagation.

Cacti can be broadly divided into three groups.

There are the desert cacti with their own specific needs, grafted cacti and forest cacti. This last group might not be known to you. They are the epiphytic cacti from the tropical forests of Central and South America. They need water through the year, including winter, and a shaded or semi-shaded position. An example of this group is the *Pereskia*.

These conditions contrast completely with those of the desert cacti, which need a totally dry winter, from about the third week in September to the third week in March. At the end of this period the plants will not look at their best, but if you gradually start re-watering, you will see the withered plant regaining its former glory. This dormant period, without water prevents the plant from rotting during the colder months, and is necessary for the subsequent formation of flowers.

The desert cacti also dislike shade or semi-shade. Stand them in full sunlight and they'll be happy. In fact they are ideal plants for the lazy gardener. Even the longest period of neglect is borne without problems. When conditions improve, they grow and flower again as before. During summer these plants can be taken outside, where the fresh air and sunlight will do them good. Fresh air is something that the cactus will respond to gratefully.

The way in which cacti are watered is important. Among amateurs this is not surprising that it is sometimes thought that cacti don't ever need watering. Although this may be so for winter, it is quite different in summer. The best method of watering cacti is to place the pot in a bucket of water, so that the root ball can fully absorb the necessary water. When you take the plant out, allow all surplus moisture to drain off completely. If the soil remains too damp you run the risk of the roots rotting. The reason for watering by this method is that, in the wild cacti tend to have a shallow, spreading root system in order to benefit quickly from any shower of rain. When grown in a pot, the surface area is small and the plants are forced to grow further down into the soil than they normally would. It is to ensure that these deeper roots also benefit from watering that this method is used.

The third group of cacti, the grafted cacti, are not to be found in nature. They are entirely 'manmade'. These strange grafted spheres and cylinders in unnatural colours, on the tops of 'cactus stalks' are often found at florists and garden centres. The commonest example of these is the cherry red *Gymnocalycium mihanovichii*. As a general rule, cacti are not potted in ordinary potting soil as this is usually enriched with manures and fertilisers, and does not have a suitable structure for them. Rather buy a cactus potting mixture, which is also suitable for potting up other desert succulents. Most cacti flower relatively quickly, usually after only a couple of years. They don't then die, as in the case of *Bromeliads,* but will continue flowering year after year.

*Aporocactus
flagilliformis*

Aporocactus
Rat's-tail cactus
An old favourite, usually grown in hanging baskets to allow its long trailing green stems to spread and hang. Flowers are bright, rose pink, and trumpet shaped. Freely borne in April and May on the long stems. Place outdoors after flowering. Grow as an epiphytic cactus, in a leaf mould, garden soil and sharp sand mixture. Water regularly but moderately, not allowing the plant to dry out completely. Can be propagated from cuttings.

*Echinocactus
grusonii*

Echinocactus
Originally from Mexico, these round or cylindrical cacti are grown for their attractive spines. They have prominent, vertical ribs, with large curved spines. *E. grusonii*, is almost spherical, of a bright green colour, with prominent ribs and bright yellow spines. Needs very good light, and warm temperatures. Temperature not below 10°C (50°F) in winter. Water regularly in summer, allowing it to dry out in between. No water in winter, or rotting can occur. Feed during the growing season. Propagated from seed, but are very slow.

*Cereus
peruvianus*

Cereus
Torch thistle
Columnar cacti with marked ribs bearing spines. Many species have a waxy 'bloom', which gives them a blue-green appearance. *C. chalybaeus* has a blue sheen, *C. peruvianus* is a greyish-green and jade-like. Some varieties have a multiple branching habit. *C. jamacaru* has greenish-blue stems and five ribs, with yellow spines. They have white flowers, but these are very rarely found in cultivation. A well ventilated sunny position, warm in summer, and cool in winter suits them best. Water in summer allowing them to dry out in between. Keep dry in winter. Feed once, at start of summer.

*Echinocereus
hybrid*

Echinocereus
Another easily cared for cactus, which has many different species and varieties. It has a strange form of growth, as branches form inside the trunk and grow through the outer skin. They are either round or cylindrical, deeply-ribbed, with spines forming on the areoles. Flowers are funnel shaped and either red, pink or purple depending on the variety. A well ventilated position with good light outside in the sun, if possible in summer. Much cooler in winter, and do not water. Water in summer, allowing soil to dry out in between. Propagate from stem cuttings in spring, and grow in a low humus, loamy soil.

*Chamaecereus
silvestrii*

Chamaecereus silvestrii
Peanut cactus
About the easiest cactus to grow, with its loose collection of thin stems 2–6cm (1–3ins) long, and 1cm (½in) thick, and short whitish spines. Stems are bright green, and have orange-scarlet, trumpet shaped flowers in summer. Handle with care as pieces are easily broken off, each piece will soon produce roots. Provide a warm, sunny position in summer, but cool in winter (even a bit of frost is tolerated). Water regularly in summer allowing the soil to dry out in between. Keep dry in winter. Soil should be light and airy. Propagate by removing shoots.

*Echinopsis
hybrid*

Echinopsis
Sea urchin cactus
Small round cacti from South America. They produce beautiful large flowers that open in the evening and last several days. They range in colour from white to yellow, and from pink to scarlet, and many more as they are easy to hybridize. Some are fragrant *E. calachlora* is a bright green ball with short spines and white flowers. *E. eyriesii* is dark green, deeply ribbed and has white areoles, with dark spines. It also has white flowers. They need good light, and some protection from strong sunlight. Warm in summer, cool in winter (almost to freezing point). Water regularly in summer, and feed well, dry in winter.

Epiphyllum

Epiphyllum hybrid

Another easy to care for, but most attractive flowering plant for indoors, this group of epiphytic cacti have spectacular flowers, some of which are perfumed. The colours range from white through pink red, purple and yellow. They have flattened stems that look like fleshy leaves, usually mid-green in colour but without sharp spines. Some bloom during the day and others at night. As these are epiphytes they should be planted in a compost rich in leaf mould and sand. Though they need good light they do need to be shaded from direct sun and prefer a ventilated situation. They grow very well in hanging containers and can go outdoors after flowering. They need warm summer temperatures and cooler 10°C (50°F) in winter. Water generously during flowering but sparingly in winter. Re-pot only when strictly necessary.

Mammillaria

Mammillaria zeilmanniana

This extensive genus of mostly round cacti with a symmetrical, 'warty' surface arranged spirally around the stems, does not have the pronounced vertical ribs of so many cacti. Short, bell-like flowers are borne in a ring at the top of the plant in summer, and the resultant fruits often remain in place until the following season's flowers appear. Blooms are mostly white, red or pink. The thorns in many varieties are decorative too. Offsets which develop at the base of older plants are easily removed and rooted. If given adequate sized pots, they can form their typical cluster of plants, which looks impressive in bloom. They need hot summer temperatures and regular watering, but do allow soil to dry out in between. Apply very little water in winter when lower temperatures are preferred. Soils may be loamy and chalky.

Gymnocalycium

Gymnocalycium mihanovichii 'Friedrichii'

Within this group of cacti there is an oddity: *G. mihanovichii 'Friedrichii'*, which is an orange-red ball with prominent ribs, and clearly contains no chlorophyll. For this reason it has to be grafted onto a green cactus stem to be able to survive. The bright colour certainly stands out from amongst a collection of plants. It can flower, bearing pink blooms, but this is very rare. Another cactus oddity is the yellow, grafted *Chamaecereus*. They need a good light, shaded from direct sun in summer, with cool, light and dry conditions in winter. Water sparingly in summer and not at all in winter.

Notocactus

Notocactus ottonis

A genus of smaller, easily grown cacti which are either spherical or columnar. They have attractive spines, light green stems and beautiful, multi-petalled flowers. Blooms are usually yellow, but this varies according to the species. Blooms last for several weeks. They need good light, and are happiest if placed outside during summer, so long as some shade can be given from the midday sun. Water and feed regularly with soft water. Will tolerate higher humidity. In winter temperatures should not be allowed to drop below 10°C (50°F), and no water must be given. Plants may be grown from seed.

Lobivia

Lobivia

These are spherical, small cacti, seldom larger than 15cm (6ins) in diameter, and many are smaller than 5cm (2ins). They have large spines and hairs. They produce large blooms in yellow or red which open by day and close during the night. Most species are from Bolivia. They need a well ventilated situation, with plenty of sun in summer, and regular feeding and watering. No water must be given in winter and the temperature should be kept just above freezing. Propagate from offsets or seed.

Opuntia

Opuntia bergeriana

Prickly pear

This is a genus of 'jointed' cacti, the best known of which are the types with flattened paddle-shaped stems, though some stems are cylindrical. They vary in size from very large tree-like species to others only a few centimetres tall. Besides their spines, all the species have tufts of microscopically fine barbed hairs, which are very difficult to remove, and quite painful when they get into the skin. Some of the species will flower in cultivation, but not all. They need good light and warmth and preferably an outdoor situation during summer. Water moderately and feed well. Keep totally dry in winter when cooler conditions are needed. Propagate from seed or from stems cut from the parent, usually at a 'joint'. Allow them to dry for a few days before planting.

Oroya

Oroya

These small spherical cacti originate in the Andes. Growing to about 8cm (3ins) high, they have pronounced vertical ribs and broadened tubercles, from which rise rosettes of longish spines, in colours which range from yellow to black. Flowers are shades of red, pink, or yellow. The situation for these plants should be well-lit, and slightly shaded from the midday sun. Water moderately in summer, allowing the soil to dry out in between. Keep dry in winter, with accompanying lower temperatures. Soil should be a well drained loam, with sharp sand added. Difficult species are frequently grafted.

Parodia

Parodia

The main characteristic of this fine-spined genus is its very slow rate of growth. Plants are globe-shaped with the ribs arranged spirally, and the tubercles and spines on the ridges. Spines are often tinged red. The blooms are wide open and daisy-like, arranged on the top of the plant; they can be yellow, pink, or red, depending on the species. They require a sunny position with plenty of water in summer but none in winter. Ensure that the soil dries out fairly quickly after each watering to prevent rotting. Over wintering requires a light spot with temperatures around 5°C (40°F). They are grown from seed.

Rebutia

Rebutia

This small cactus group from South America is one of the easiest but most rewarding to grow. All the species form 'clumps' of stems by sending up side shoots, and can soon fill a pot completely. They will also flower remarkably early (after only a year or so). Their blooms occur in a range of bright colours, and each lasts for about a week. They open in the morning and close each evening. Some plants may bloom twice in the same year. Grow *Rebutias* out of doors in summer, in full sun, but with a little shading when it is very hot. Spraying the stems in warm weather is beneficial. In winter, plants must remain dry, and be kept at temperatures between 5 and 10°C (40 and 50°F). Feed only once in spring. Soil should be fertile and drainage good. Propagate from seed or by division.

Cacti are not plants that can be handled without gloves. The jointed cactus group have vicious thorns with hooked points, which are difficult to remove once they have hooked into a finger; infection is another likely result. When such a cactus is to be re-potted, wear thick gloves, and make 'ropes' of rolled newspaper to wrap around the stems.

Cacti are plants that don't produce leaves. They have the ability to store moisture, and so survive dry periods. They lose hardly any water through transpiration. There are even cacti covered with white hairs, which further reduce transpiration. The Epostao's are cacti with long hairs, hence the name 'bearded'. These hairs also protect the plant from sunlight, so they can tolerate the very warmest of situations.

Succulents

Succulent leaved plants can usually be propagated fairly easily from cuttings or even leaf-sections. Allow the cut parts to dry off, before inserting them into sand, to prevent rotting.

Because of their fairly close similarity to cacti, succulents are not nearly as bothered by a sunny position indoors as are other normal houseplants. The temperature does not have to be high and they appreciate fresh air rather than a stale atmosphere. Even in summer a cooler temperature will suit most types better. In winter, temperatures can be allowed to drop to about 10°C (50°F), and still lower if the soil is fairly dry and humidity low. There is often some misunderstanding over how much water to give these plants. It is not true that they need little or no water. It is a fact that they can survive for long periods without water, as happens in their natural habitats. This is why they have a shallow, but extensive root system which can make the best use of the smallest shower. That is also why they have thickened leaves with tough skin especially adapted to store moisture as a reserve for dry times.

The plants will grow better indoors if they are regularly watered, but if they skip a turn it need not be the disaster it could well be with softer plants. In the winter allow the plants to become fairly dry. The cooler the position the less water they need. In fact, a wet root system soon results in a dead plant. To accommodate the plant's tendency towards shallow rooting they should be planted in wide, shallow pots. There are exceptions to this rule, species such as *Lithops* prefer their roots to be much deeper. Re-potting is done in spring, using an ordinary potting mixture provided a quantity of coarse sand or grit is mixed into it. This ensures better drainage and aeration of the soil. Potting mixtures specially designed for succulents can usually be bought. Normal houseplant mixtures that have fertiliser already added are often too rich in nitrogen and should be diluted by adding sand or clean soil.

Succulents generally need low dilutions of fertiliser at each application. Specially formulated feeds for cacti and succulents are the safest to use. Succulents and cacti have much in common as regards requirements and growth habits. But the external appearances provide the more obvious distinctions. Cacti are characterised by their thorns, while most succulents have leaves with smooth surfaces.

Echeveria is one of many easily propagated succulents.

Agave

Agave victoria-reginae

These tough and hardy dryland plants have long, rigid leaves with sharp tips, and some have rather sharp thorns up the edges as well. They grow in symmetrical rosettes and vary in length from a few centimetres up to 3m (10ft). A smaller type, *Agave victoria-reginae* makes a very decorative pot plant. It has thick, rounded leaves with white edges, and these are tipped with a sharp, hard spine. After flowering, the plant will gradually die off, but not before producing several young shoots (suckers) from its base. Good light and warm temperatures in summer are necessary, with generous watering and occasional feeding. Over wintering requires cool, unheated conditions, but not frost and virtually no water. *Agaves* are all good tub plants, and can be very dramatic on a patio in summer *(but beware of the sharp spines)*. Other suitable species include *A. filifera, A. parasana* and *A. americana*, which becomes large and also has a variegated variety.

Echeveria

Echeveria metallica

A large genus of easily grown succulents. The leaves are arranged in rosettes, and often have a white, waxy sheen. Several different types can be grown indoors. These plants are grown for their beautiful leaves, and light intensity is very important for the maintenance of good colouring. Good light is essential, or the plants tend to 'green' and stretch. They can be taken outside during summer, but those with a waxy 'bloom' should be kept indoors. Warm summer temperatures with generous watering but cooler in winter with very little water. Drainage must be good to prevent roots rotting. Do not water over the leaves as they tend to scorch. Try not to touch them either for the same reason. Young rosettes are produced as suckers.

Aloe

Aloe arborescens

A large genus, mostly from Africa, that includes many different forms; some have stems and grow tall, others are stemless and small. They have typical fleshy leaves, in rosettes like the *Agave*, but these plants do not die off after flowering, and can be very long-lived. Tall spikes of tubular or bell-shaped flowers are produced from the leaf axils. It is the smaller species that are suitable as houseplants. One of the most popular is *Aloe variegata*, which has narrow, pointed overlapping leaves of dark-green, with irregular bands of white. They produce a spike of orange tubular flowers. Other species, such as *A. arborescens* are grown more for the 'octopus-like' foliage. Good light and a dry atmosphere suit them best in summer, with cooler winters but no frost. Water well in summer, but sparingly in winter, and don't overfeed them. Many species produce small shoots from the stem base, which are easily removed and rooted in sand.

Euphorbia

Euphorbia trigona

Spurge

This genus covers a wide range of plants including shrubby, herbaceous and succulents. The succulents are grown for their interesting shapes. Many closely resemble cacti and even have thorns. Often the only way of telling whether they are cacti or not is to wound them slightly, to see if they contain a milky sap, which is characteristic of all *Euphorbias*. *E. pseudocactus* is particularly popular, for its rapid upright growth, and it's often used with cactus groups. The care of these larger succulents is also very similar to that for cacti. Watering, sun and shading and feeding requirements are the same, as are over wintering requirements. Propagate by seed and cuttings.

Crassula arborescens

Gasteria

Crassula

A genus of 300 species of succulents from Southern Africa. The thickened leaves are often covered in hair or 'bloom'. Most species produce panicles of starry flowers. *C. arborescens*, sometimes called the Jade plant, has silvery, grey-green leaves that sometimes have red margins. It can grow indoors for many years. Good light, shaded slightly in summer and a sunny window sill in winter are suitable. Warmer summer temperatures, but cool in winter, suit it best. Water regularly all year round but somewhat less in winter. Can be kept outdoors for much of the year, but frost may well be harmful. Other smaller species suitable for the home are *C. falcata*, and *C. lycopodoides*. They have a totally different appearance but care is similar to that given to *C. arborescens*.

Gasteria

Gasterias are true succulents; long, narrow fleshy leaves, many with interesting markings, arise as almost stemless clumps, typically in one flattened plane. They do well as indoor plants, and their needs are simple. *G. liliputana* is the smallest species and the opposing leaves grow in a spiral as they increase in number. They are dark green mottled white. *Gasterias* need a sunny position and can be kept on a window sill throughout the year. Water freely during summer. During the winter allow the soil to dry out to prevent rotting. Feed sparingly in summer, using a 'cactus type' fertiliser. Soils should be light and well drained. Propagate either with seed or side shoots.

*Graptopetalum
paraguayense*

Graptopetalum

There are, once again, a variety of colours, shapes and sizes, amongst these succulents from Central America. They are grown for their attractive leaves rather than their blooms. Closely related to *Sedum* their fleshy leaves are borne in rosettes, and are often greeny-blue in colour with a waxy sheen. *G. filliferum* has pointed leaves and grows in a tight rosette. The small white flowers are tinted red on the tips of the petals. *G. paraguayense* has club-shaped grey-green leaves on fleshy stems. They need good light and warm temperatures in summer, and can be placed outside. Water regularly but sparingly in summer, even less frequently in winter. A cool winter situation is one of its few essential needs, to prevent pests and spoiling of foliage. They are useful in groups with *Sedums* and *Echeverias*.

*Kalanchoë
blossfeldiana*

Kalanchoë

As with all the *Kalanchoës*, *K. blossfeldiana* is a 'short-day' plant. This means that if it is to bloom, it must be kept for a while with less than 10 hours of light per day. This induces the plant to produce flower buds. It is a winter and spring flowering plant, and grows about 25cm (10ins) tall, has glossy, dark green leaves and orange-red flowers on branched stems. It requires semi-shade in summer, but full light in winter if the best flowering is to be achieved. Warm summer temperatures and moderate winters, not below 15°C (60°F). Water regularly throughout the year and this tough plant will give few problems. It is commonly thrown out after blooming, but this seems pointless.

*Glottiphyllum
oligocarpum*

Glottiphyllum

A desert genus from Southern Africa, they have pairs of opposite leaves like the stone plant, *Lithops*, but with larger leaves. Leaves are fleshy and grey-green, though too much sun can turn them mauve. They have yellow daisy-like flowers, appearing from the centre of the plant. They need good light, with some shading from direct sun. Water sparingly in summer, but keep them dry in winter. During winter they prefer a cooler situation. Problems can arise with watering, literally! During summer they need virtually no water, and in winter none at all. They need a fairly poor loamy soil, and no fertilising, and shade will cause them to become rather soft.

*Kalanchoë
daigremontiana*

Kalanchoë (Bryophyllum)

This genus is divided into two sections, members of the first group produce plantlets on the edges of their leaves as their means of reproduction. They are an undemanding group, accepting dry or humid conditions, and their only dislike is too much water. Some examples from this group include: *K. daigremontiana*, which grows to over 70cm (2ft) tall and has attractive leathery green leaves, with brown markings. *K. laxiflora* has grey-green leaves, while *K. tubiflora* has lance-shaped grey-green leaves with brown flecks. Over winter these plants at temperatures over 10°C (50°F). Winter flowering species belong in the second group and have plain, leathery leaves (as in the case of *K. blossfeldiana*).

Haworthia

Haworthia

These succulents, belonging to the Lily family, are grown mainly for their attractive foliage. One section of this genus has thickened, scaly leaves of various colours, usually heavily marked or spotted with white. The second group has softer, succulent green leaves that grow in rosettes. They all bear tiny white flowers on a tall slender stem in summer. They all need good light and feeding during the spring growing period. Cool winter temperatures are preferred. Water generously in summer but keep drier in winter. If they are kept in a very dry atmosphere water them occasionally. Propagate by seed or side-shoots.

*Pachyphytum
oviferum*

Pachyphytum

Moon stones

This genus has very thick leaves, either in rosettes or on stems. In the search for new plants, hybrids between *Pachyphytum* and *Echeveria* have been developed, and called *X Pachyveria* (see the next entry). The leaves have a typical bloom which can be damaged by water or handling. *P. oviferum* has a short stem and egg-shaped leaves, covered in silvery bloom. The flowers are bell-shaped and red, but almost completely covered by white sepals. These appear in May. *P. hookeri* is more shrub-like, growing to about 60cm (2ft). They need a sunny and airy position. Water carefully in summer but keep almost dry in winter, when cooler conditions are needed. Feed once per month in summer. Propagate by seed or leaves.

266

× Pachyveria

× Pachyveria

The × *Pachyveria* is a cross (the × indicates a hybrid) between *Echeveria* and *Pachyphytum*. The improved plants have attractive features, combining the better points of both parents. There are several hybrid varieties. They all require plenty of light both in summer and winter but no direct sunlight. Provide them with cool winter temperatures and very little water. Moderate watering in summer and an occasional feeding with a cactus type fertiliser. These plants can be taken outside in the summer if a protected spot is available. Propagate from seed which germinates quickly.

Sedum sieboldii 'Medio-Variegatum'

Sedum

Stone crop

Amongst the *Sedums* you have a very wide choice of interesting and pretty little plants. Fleshy, attractive leaves, terminal panicles of flowers in yellow, pink or white, make this a most popular rock garden plant. The Mexican varieties are grown as pot plants. *S. sieboldii* has purplish stems and spirally arranged leaves which are round, blue-green with wavy margins. It dies down in winter. Other well known species include *S. morganianum*, *S. pachyphyllum*, and *S. rubrotinctum*, but there are many more well-worth growing. Most species prefer full sun and can be placed in sheltered spots outside in summer. Over winter without heat and with hardly any water. Only feed them if soil is poor, which must drain freely and be light. Propagate with leaf or stem cuttings.

Rhipsalidopsis gaertneri

Rhipsalidopsis

Easter cactus

These are epiphytic cacti from tropical Brazil, and have flattened leaf-like stems that branch at the ends. The two best known types are *R. gaertneri*, with its scarlet-red blooms, and *R.* × *graeseri*, with more orange shades. These 'Easter' cacti appear similar to the 'Christmas' cacti, but are treated differently. They are sensitive to lime, and to lack of water and need a higher humidity. In the growing season, from August to January, water them normally. Then reduce water until flower buds form and then water more often. Don't turn the plant once flowers start showing. Feed sparingly. Propagate from seed and cuttings.

Rochea coccinea

Rochea

Of the many members of this genus of tender succulents, *R. coccinea* is the best known. It grows to about 40cm (16ins) in height. The leathery, diamond-shaped leaves are closely packed and symmetrically arranged up the stems. Terminal clusters of flowers are carmine-red and produced from July to September. They like some sun in summer and can be placed outside. Its watering, feeding and humidity needs are average. In winter temperatures should not be lower than 5°C (40°F). Cut back stems that have flowered to make space for new shoots.

Some exceptional and weird plants make up the group of desert succulents known as 'living stones'. Some allied types, such as Argyroderma, Conophytum *and* Glottiphyllum *are also included, but the main family is* Lithops, *with its many different and strange species, with their natural 'stony' colourings and, more surprisingly, bright little flowers. They are usually grown in small individual pots, with matching gravel ground-cover. They appear best in groups in larger, flat trays, with other species, in the form of a mini desert. The biggest enemy of these plants is water and also lack of light.*

Orchids and Bromeliads

Orchids

Once you start collecting orchids . . .

If you want to display orchids indoors, you must be prepared to buy adult plants that are already blooming, or are of flowering age. Most species will not happily develop from juvenile to adult stage under normal home conditions. Larger, established plants will have built up their reserves of food and water, and will be more tolerant of the climatic changes. Most orchids will probably be happiest in glasshouses.

Orchids have such 'exotic' and beautiful blooms that one tends to imagine that they must be difficult to grow. Fortunately, this is not strictly true, and a variety of different tropical orchids can be grown on a home window sill without too much special care.

Propagation of orchids, other than by division, should be left to experts, as it is a complex and exacting business. Sowing of fertile seed must be done under sterile conditions, on special growing mediums in airtight glass flasks, and temperatures have to be watched carefully. If you develop an interest in orchid cultivation, you will need to obtain some of the specialized books on the subject. There is a great deal that can be learnt: this is not surprising when you consider that there are between 50,000 and 75,000 species and varieties in this extremely diverse plant order.

It is certainly possible to create suitable conditions on a window sill for those species that are able to adapt to the environment to be found in your home. It is here, on a window sill, that most of the plant's main needs can be best met. These are light, warmth and humidity. Orchids generally need good light, but must be protected from direct sunlight. Throughout the year they need daylight of at least 10 hours' duration (as would be the case in the countries of origin). This is not a problem in summer, but in winter the day's 'length' will have to be artificially extended through the use of electric lighting. Because it is supplementary lighting, you don't have to use a special growing-lamp; an ordinary light will do just as well. During summer, warmth originates from the sun, via the glass, while in winter it can be supplied by a regulated radiator. Humidity can be provided and maintained with the assistance of the same heat sources: you will need a shallow tray or dish, of metal or plastic, into which you place a relatively thick layer of clean, fine gravel. Place the plant pots on stands over this gravel, which is then well watered, and kept perpetually damp. Provided the radiator is situated beneath the window, the water will evaporate, and the water vapour will provide the necessary micro-climate to surround the plants.

If you doubt this you can measure the moisture with a hygrometer; you will see that the humidity reading will show about 50%, which is what the plant needs.

For these reasons, window sills will provide the most favourable situations in most homes. Ensure that the sill is completely draught-free, as this is one condition that orchids will not tolerate. Double-glazing and screening from the midday sun are also beneficial.

You can, if you wish, provide more refined conditions for smaller orchids by using a terrarium, or an old aquarium, as a mini environment. If you become keener, or wish to grow more difficult species, you can install special heating and lighting fixtures, and possibly enclose the plants more, so that the various conditions can be better controlled. Re-potting is done to stimulate root growth; obviously, a healthily growing plant will also flower better. Re-pot into a slightly larger pot, after removing all dead roots, and any of the growing medium that appears too damp or spongy. Refill carefully around the root ball with the appropriate mixture for that particular species.

Epiphytic orchids need very airy, coarse materials, while ground orchids prefer a heavier mixture containing loam and compost.

After blooming, orchids need a rest period, when less water is given, and lower temperatures are needed. In fact, this cool situation is an essential prerequisite for the formation of the next season's flower buds.

Brassia

Brassia

These hardy and easily grown orchids have flower spikes that grow up to 50cm (20ins) in length. A few species suitable for home growing are: *B. verrucosa*, and *B. maculata*, which has closely packed yellow flowers, with triangular lips and spidery petals. It flowers in early summer. These plants need a semi-shaded position, and warm temperatures, 18–20°C (64–70°F). Water generously, with lime-free water during the growing period, and feed with a very diluted fertiliser. Re-pot, if needed, in early spring in a coarse mix containing peat, bark and charcoal. Water sparingly in winter and keep in a cooler spot.

Cymbidium

Cymbidium

This is the best orchid for the beginner. *Cymbidiums* are comparatively easy to grow, and there are many smaller sized hybrids that would be happy in a sunny room, or in window case. The miniature varieties have flower spikes from 15cm (6ins) to about 60cm (2ft) long, each with a dozen or more blooms; these occur in a wide range of colours. The plants can be placed outside in summer in a shady spot. Indoors they need a very good light, but also without direct sun. Cool winter temperatures, 8–12°C (46–54°F) are needed, with less water. Water and feed generously in summer, but allow the soil to dry out in between. Re-pot directly after flowering in spring. Blooms will last for several weeks in a vase.

Cattleya

Cattleya

It is usually recommended that these tropical, epiphytic orchids only be grown in heated greenhouses. However, with some care and attention, some of the species can be grown in the home provided you can accommodate their particular needs. Both temperature and humidity must be kept as high as possible during the growing period in summer. Stand the plants over a damp gravel tray, and screen them from draughts. Plants should be grown in a very coarse, open mixture, in open-sided containers, so that air can readily reach the roots. During the resting period, which varies according to the species, limit watering and provide a cool situation, at about 15°C (60°F). Water with soft water and always avoid wetting leaves or blooms. Propagate by division.

Epidendrum

Epidendrum

This is a large and extremely diverse genus of epiphytes, with all manner of blooms, colours and growth forms. There are many types with interesting blooms that could be chosen for growing at home; one could select different types to provide colour at all times of the year. Flowers are usually brightly coloured, and borne on terminal spikes or clusters. *E. radicans* is a cane-like species with several bright colour varieties, and will grow happily amongst other tropical houseplants. Their leafy stems grow to 1m or more (3–4ft), and may well need support. They can go outside, into semi-shade in summer, and should be kept cool in winter at about 13°C (56°F). They need watering throughout the year and a light feed during the warmer months.

Coelogyne cristata

Odontoglossum

Coelogyne

Amongst this tropical epiphytic genus from Asia, there are a few species that will tolerate home conditions. *C. fimbriata, C. massangeana* and *C. cristata* are the easiest to handle. The plants prefer to be overcrowded in their pots with roots in a solid mass. For the growing season, place the plants on a warm, shaded sill, and keep humidity high. Spray and ventilate on hot days. They bloom in early spring, and can then be re-potted, using a coarse mix. Select a cooler spot for winter, when they prefer a temperature of 10–12°C (50–54°F) and much less water.

Odontoglossum

Amongst the species of this beautiful orchid there are several that are suitable for indoor culture. One of the easiest to grow is *O. grande*, which has broad pseudobulbs (leaf bases), with pairs of leaves. Its 'butterfly-like' blooms are carried on long, slender spikes. These plants like cooler, airy, moist conditions, with regular watering and humidifying using soft water. After flowering in late autumn or winter, allow plants to rest by drastically reducing the watering and keeping temperatures slightly below normal room temperature. Re-pot in spring only when they are totally root-bound, using a very coarse mixture. The blooms make excellent cut flowers.

Oncidium

Oncidium

Another very large group, and is closely related to the *Odontoglossum*. In fact, a book could be written on these alone. Below are two species that can be home-grown. The better known of the two is *O. ornithorhynchum*, which flowers in autumn, producing masses of scented, pale pink and rose flowers on the slender twigs of the flower spike. The second species, *O. varicosum*, blooms in winter, with very branched spikes of up to 1.3m (5ft) in length, bearing anything up to 90 individual yellow flowers, each about 3cm (1in) across. The major disadvantage with these plants is that they will only bloom in alternate years. They need a plentiful supply of water in summer, but very little in winter and, as with most species, they enjoy both warmth and humidity. Re-pot when pots become overcrowded. Blooms last very well in water.

Paphiopedilum

Paphiopedilum

Paphiopedilum
Slipper orchid
These are mainly terrestrial orchids without pseudobulbs. They have been popular for many years, and a great variety of hybrids are available, many of which can be easily kept in the home throughout the year. Their main requirements are plentiful shaded light and high humidity. *P. hirsutissimum* and *P. insigne* and their many hybrids prefer a rest period after blooming, with somewhat lower temperatures. Many other types will grow in the same spot all the year round, as they have no need of rest. Do keep an eye on humidity and their drying-out during winter when the heating is turned up high.

Vanda

Vanda coerulea

Vanda
These species are only really successful in a heated greenhouse, but there is an exception: this is *V. coerulea*, which bears incredible sky-blue blooms in clusters on slender spikes in autumn. They do need to be rested at a lower temperature after flowering. In summer the plant needs a semi-shaded position, with regular watering and light feeding, using lime-free water. Temperatures over 20°C (68°F) are preferred, and provision must be made for humidifying when air becomes too dry. Re-pot in spring at the start of the growing period. Propagate by division.

Growing and resting periods differ greatly between the various orchid families, and even between members of the same family. Usually, the foliage becomes limp at the start of a rest-period; this is most commonly during February, when any necessary re-potting should be done. During the summer, plants store reserves of food, before their dormant period commences. Some species flower before the resting stage, and others soon after they 'awaken' in the spring.

In many instances, orchids are hung up, as their leaves and/or blooms are fairly extensive, and inclined to 'cascade'. They are also rather brittle. One can obtain special orchid cases, for more tropical species, which may contain a tree stump onto which certain epiphytic species can be attached. These plants often require additional heating and humidity. Most orchids cannot be grown in normal potting soils but require various specific mixtures. Unless you have the facilities, and many plants to re-pot, it is easier to purchase small quantities of orchid-mix from a garden centre.

Bromeliads

As epiphytes, these attractive Bromeliads need special treatment.

The Bromeliad family has two major divisions. On the one hand there is the larger, better known group of epiphytic species, which grow on tree trunks, mainly in tropical jungles. The other group comprises terrestrial plants (those that grow on the ground), but many of these are still closer to the tree-types in habit, than to normal plants.

Epiphytic Bromeliads obtain their food and water mainly via the central heart of the plant and not from the roots which serve mainly to anchor the plant to a branch. Rainwater direct, or splashed from surrounding foliage, collects in the centre cone of these plants whose leaves form a rosette around it. The reservoir of water and nutrient provides for the plant's needs until the next shower replenishes it. Should this source dry up temporarily, then the roots are able to absorb a limited amount of moisture from the host's bark.

Bromeliads prefer pure water and are not too keen on our chlorinated supplies, which often contain a high proportion of lime. These facts apply broadly to the terrestrial species as well.

In general, Bromeliads can be grown successfully if the following conditions and requirements are met: for plants that are blooming, or simply growing, a temperature of 15°C (60°F) is sufficient.

To induce mature plants to bloom (at the correct time of year) the temperature will need to be increased to anything between 25°C and 30°C (76°F and 86°F). There is always a close relationship between the plant's moisture requirements and the temperature. Atmospheric humidity should preferably also be fairly high, although many species will tolerate the drier conditions to be found in our homes. What they do appreciate is regular spraying with water, and the topping-up of the central cone with tepid water. The soil mixture in the pot should be kept slightly damp. During winter, the central 'vase' should be kept empty, and only dampen the soil now and then.

The next factor, after water and temperature, is light. These plants must have good light conditions, but *never* direct sunlight. Situations that are too dark will cause the foliage to lose its colouring, and will discourage flowering, whilst direct sunlight can often cause scorching of foliage.

For feeding, you must only add a very small amount of a balanced houseplant fertiliser to the water used for topping up the plant's reservoir, or to the water used for spraying the foliage.

Aechmea

The *Aechmea* is a genus of true epiphytes that can be grown without a pot. A branch or a piece of tree trunk upon which it can be fastened is quite sufficient. The plant's roots serve more to anchor it in position that to feed it, although they can do so if necessary. Easiest to cultivate are *A. fasciata*. *Aechmea* will only flower once from each leaf rosette. After flowering new plants will form at the base. The 'base' should be kept slightly damp throughout the year with lime-free water and the rosette 'vase' topped-up with water in summer. The plant can be fed with well-diluted liquid fertiliser as a foliar feed. If temperatures become cooler, remove the water from the 'vase'. High humidity and temperatures above 15°C (60°F) are preferred.

Achmea fasciata

Ananas

A. comosus is the commercial pineapple you can buy at the market. Several decorative hybrids have been developed as houseplants. Some have variegated leaves in various shades and patterns. They produce a short, strong flower stalk with a tufty flower. The fruit develops as a typical pineapple. Only mature plants will bear flowers and will then decline gradually, but they will develop new side shoots. The hard, pointed leaves can inflict a nasty wound if you do not take sufficient care. Water generously with lime-free water but allow plant to dry out in between. Winter temperatures should not drop below 15°C (60°F) and they need a bright, humid spot throughout the year. Feed and water as you would other *Bromeliads*.

Ananas comosus

Billbergia

In contrast to most species of *Bromeliad*, plants of the genus *Billbergia* grow in the soil. Two of them are well suited for indoor situations. *B. nutans* has dark-green, grass-like leaves; the flowers have rose-pink bracts, and hanging green and purple tubular flowers. B. windii has grey-green foliage, its arching flowers have deep pink bracts and greenish-blue flowers. Both these types are best grown as a 'clump', with a potful of flowering and younger stems. They will not tolerate temperatures much below 10°C (50°F), but are otherwise treated in the same way as any normal houseplant. Higher winter temperatures will do no harm, but a temperature of around 15°C (60°F) suits best. They are tolerant of lime both in soil and water. Propagate by division, during annual re-potting, when flowered-out stems can also be removed.

Billbergia nutans

Cryptanthus
Earth stars

A genus of dwarf, evergreen *Bromeliads*, which differ from other types in that their foliage does not form a watertight 'vase' for the retention of water, but rather a simple rosette. They are highly suited for growing in the home and are easy to grow and handle. The foliage of most varieties is very decorative, with bars, stripes, all manner of mottling, and several very distinctive variegations. Flowers are generally small and insignificant. After flowering, the adult plant produces new plantlets from the axils of its lower leaves; these break off easily and will root if placed on a damp surface. Plant in a light peaty potting mix. Use soft water regularly for watering them during the growing season, and also for spraying the foliage. In winter, soil must be kept barely moist, and temperatures kept at 15–20°C (50–68°F). Plants may be grown on tree-trunks as epiphytes, and are excellent in cases and bottle gardens.

Cryptanthus

One of many fantastic blooms.

Guzmania

Guzmania

Another genus of tropical epiphytes, with a great number of species, ranging from giants to the small 25cm (10ins) *G. minor*. The foliage is typically rolled to form a central 'vase', and the flower rises from the very centre of the rosette and is surrounded by brightly coloured bracts of yellow, orange or red which last a long time on the plant. These species will do well if a constant temperature and humidity can be maintained. A plant window, or large case, would be ideal. Place in bright shaded light, avoid draughts and sharp temperature changes. Water generously during the growing season from March to August onto soil, foliage and 'vase', using soft water. Fertilise with a diluted foliar spray. Keep plants dry during winter, and with an empty 'vase'.

Vriesea

Vriesea

Both terrestrial and epiphytic types are found in this group; those species with plain green foliage are usually kept for their brightly coloured blooms, while the equally large group with variegations and markings on their foliage tend to be kept for their foliage. All the species have the typical leaf rosettes with their central 'reservoir' of water. The flowers of some species are so bright and colourful that they seem quite improbable. Most species are too 'tropical' to be kept in the home though the green-foliaged types are hardier, such as *V. psittacina* and *V. hybrid Rex*. The most likely problems that will be encountered are not diseases but sunburn and rotting. General care is similar to that needed by *Aechmea's*.

Neoregelia

Neoregelia

Neoregelia and *Nidularium* are closely related genera, and are usually described together as their needs are so similar. Growing and blooming conditions are similar to those of *Aechmea*, as these are also epiphytes. The *Nidularium* is difficult to grow without the controlled environment of a heated greenhouse or large case. *Neoregelia* has several species and their varieties that are suitable for normal home conditions, notably *N. carolinae* and *N. princeps*. They require good indirect light, hot summer temperatures, with regular watering and feeding. During the winter rest period, the temperature should not drop below 15°C (60°F), and very little water must be applied.

Bromeliads need their own particular types of potting-mixture, which provides for their manner of feeding and growing. A balanced mixture can be made up of: 1 part half-rotted Beech compost, 1 part coarse peat, 1 part fern fibre, a small quantity of mature manure, and some river sand. Epiphytic Bromeliads *can also be grown on a tree stump.*

Tillandsia

Tillandsia usneoides

This large genus also has a diversity of species, originating in different continents, and with differing growing and climatic needs. There are both terrestrial and epiphytic types, and a large group that are neither. These are the weird 'air plants', which have simply to be hung up in a moist location. If they receive no rain (or watering) their wiry or mossy leaves shrivel a bit. When they are wetted they simply carry on growing. A typical example is Spanish Moss, *T. usneoides*, which hangs in large bunches from trees in its tropical habitat. During summer, it may produce small yellow-green flowers. To propagate them simply pull off a small tuft of stems. Mist spray frequently in summer with soft water, provide good light levels, and keep humidity high. Most 'air plants' need to be kept in a case or terrarium, where the humidity will be adequate.

Index